ASSET LIABILITY MANAGEMENT
POLICIES, STRATEGIES AND OPTIONS

ASSET LIABILITY MANAGEMENT
POLICIES, STRATEGIES AND OPTIONS

Darpan Verma

RANDOM

RANDOM PUBLICATIONS

NEW DELHI - 110 002 (INDIA)

Asset Liability Management: Policies, Strategies and Options

ISBN 978-93-51117-15-5

Published in 2015 in India by

RANDOM PUBLICATIONS

4376-A/4B, Gali Murari Lal, Ansari Road
New Delhi-110 002
Phone: +9111-43580356, 23289044
E-mail: randomexports@gmail.com; sales@randompublications.com; info@randompublications.com

Reprinted 2018

Type Setting by: Friends Media, Delhi-110089
Digitally Pritnted at : Replika Press Pvt. Ltd.

Preface

Initially pioneered by Anglo-Saxon financial institutions during the 1970s as interest rates became increasingly volatile, asset and liability management (often abbreviated ALM) is the practice of managing risks that arise due to mismatches between the assets and liabilities. The process is at the crossroads between risk management and strategic planning. It is not just about offering solutions to mitigate or hedge the risks arising from the interaction of assets and liabilities but is focused on a long-term perspective: success in the process of maximising assets to meet complex liabilities may increase profitability. The exact roles and perimeter around ALM can vary significantly from one bank to another depending on the business model adopted and can encompass a broad area of risks.

The traditional ALM programmes focus on interest rate risk and liquidity risk because they represent the most prominent risks affecting the organization balance-sheet. But ALM also now seeks to broaden assignments such as foreign exchange risk and capital management. According to the Balance sheet management benchmark survey conducted in 2009 by the audit and consulting company PricewaterhouseCoopers (PwC), 51% of the 43 leading financial institutions participants look at capital management in their ALM unit. The ALM function scope covers both a prudential component (management of all possible risks and rules and regulation) and an optimization role (management of funding costs, generating results on balance sheet position), within the limits of compliance (implementation and monitoring with internal rules and regulatory set of rules). ALM intervenes in these issues of current business activities but is also consulted to organic development and external acquisition to analyse and validate the funding terms options, conditions of the projects and any risks. Today, ALM techniques and processes have been extended and adopted by corporations other than financial institutions; e.g., insurance. The objective is to measure the direction and extent of asset-liability mismatch through the funding or maturity gap. This aspect of ALM stresses the importance of balancing maturities as well as cash-flows or interest rates for a particular set time horizon. For the management of interest rate risk it may take the form of matching the maturities and interest rates of loans and investments with the maturities and interest rates of deposit, equity and external credit in order to maintain adequate profitability. In other words, it is the management of the spread between interest rate sensitive assets and interest rate sensitive liabilities. The role of the bank in the context of the maturity transformation that occurs in the banking book (as traditional activity of the bank is to borrow short and lend long) lets inherently the institution vulnerable to liquidity risk and can even conduct to the so-call risk of 'run of the bank' as depositors, investors or insurance policy holders can withdraw their funds/ seek for cash in their financial claims and thus impacting current and future cash-flow and collateral needs of the bank (risk appeared if the bank is unable to meet in good conditions these obligations as they come due). This aspect of liquidity risk is named funding liquidity risk and arises because of liquidity mismatch of assets and liabilities (unbalance in the maturity term creating liquidity gap). Even if market liquidity risk is not covered into the conventional techniques of ALM (market liquidity risk as the risk to not easily offset or eliminate a position at the prevailing market price because of inadequate market depth or market disruption), these 2 liquidity risk types are closely interconnected. As an echo to the deficit of funds resulting from gaps between assets and liabilities the bank has also to address its funding requirement through an effective, robust and stable funding model. As the bank should not assume that business will always continue as it is the current business process, the institution needs to explore emergency sources of funds and formalise a contingency plan. The purpose is to find alternative backup sources of funding to those that occur within the normal course of operations.

This book is a comprehensive and authoritative presentation of ALM techniques and issues. Written in accessible style, this book is essential reading for market practitioners, bank regulators and graduate students in banking and finance.

I thank all members of my team who have helped in the preparation of the book. My special thanks go to "Random Publications" who have published the book.

— Darpan Verma

Contents

Chapter 1

Introduction

In financial accounting, assets are economic resources. Anything tangible or intangible that is capable of being owned or controlled to produce value and that is held to have positive economic value is considered an asset. Simply stated, assets represent ownership of value that can be converted into cash (although cash itself is also considered an asset). The balance sheet of a firm records the monetary value of the assets owned by the firm. It is money and other valuables belonging to an individual or business. Two major asset classes are tangible assets and intangible assets. Tangible assets contain various subclasses, including current assets and fixed assets. Current assets include inventory, while fixed assets include such items as buildings and equipment. Intangible assets are nonphysical resources and rights that have a value to the firm because they give the firm some kind of advantage in the market place. Examples of intangible assets are goodwill, copyrights, trademarks, patents and computer programs, and financial assets, including such items as accounts receivable, bonds and stocks.

Formal Definition

An asset is a resource controlled by the entity as a result of past events and from which future economic benefits are expected to flow to the entity.

Asset Characteristics

It should be noted that-other than software companies and the like-employees are not considered as assets, like machinery is, even though they are capable of producing value.

- The probable present benefit involves a capacity, singly or in combination with other assets, in the case of profit oriented enterprises, to contribute directly or indirectly to future net cash flows, and, in the case of not-for-profit organizations, to provide services;
- The entity can control access to the benefit;
- The transaction or event giving rise to the entity's right to, or control of, the benefit has already occurred.

In the financial accounting sense of the term, it is not necessary to be able to legally enforce the asset's benefit for qualifying a resource as being an asset, provided the entity can control its use by other means.

It is important to understand that in an accounting sense an asset is not the same as ownership. Assets are equal to "equity" plus "liabilities."

The accounting equation relates assets, liabilities, and owner's equity:

Assets = Liabilities + Stockholder's Equity (Owner's Equity).

The accounting equation is the mathematical structure of the balance sheet.

Assets are listed on the balance sheet. Similarly, in economics an asset is any form in which wealth can be held.

Probably the most accepted accounting definition of asset is the one used by the International Accounting Standards Board. The following is a quotation from the IFRS Framework: "An asset is a resource controlled by the enterprise as a result of past events and from which future economic benefits are expected to flow to the enterprise."

Assets are formally controlled and managed within larger organizations via the use of asset tracking tools. These monitor the purchasing, upgrading, servicing, licensing, disposal etc., of both physical and non-physical assets. In a company's balance sheet certain divisions are required by generally accepted accounting principles (GAAP), which vary from country to country.

Current Assets

Current assets are cash and other assets expected to be converted to cash, sold, or consumed either in a year or in the operating cycle (whichever is longer), without disturbing the normal operations of a business. These assets are continually turned over in the course of a business during normal business activity. There are 5 major items included into current assets:

1. Cash and cash equivalents — it is the most liquid asset, which includes currency, deposit accounts, and negotiable instruments (e.g., money orders, cheque, bank drafts).
2. Short-term investments — include securities bought and held for sale in the near future to generate income on short-term price differences (trading securities).
3. Receivables — usually reported as net of allowance for uncollectable accounts.
4. Inventory — trading these assets is a normal business of a company. The inventory value reported on the balance sheet is usually the historical cost or fair market value, whichever is lower. This is known as the "lower of cost or market" rule.
5. Prepaid expenses — these are expenses paid in cash and recorded as assets before they are used or consumed (a common example is insurance).

The phrase *net current assets* (also called *working capital*) is often used and refers to the total of current assets less the total of current liabilities.

Long-term Investments

Often referred to simply as "investments". Long-term investments are to be held for many years and are not intended to be disposed of in the near future. This group usually consists of four types of investments:

1. Investments in securities such as bonds, common stock, or long-term notes.
2. Investments in fixed assets not used in operations (e.g., land held for sale).
3. Investments in special funds (e.g. sinking funds or pension funds).

Different forms of insurance may also be treated as long term investments.

Fixed Assets

Fixed assets, also known as a non-current asset or as property, plant, and equipment (PP&E), is a term used in accounting for assets and property which cannot easily be converted into cash. This can be compared with current assets such as cash or bank accounts, which are described as liquid assets. In most cases, only tangible assets are referred to as fixed.

Moreover, a fixed/non-current asset can also be defined as an asset not directly sold to a firm's consumers/end-users. As an example, a baking firm's current assets would be its inventory (in this case, flour, yeast, etc.), the value of sales owed to the firm via credit (i.e. debtors or accounts receivable), cash held in the bank, etc. Its non-current assets would be the oven used to bake bread, motor vehicles used to transport deliveries, cash registers used to handle cash payments, etc. Each aforementioned non-current asset is not sold directly to consumers.

These are items of value which the organization has bought and will use for an extended period of time; fixed assets normally include items such as land and buildings, motor vehicles, furniture, office equipment, computers, fixtures and fittings, and plant and machinery. These often receive favorable tax treatment (depreciation allowance) over short-term assets. According to International Accounting Standard (IAS) 16, Fixed Assets are assets whose future economic benefit is probable to flow into the entity, whose cost can be measured reliably.

It is pertinent to note that the cost of a fixed asset is its purchase price, including import duties and other deductible trade discounts and rebates. In addition, cost attributable to bringing and installing the asset in its needed location and the initial estimate of dismantling and removing the item if they are eventually no longer needed on the location.

The primary objective of a business entity is to make profit and increase the wealth of its owners. In the attainment of this objective it is required that the management will exercise due care and diligence in applying the basic accounting concept of "Matching Concept". Matching concept is simply matching the expenses of a period against the revenues of the same period.

The use of assets in the generation of revenue is usually more than a year-that is long term. It is therefore obligatory that in order to accurately determine the net income or profit for a period depreciation is charged on the total value of asset that contributed to the revenue for the period in consideration and charge against the same revenue of the same period. This is essential in the prudent reporting of the net revenue for the entity in the period.

Net book value of an asset is basically the difference between the historical cost of that asset and it associated depreciation. From the foregoing, it is apparent that in order to report a true and fair position of the financial jurisprudence of an entity it is relatable to record and report the value of fixed assets at its net book value. Apart from the fact that it is enshrined in Standard Accounting Statement (SAS) 3 and IAS 16 that value of asset should be carried at the net book value, it is the best way of consciously presenting the value of assets to the owners of the business and potential investor.

Depreciating a Fixed Asset

Depreciation is, simply put, the expense generated by the use of an asset. It is the wear and tear of an asset or diminution in the historical value owing to usage. Further to this; it is the cost of the asset less any salvage value over its estimated useful life. It is an expense because it is matched against the revenue generated through the use of the same asset. Depreciation is usually spread over the economic useful life of an asset because it is regarded as the cost of an asset absorbed over its useful life. Invariably the depreciation expense is charged against the revenue generated through the use of the asset. The method of depreciation to be adopted is best left for the management to decide in consideration to the peculiarity of the business, prevailing economic condition of the assets and existing accounting guideline and principles as implied in the organizational policies.

It is worth noting that not all fixed assets depreciate in value year-over-year. Land and buildings, for example, may often increase in value depending on local real-estate conditions.

A long-term tangible piece of property that a firm owns and uses in the production of its income and is not expected to be consumed or converted into cash any sooner than at least one year's time.

Fixed assets are sometimes collectively referred to as "plant".

Also referred to as PPE (property, plant, and equipment), these are purchased for continued and long-term use in earning profit in a business. This group includes as an asset land, buildings, machinery, furniture, tools, and certain wasting resources e.g., timberland and minerals. They are written off against profits over their anticipated life by charging depreciation expenses (with exception of land assets). Accumulated depreciation is shown in the face of the balance sheet or in the notes.

These are also called capital assets in management accounting.

Fixed Assets Register

A Fixed Asset Register (FAR) is an accounting method used for major resources of a business.

Fixed Assets are assets such as land, machines, office equipments, buildings, patents, trademarks, copyrights, etc. held for the purpose of production of goods or rendering of services and are not held for the purpose of sale in the ordinary course of business.

Fixed assets constitute a major chunk of the total assets in the case of all manufacturing entities. Even in the case of service entities such as hotels, banks, financial institutions, insurers, mobile/telephone service providers etc. it has become imperative to invest heavily in furnishing, equipment, and technology to attract, and retain customers.

Just as it is important for a person investing on the NASDAQ to know those investments, so it is important for a business entity to have a list of its fixed assets. A Fixed Asset Register is that list of assets.

Objectives in Maintaining a Fixed Asset Register (FAR)

A FAR must be kept in order to be in compliance with legislation governing corporations, companies, etc. It allows a company to keep track of details of each fixed asset, ensuring control and preventing misappropriation of assets. It also keeps track of the correct value of assets, which allows for computation of depreciation and for tax and insurance purposes. The FAR generates accurate, complete, and customized reports that suits the needs of management.

A FAR also allows a company to keep track of fixed assets that are not under simple, direct control of the company. This means owned and leased assets, assets under construction, and imported assets.

The FAR can also be used to aid in capital budgeting and to keep track of amount provided for Asset Retirement Obligation (ARO) in respect of each asset as required by US GAAP (FAS – 143).

Making Entries in the FAR

Not all assets are capitalized. Keeping in view the concept of materiality, a company may have a policy to capitalize only those assets which cost more than a specified amount. In the US, government agencies are required to expense all equipment whose value is below a threshold limit. Similarly, fixed assets which have a useful life of less than one year are not capitalized.

In some companies, improvements or alterations made to an asset are capitalized separately in the FAR. This is not correct. If such mistakes are made, it is highly probable that the auditors while undertaking physical verification of assets will notice irreconcilable differences. Where improvements or alterations made to an existing asset justifying capitalization, such additions should be made to the cost of the original asset.

The Format of FAR Entries

The format/details to be provided in a FAR generally depends upon the following factors:

a) Nature of assets.
   i. If moveable assets constitute a significant portion of total fixed assets, details will be necessary on their movement from one department/cost center/people to another.
   ii. Cost of assets. Greater control and security is required for costly equipment.

b) Customized Reports on fixed assets required by management.

c) Disclosure norms/regulatory compliances as per statutory laws applicable to the entity.

d) Extent of owned, and assets taken on lease/hire purchase.

e) Requirements of insurance company.

f) Location of fixed assets. If fixed assets are located at numerous locations, greater details will have to be given. In the case of a construction company, the assets are located at different work sites. These work sites maybe in different cities/countries/ continents.

g) Maintenance costs. Some fixed assets require regular servicing to keep them running in an efficient and satisfactory manner. It would be necessary to keep a tab on the maintenance costs, dates of servicing etc. during a stated period.

Maintenance of a FAR in a Multi-National Corporation (MNC) can be onerous and complex due to different regulatory and compliance requirements in each country and different currencies.

Generally, an MNC sets up a subsidiary in the country in which it intends to start operations. Maintenance of FAR is decentralized. The FAR is maintained per the company's policy, and regulatory requirements which are country specific. If consolidation of holding company and its subsidiaries (whether domestic or foreign) is required by the law applicable to companies, and relevant Accounting Standards, the task may become a bit complex. The crucial point is related to selection of exchange rate for conversion of fixed assets. Most companies either use average annual rate or year-end exchange rate.

Similarly, for companies having their shares listed on American Stock Exchanges, the fixed assets are required to be stated in accordance with the requirements of US generally accepted accounting principles (US GAAP).

Identification of a Fixed Asset

In a large corporation, the task of identifying and locating a specific fixed asset can be difficult unless numbering is scientific, systematic, and up-to-date. A common problem in most companies is the improper maintenance of the FAR. Physical verification of fixed assets becomes a futile exercise unless the FAR is properly maintained.

It would be advisable to use a scientific numbering technique to identify fixed assets. The process of numbering fixed assets is called tagging. An identification number (combination of alphabets, and numbers) is written on the asset. Engraving the identification number on the asset is advisable in the case of Plant & Machinery where there is heavy wear and tear. A tag verifies the existence of assets and their location, aids in maintenance, provides a common ground for communication between the Accounts Department and the end-users and recording the net book value of asset in case of sale/scrapping.

It is not necessary to tag all fixed assets. Land, buildings and vehicles all have independent systems of tracking in registration papers and survey numbers.

Fixed Assets Management

Fixed assets management is an accounting process that seeks to track fixed assets for the purposes of financial accounting, preventive maintenance, and theft deterrence.

Many organizations face a significant challenge to track the location, quantity, condition, maintenance and depreciation status of their fixed assets. A popular approach to tracking fixed assets utilizes serial numbered Asset Tags, often with bar codes for easy and accurate reading. Periodically, the owner of the assets can take inventory with a mobile barcode reader and then produce a report.

Off-the-shelf software packages for fixed asset management are marketed to businesses small and large. Some Enterprise Resource Planning systems are available with fixed assets modules.

Some tracking methods automate the process, such as by using fixed scanners to read bar codes on railway freight cars or by attaching a radio-frequency identification (RFID) tag to an asset.

Fixed Asset Tracking Software

Tracking assets is an important concern of every company, regardless of size. Fixed assets are defined as any 'permanent' object that a business uses internally including but not limited to computers, tools, software, or office equipment. While employees may utilize a specific tool or tools, the asset ultimately belongs to the company and must be returned. And therefore without an accurate method of keeping track of these assets it would be very easy for a company to lose control of them.

With advancements in technology, asset tracking software is now available that will help any size business track valuable assets such as equipment and supplies. According to a study issued in December, 2005 by the ARC Advisory Group, the worldwide market for Enterprise Asset Management (EAM) was then at an estimated $2.2 billion and was expected to grow at about 5.0 percent per year reaching $2.8 billion in 2010.

Asset tracking software allows companies to track what assets it owns, where each is located, who has it, when it was checked out, when it is due for return, when it is scheduled for maintenance, and the cost and depreciation of each asset.

The reporting option that is built into most asset tracking solutions provides pre-built reports, including assets by category and department, check-in/check-out, net book value of assets, assets past due, audit history, and transactions.

All of this information is captured in one program and can be used on PCs as well as mobile devices. As a result, companies reduce expenses through loss prevention and improved equipment maintenance. They reduce new and unnecessary equipment purchases, and they can more accurately calculate taxes based on depreciation schedules.

The most commonly tracked assets are:

- Plant and equipment
- Buildings
- Fixtures and fittings.

Intangible Assets

Intangible assets are defined as identifiable non-monetary assets that cannot be seen, touched or physically measured, which are created through time and/or effort and that are identifiable as a separate asset. There are two primary forms of intangibles-legal intangibles (such as trade secrets (e.g., customer lists), copyrights, patents, and trademarks) and competitive intangibles (such as knowledge activities (know-how, knowledge), collaboration activities, leverage activities, and structural activities). Legal intangibles are known under the generic term intellectual property and generate legal property rights defensible in a court of law.

Competitive intangibles, whilst legally non-ownable, directly impact effectiveness, productivity, wastage, and opportunity costs within an organization-and therefore costs, revenues, customer service, satisfaction, market value, and share price. Human capital is the primary source of competitive intangibles for organizations today. Competitive intangibles are the source from which competitive advantage flows, or is destroyed. The area of finance that deals with intangible assets is known as Intangible Asset Finance.

The Uniform Commercial Code (Section 9-102(a)(42)) defines "general intangibles" as;

> *"any personal property...other than accounts, chattel paper, commercial tort claims, deposit accounts, documents, goods, instruments, investment property, letter of credit rights, letters of credit, money, and oil, gas, or other minerals before extraction. The term includes payment intangibles and software."*

Intangible assets lack of physical substance and usually are very hard to evaluate. They include patents, copyrights, franchises, goodwill, trademarks, trade names, etc. These assets are (according to US GAAP) amortized to expense over 5 to 40 years with the exception of goodwill.

Websites are treated differently in different countries and may fall under either tangible or intangible assets.

Tangible Assets

Tangible assets are those that have a physical substance and can be touched, such as currencies, buildings, real estate, vehicles, inventories, equipment, and precious metals.

Other Related Meanings

Information Asset

In Information technology, chiefly in Information security, data needed to conduct the organization business and the technical equipment to manage (input, store, display, print) are called information asset.

They can represent a large portion of intangible and tangible asset of an organization.

If these assets become unavailable, business operations can be disrupted. Confidential information disclosure can represent a huge liability.

While evaluating the potential loss tied to an asset or a group of assets, the value tied to the largest sum between the related asset and their value should be considered.

Property

Property is any physical or intangible entity that is owned by a person or jointly by a group of people. Depending on the nature of the property, an owner of property has the right to consume, sell, rent, mortgage, transfer, exchange or destroy it, or to exclude others from doing these things. Important widely recognized types of property include real property (the combination of land and any improvements to or on the land), personal property (physical possessions belonging to a person), private property (property owned by legal persons or business entities), public property (state owned or publicly owned and available possessions) and intellectual property (exclusive rights over artistic creations, inventions, etc.), although the latter is not always as widely recognized or enforced. A title, or a right of ownership, establishes the relation between the property and other persons, assuring the owner the right to dispose of the property as the owner sees fit. Some philosophers assert that property rights arise from social convention. Others find origins for them in morality or natural law.

Use of the Term

Various scholarly disciplines (such as law, economics, anthropology or sociology) may treat the concept more systematically, but definitions vary within and between fields. Scholars in the social sciences frequently conceive of property as a bundle of rights. They stress that property is not a relationship between people and things, but a relationship between people *with regard to* things.

Property is usually thought of as being defined and protected by the local sovereignty. Ownership, however, does not necessarily equate with sovereignty. If ownership gave supreme authority, it would be sovereignty, not ownership. These are two different concepts.

Public property is any property that is controlled by a state or by a whole community. *Private property* is any property that is not public property. Private property may be under the control of a single person or by a group of persons jointly.

General Characteristics

Modern property rights are based on conceptions of owners and possession as belonging to legal persons, even if the legal person is not a natural person. In most countries, corporations, for example, have legal rights similar to those of citizens. Therefore, the corporation is a juristic person or artificial legal entity, under a concept that some refer to as "corporate personhood".

Traditional principles of property rights include:

1. control of the use of the property
2. the right to any benefit from the property (examples: mining rights and rent)
3. a right to transfer or sell the property
4. a right to exclude others from the property.

Traditional property rights do not include:

1. uses that unreasonably interfere with the property rights of another private party (the right of quiet enjoyment)
2. uses that unreasonably interfere with public property rights, including uses that interfere with public health, safety, peace or convenience.

Not every person or entity with an interest in a given piece of property may be able to exercise all possible property rights. For example, as a lessee of a particular piece of property, you may not sell the property, because a tenant is only in possession and does not have title to transfer. Similarly, while you are a lessee, the owner cannot use their right to exclude to keep you from the property, or, if they do, you may be entitled to stop paying rent or sue for access.

Further, property may be held in a number of forms, such as through joint ownership, community property, sole ownership or lease. These different types of ownership may complicate an owner's ability to exercise property rights unilaterally. For example, if two people own a single piece of land as joint tenants then, depending on the law in the jurisdiction, each may have limited recourse for the actions of the other. For example, one of the owners might sell their interest in the property to a stranger whom the other owner does not particularly like.

Legal systems have evolved to cover transactions and disputes that arise over the possession, use, transfer, and disposal of property, most particularly involving contracts. Positive law defines such rights, and the judiciary is used to adjudicate and to enforce property rights.

According to Adam Smith, the expectation of profit from "improving one's stock of capital" rests on private property rights. It is an assumption central to capitalism that property rights encourage their holders to develop the property, generate wealth, and efficiently allocate resources based on the operation of markets. From this has evolved the modern conception of property as a right enforced by positive law, in the expectation that this will produce more wealth and better standards of living.

In his text *The Common Law*, Oliver Wendell Holmes describes property as having two fundamental aspects. The first is possession, which can be defined as control over a resource based on the practical inability of another to contradict the ends of the possessor. The second is title, which is the expectation that others will recognize rights to control resource, even when it is not in possession. He elaborates the differences between these two concepts, and proposes a history of how they came to be attached to persons, as opposed to families or entities such as the church.

Classical Liberals, Objectivists, and Related Traditions

Most thinkers from these traditions subscribe to the labor theory of property. They hold that you own your own life, and it follows that you must own the products of that life, and that those products can be traded in free exchange with others.

> *"Every man has a property in his own person. This nobody has a right to, but himself." (John Locke, Second Treatise on Civil Government)*
>
> *"The reason why men enter into society is the preservation of their property." (John Locke, Second Treatise on Civil Government)*
>
> *"Life, liberty, and property do not exist because men have made laws. On the contrary, it was the fact that life, liberty, and property existed beforehand that caused men to make laws in the first place." (Frédéric Bastiat, The Law)*

- Socialism's fundamental principles are centered on a critique of this concept, stating, among other things, that the cost of defending property is higher than the returns from private property ownership, and that, even when property rights encourage their holders to develop their property or generate wealth, they do so only for their own benefit, which may not coincide with benefit to other people or to society at large.

- Libertarian socialism generally accepts property rights, but with a short abandonment period. In other words, a person must make (more or less) continuous use of the item or else lose ownership rights. This is usually referred to as "possession property" or "usufruct". Thus, in this usufruct system, absentee ownership is illegitimate and workers own the machines or other equipment that they work with.
- Communism argues that only collective ownership of the means of production through a polity (though not necessarily a state) will assure the minimization of unequal or unjust outcomes and the maximization of benefits, and that therefore private ownership of capital should be abolished.

Both communism and some kinds of socialism have also upheld the notion that private ownership of capital is inherently illegitimate. This argument centers mainly on the idea that private ownership of capital always benefits one class over another, giving rise to domination through the use of this privately owned capital. Communists are not opposed to personal property that is "hard-won, self-acquired, self-earned" (Communist Manifesto) by members of the proletariat. Both socialism and communism are careful to make the distinction between private ownership of capital (land, factories, resources, etc...) and private property (homes, material objects, and so forth).

Theories of Property

There exist many theories. One is the relatively rare first possession theory of property, where ownership of something is seen as justified simply by someone seizing something before someone else does. Perhaps one of the most popular, is the natural rights definition of property rights as advanced by John Locke. Locke advanced the theory that when one mixes one's labor with nature, one gains a relationship with that part of nature with which the labor is mixed, subject to the limitation that there should be "enough, and as good, left in common for others."

From the Rerum Novarum, Pope Leo XIII wrote "It is surely undeniable that, when a man engages in remunerative labor, the impelling reason and motive of his work is to obtain property, and thereafter to hold it as his very own."

Anthropology studies the diverse systems of ownership, rights of use and transfer, and possession under the term "theories of property." Western legal theory is based, as mentioned, on the owner of property being a legal person. However, not all property systems are founded on this basis.

In every culture studied ownership and possession are the subject of custom and regulation, and "law" where the term can meaningfully be applied. Many tribal cultures balance individual ownership with the laws of collective groups: tribes, families, associations and nations. For example the 1839 Cherokee Constitution frames the issue in these terms:

The lands of the Cherokee Nation shall remain common property; but the improvements made thereon, and in the possession of the citizens respectively who made, or may rightfully be in possession of them: Provided, that the citizens of the Nation possessing exclusive and indefeasible right to their improvements, as expressed in this article, shall possess no right or power to dispose of their improvements, in any manner whatever, to the United States, individual States, or to individual citizens thereof; and that, whenever any citizen shall remove with his effects out of the limits of this Nation, and become a citizen of any other government, all his rights and privileges as a citizen of this Nation shall cease: Provided, nevertheless, That the National Council shall have power to re-admit, by law, to all the rights of citizenship, any such person or persons who may, at any time, desire to return to the Nation, on memorializing the National Council for such readmission.

Communal property systems describe ownership as belonging to the entire social and political unit. Such arrangements can under certain conditions erode to open access resources. This development has been critiqued by the tragedy of the commons.

Corporate systems describe ownership as being attached to an identifiable group with an identifiable responsible individual. The Roman property law was based on such a corporate system.

Different societies may have different theories of property for differing types of ownership. Pauline Peters argued that property systems are not isolable from the social fabric, and notions of property may not be stated as such, but instead may be framed in negative terms: for example the taboo system among Polynesian peoples.

Property in Philosophy

In medieval and Renaissance Europe the term "property" essentially referred to land. Much rethinking has come to be regarded as only a special case of the property genus. This rethinking was inspired by at least three broad features of early modern Europe: the surge of commerce, the breakdown of efforts to prohibit interest (then called "usury"), and the development of centralized national monarchies.

Ancient Philosophy

Urukagina, the king of the Sumerian city-state Lagash, established the first laws that forbade compelling the sale of property.

The Ten Commandments shown in Exodus 20:2-17 and Deuteronomy 5:6-21 stated that the Israelites were not to steal, a blanket early protection of private property.

Aristotle, in *Politics,* advocates "private property" He argues that self-interest leads to neglect of the commons. "[T]hat which is common to the greatest number has the least care bestowed upon it. Every one thinks chiefly of his own, hardly at all of the common interest; and only when he is himself concerned as an individual."

In addition he says that when property is common, there are natural problems that arise due to differences in labor: "If they do not share equally enjoyments and toils, those who labor much and get little will necessarily complain of those who labor little and receive or consume much. But indeed there is always a difficulty in men living together and having all human relations in common, but especially in their having common property."

Pre-industrial English Philosophy

Thomas Hobbes (17th Century): The principal writings of Thomas Hobbes appeared between 1640 and 1651—during and immediately following the war between forces loyal to King Charles I and those loyal to Parliament. In his own words, Hobbes' reflection began with the idea of "giving to every man his own," a phrase he drew from the writings of Cicero. But he wondered: How can anybody call anything his own? He concluded: My own can only truly be mine if there is one unambiguously strongest power in the realm, and that power treats it as mine, protecting its status as such.

James Harrington (17th century): A contemporary of Hobbes, James Harrington, reacted differently to the same tumult; he considered property natural but not inevitable. The author of 'Oceana', he may have been the first political theorist to postulate that political power is a consequence, not the cause, of the distribution of property. He said that the worst possible situation is one in which the commoners have half a nation's property, with crown and nobility holding the other half—a circumstance fraught with instability and violence. A much better situation (a stable republic) will exist once the commoners own most property, he suggested.

In later years, the ranks of Harrington's admirers included American revolutionary and founder John Adams.

Robert Filmer (17th Century): Another member of the Hobbes/Harrington generation, Sir Robert Filmer, reached conclusions much like Hobbes', but through Biblical exegesis. Filmer said that the institution of kingship is analogous to that of fatherhood, that subjects are but children, whether obedient or unruly, and that property rights are akin to the household goods that a father may dole out among his children—his to take back and dispose of according to his pleasure.

John Locke (17th Century): In the following generation, John Locke sought to answer Filmer, creating a rationale for a balanced constitution in which the monarch had a part to play, but not an overwhelming part. Since Filmer's views essentially require that the Stuart family be uniquely descended from the patriarchs of the Bible, and since even in the late 17th century that was a difficult view to uphold, Locke attacked Filmer's views in his First Treatise on Government, freeing him to set out his own views in the Second Treatise on Civil Government. Therein, Locke imagined a pre-social world, the unhappy residents of which create a social contract. They would, he allowed, create a monarchy, but its task would be to execute the will of an elected legislature.

"To this end" he wrote, meaning the end of their own long life and peace, "it is that men give up all their natural power to the society they enter into, and the community put the legislative power into such hands as they think fit, with this trust, that they shall be governed by declared laws, or else their peace, quiet, and property will still be at the same uncertainty as it was in the state of nature." Even when it keeps to proper legislative form, though, Locke held that there are limits to what a government established by such a contract might rightly do.

"It cannot be supposed that [the hypothetical contractors] they should intend, had they a power so to do, to give any one or more an absolute arbitrary power over their persons and estates, and put a force into the magistrate's hand to execute his unlimited will arbitrarily upon them; this were to put themselves into a worse condition than the state of nature, wherein they had a liberty to defend their right against the injuries of others, and were upon equal terms of force to maintain it, whether invaded by a single man or many in combination. Whereas by supposing they have given up themselves to the absolute arbitrary power and will of a legislator, they have disarmed themselves, and armed him to make a prey of them when he pleases..."

Note that both "persons *and* estates" are to be protected from the arbitrary power of any magistrate, inclusive of the "power and will of a legislator." In Lockean terms, depredations against an estate are just as plausible a justification for resistance and revolution as are those against persons. In neither case are subjects required to allow themselves to become prey.

To explain the ownership of property Locke advanced a labor theory of property.

William Blackstone (18th Century): In the 1760s, William Blackstone sought to codify the English common law. In his famous *Commentaries on the Laws of England* he wrote that "every wanton and causeless restraint of the will of the subject, whether produced by a monarch, a nobility, or a popular assembly is a degree of tyranny."

How should such tyranny be prevented or resisted? Through property rights, Blackstone thought, which is why he emphasized that indemnification must be awarded a non-consenting owner whose property is taken by eminent domain, and that a property owner is protected against physical invasion of his property by the laws of trespass and nuisance. Indeed, he wrote that a landowner is free to kill any stranger on his property between dusk and dawn, even an agent of the King, since it isn't reasonable to expect him to recognize the King's agents in the dark.

David Hume (18th Century): In contrast to the figures discussed in this section thus far, David Hume lived a relatively quiet life that had settled down to a relatively stable social and political structure. He lived the life of a solitary writer until 1763 when, at 52 years of age, he went off to Paris to work at the British embassy.

In contrast, one might think, to his outrage-generating works on religion and his skeptical views in epistemology, Hume's views on law and property were quite conservative.

He did not believe in hypothetical contracts, or in the love of mankind in general, and sought to ground politics upon actual human beings as one knows them. "In general," he wrote, "it may be affirmed that there is no such passion in human mind, as the love of mankind, merely as such, independent of personal qualities, or services, or of relation to ourselves." Existing customs should not lightly be disregarded, because they have come to be what they are as a result of human nature. With this endorsement of custom comes an endorsement of existing governments, because he conceived of the two as complementary: "A regard for liberty, though a laudable passion, ought commonly to be subordinate to a reverence for established government."

These views led to a view on property rights that might today be described as legal positivism. There are property rights because of and to the extent that the existing law, supported by social customs, secure them. He offered some practical home-spun advice on the general subject, though, as when he referred to avarice as "the spur of industry," and expressed concern about excessive levels of taxation, which "destroy industry, by engendering despair."

Critique and Response

> *"Civil government, so far as it is instituted for the security of property, is, in reality, instituted for the defence of the rich against the poor, or of those who have property against those who have none at all."*
>
> —*Adam Smith, The Wealth of Nations, 1776*

By the mid 19th century, the industrial revolution had transformed England and had begun in France. The established conception of what constitutes property expanded beyond land to encompass scarce goods in general. In France, the revolution of the 1790s had led to large-scale confiscation of land formerly owned by church and king. The restoration of the monarchy led to claims by those dispossessed to have their former lands returned. Furthermore, the labor theory of value popularized by classical economists such as Adam Smith and David Ricardo were utilized by a new ideology called socialism to critique the relations of property to other economic issues, such as profit, rent, interest, and wage-labor. Thus, property was no longer an esoteric philosophical question, but a political issue of substantial concern.

Charles Comte – Legitimate Origin of Property

Charles Comte, in *Traité de la propriété* (1834), attempted to justify the legitimacy of private property in response to the Bourbon Restoration. According to David Hart, Comte had three main points: "firstly, that interference by the state over the centuries in property ownership has had dire consequences for justice as well as for economic productivity; secondly, that property is legitimate when it emerges in such a way as not to harm anyone; and thirdly, that historically some, but by no means all, property which has evolved has done so legitimately, with the implication that the present distribution of property is a complex mixture of legitimately and illegitimately held titles." (*The Radical Liberalism of Charles Comte and Charles Dunoyer*

Comte, as Proudhon later did, rejected Roman legal tradition with its toleration of slavery. He posited a communal "national" property consisting of non-scarce goods, such as land in ancient hunter-gatherer societies. Since agriculture was so much more efficient than hunting and gathering, private property appropriated by someone for farming left remaining hunter-gatherers with more land per person, and hence did not harm them. Thus this type of land appropriation did not violate the Lockean proviso – there was "still enough, and as good left." Comte's analysis would be used by later theorists in response to the socialist critique on property.

Pierre Proudhon – Property is Theft

In his 1849 treatise *What is Property?*, Pierre Proudhon answers with "Property is theft!" In natural resources, he sees two types of property, *de jure* property (legal title) and *de facto* property (physical possession), and argues that the former is illegitimate. Proudhon's conclusion is that "property, to be just and possible, must necessarily have equality for its condition."

His analysis of the product of labor upon natural resources as property (usufruct) is more nuanced. He asserts that land itself cannot be property, yet it should be held by individual possessors as stewards of mankind with the product of labor being the property of the producer. Proudhon reasoned that any wealth gained without labor was stolen from those who labored to create that wealth. Even a voluntary contract to surrender the product of labor to an employer was theft, according to Proudhon, since the controller of natural resources had no moral right to charge others for the use of that which he did not labor to create and therefore did not own.

Proudhon's theory of property greatly influenced the budding socialist movement, inspiring anarchist theorists such as Mikhail Bakunin who modified Proudhon's ideas, as well as antagonizing theorists like Karl Marx.

Frédéric Bastiat – Property is Value

In a radical departure from traditional property theory, he defines property not as a physical object, but rather as a relationship between people with respect to an object. Thus, saying one owns a glass of water is merely verbal shorthand for *I may justly gift or trade this water to another person.* In essence, what one owns is not the object but the value of the object. By "value," Bastiat apparently means *market value*; he emphasizes that this is quite different from utility. *"In our relations with one another, we are not owners of the utility of things, but of their value, and value is the appraisal made of reciprocal services."*

Strongly disputing Proudhon's equality-based argument, Bastiat theorizes that, as a result of technological progress and the division of labor, the stock of communal wealth increases over time; that the hours of work an unskilled laborer expends to buy e.g. 100 liters of wheat decreases over time, thus amounting to "gratis" satisfaction. Thus, private property continually destroys itself, becoming transformed into communal wealth. The increasing proportion of communal wealth to private property results in a tendency toward equality of mankind. *"Since the human race started from the point of greatest poverty, that is, from the point where there were the most obstacles to be overcome, it is clear that all that has been gained from one era to the next has been due to the spirit of property."*

This transformation of private property into the communal domain, Bastiat points out, does not imply that private property will ever totally disappear. This is because man, as he progresses, continually invents new and more sophisticated needs and desires.

Contemporary Views

Among contemporary political thinkers who believe that natural persons enjoy rights to own property and to enter into contracts, there are two views about John Locke. On the one hand there are ardent Locke admirers, such as W.H. Hutt (1956), who praised Locke for laying down the "quintessence of individualism." On the other hand, there are those such as Richard Pipes who think that Locke's arguments are weak, and that undue reliance thereon has weakened the cause of individualism in recent times. Pipes has written that Locke's work "marked a regression because it rested on the concept of Natural Law" rather than upon Harrington's sociological framework.

Hernando de Soto has argued that an important characteristic of capitalist market economy is the functioning state protection of property rights in a formal property system where ownership and transactions are clearly recorded. These property rights and the whole formal system of property make possible:

- Greater independence for individuals from local community arrangements to protect their assets;

- Clear, provable, and protectable ownership;
- The standardization and integration of property rules and property information in the country as a whole;
- Increased trust arising from a greater certainty of punishment for cheating in economic transactions;
- More formal and complex written statements of ownership that permit the easier assumption of shared risk and ownership in companies, and insurance against risk;
- Greater availability of loans for new projects, since more things could be used as collateral for the loans;
- Easier access to and more reliable information regarding such things as credit history and the worth of assets;
- Increased fungibility, standardization and transferability of statements documenting the ownership of property, which paves the way for structures such as national markets for companies and the easy transportation of property through complex networks of individuals and other entities;
- Greater protection of biodiversity due to minimizing of shifting agriculture practices.

All of the above enhance economic growth.

Most legal systems distinguish different types (immovable property, estate in land, real estate, real property) of property, especially between land and all other forms of property—goods and chattels, movable property or personal property. They often distinguish tangible and intangible property.

One categorization scheme specifies three species of property: land, improvements (immovable man-made things), and personal property (movable man-made things).

In common law, real property (immovable property) is the combination of interests in land and improvements thereto, and personal property is interest in movable property.

Real property rights are rights relating to the land. These rights include ownership and usage. Owners can grant rights to persons and entities in the form of leases, licenses and easements.

Later, with the development of more complex forms of non-tangible property, personal property was divided into tangible property (such as cars and clothing) and intangible property (such as financial instruments, including stocks and bonds, and intellectual property, including patents, copyrights, and trademarks).

What can be Property?

The two major justifications given for original property, or homesteading, are effort and scarcity. John Locke emphasized effort, "mixing your labor" with an object, or clearing and cultivating virgin land. Benjamin Tucker preferred to look at the telos of property, i.e. What is the purpose of property? His answer: to solve the scarcity problem. Only when items are relatively scarce with respect to people's desires do they become property.

For example, hunter-gatherers did not consider land to be property, since there was no shortage of land. Agrarian societies later made arable land property, as it was scarce. For something to be economically scarce, it must necessarily have the *exclusivity property*-that use by one person excludes others from using it. These two justifications lead to different conclusions on what can be property. Intellectual property-non-corporeal things like ideas, plans, orderings and arrangements (musical compositions, novels, computer programs)-are generally considered valid property to those who support an effort justification, but invalid to those who support a scarcity justification, since they don't have the exclusivity property (however they may still support other 'intellectual property'-laws such as Copyright, as long as these are a subject of contract instead of government arbitration). Thus even ardent propertarians may disagree about IP. By either standard, one's body is one's property.

From some anarchist points of view, the validity of property depends on whether the "property right" requires enforcement by the state. Different forms of "property" require different amounts of enforcement: intellectual property requires a great deal of state intervention to enforce, ownership of distant physical property requires quite a lot, ownership of carried objects requires very little, while ownership of one's own body requires absolutely no state intervention.

Many things have existed that did not have an owner, sometimes called the commons. The term "commons," however, is also often used to mean something quite different: "general collective ownership"-i.e. common ownership. Also, the same term is sometimes used by statists to mean government-owned property that the general public is allowed to access (public property). Law in all societies has tended to develop towards reducing the number of things not having clear owners. Supporters of property rights argue that this enables better protection of scarce resources, due to the tragedy of the commons, while critics argue that it leads to the 'exploitation' of those resources for personal gain and that it hinders taking advantage of potential network effects.

These arguments have differing validity for different types of "property"—things that are not scarce are, for instance, not subject to the tragedy of the commons. Some apparent critics advocate general collective ownership rather than ownerlessness.

Things that do not have owners include: ideas (except for intellectual property), seawater (which is, however, protected by anti-pollution laws), parts of the seafloor, gases in Earth's atmosphere, animals in the wild (though there may be restrictions on hunting etc. — and in some legal systems, such as that of New York, they are actually treated as government property), celestial bodies and outer space, and land in Antarctica.

The nature of children under the age of majority is another contested issue here. In ancient societies children were generally considered the property of their parents. Children in most modern societies theoretically own their own bodies but are not considered competent to exercise their rights, and their parents or guardians are given most of the actual rights of control over them.

Questions regarding the nature of ownership of the body also come up in the issue of abortion, drugs and euthanasia.

In many ancient legal systems (e.g. early Roman law), religious sites (e.g. temples) were considered property of the God or gods they were devoted to. However, religious pluralism makes it more convenient to have religious sites owned by the religious body that runs them.

Intellectual property and air (airspace, no-fly zone, pollution laws, which can include tradeable emissions rights) can be property in some senses of the word.

Rights of use as Property

Ownership of land can be held separately from the ownership of rights over that land, including sporting rights, mineral rights, development rights, air rights, and such other rights as may be worth segregating from simple land ownership.

Who can be an Owner?

Ownership is the state or fact of exclusive rights and control over property, which may be an object, land/real estate or intellectual property. Ownership involves multiple rights, collectively referred to as title, which may be separated and held by different parties. The concept of ownership has existed for thousands of years and in all cultures. Over the millennia, however, and across cultures what is considered eligible to be property and how that property is regarded culturally is very different. Ownership is the basis for many other concepts that form the foundations of ancient and modern societies such as money, trade, debt, bankruptcy, the criminality of theft and private vs. public property. Ownership is the key building block in the development of the capitalist socio-economic system.

The process and mechanics of ownership are fairly complex since one can gain, transfer and lose ownership of property in a number of ways. To acquire property one can purchase it with money, trade it for other property, receive it as a gift, steal it, find it, make it or homestead it. One can transfer or lose ownership of property by selling it for money, exchanging it for other property, giving it as a gift, being robbed of it, misplacing it, or having it stripped from one's ownership through legal means such as eviction, foreclosure, seizure or taking. Ownership is self-propagating in that the owner of any property will also own the economic benefits of that property.

Types of Owners

In Person

Individuals may own property directly. In some societies only adult men may own property; in other societies (such as the Haudenosaunee), property is matrilinear and passed on from mother to the son. In most societies both men and women can own property with no restrictions and limitations at all.

Structured Ownership Entities

Throughout history, nations (or governments) and religious organizations have owned property. These entities exist primarily for other purposes than to own or operate property, hence they may have no clear rules regarding the disposition of their property.

To own and operate property, structures (often known today as legal entities) have been created in many societies throughout history. The differences in how they deal with members' rights is a key factor in determining their type. Each type has advantages and disadvantages derived from their means of recognizing or disregarding (rewarding or not), contributions of financial capital or personal effort.

Cooperatives, corporations, trusts, partnerships, condominium associations are only some of the many varied types of structured ownership; each type has many subtypes. Legal advantages or restrictions on various types of structured ownership have existed in many societies past and present. To govern how assets are to be used, shared or treated, rules and regulations may be legally imposed or internally adopted or decreed.

Liability for the Group or for Others in the Group

Ownership implies responsibility, for actions regarding the property. A "legal shield" is said to exist if the entity's legal liabilities do not get redistributed among the entity's owners or members. An application of this, to limit ownership risks, is to form a new entity to purchase, own and operate each property. Since the entity is separate and distinct from others, if a problem occurs which leads to a massive liability, the individual is protected from losing more than the value of that one property. Many other properties are protected, when owned by other distinct entities.

In the loosest sense of group ownership, a lack of legal framework, rules and regulations may mean that group ownership of property places every member in a position of responsibility (liability) for the actions of each other member. A structured group duly constituted as an entity under law may still not protect members from being personally liable for each others' actions. Court decisions against the entity itself may give rise to unlimited personal liability for each and every member. An example of this situation is a professional partnership (e.g. law practice) in some jurisdictions. Thus, being a partner or owner in a group may give little advantage in terms of share ownership while producing a lot of risk to the partner, owner or participant.

Sharing Gains

At the end of each financial year, accounting rules determine a surplus or profit, which may be retained inside the entity or distributed among owners according to the initial setup intent when the entity was created.

Entities *with a member focus* will give financial surplus back to members according to the volume of financial activity that the participating member generated for the entity. Examples of this are producer cooperatives, buyer cooperatives and participating whole life policyholders in both mutual and share-capital insurance companies.

Entities *with share voting rights that depend on financial capital* distribute surplus among shareholders without regard to any other contribution to the entity. Depending on internal rules and regulations, certain classes of shares have the right to receive increases in financial "dividends" while other classes do not. After many years the increase over time is substantial if the business is profitable. Examples of this are common shares and preferred shares in private or publicly listed share capital corporations.

Entities *with a focus on providing service in perpetuam* do not distribute financial surplus; they must retain it. It will then serve as a cushion against losses or as a means to finance growth activities. Examples of this are not-for-profit entities: they are allowed to make profits, but are not permitted to give any of it back to members except by way of discounts in the future on new transactions.

Depending on the charter at the foundation of the entity, and depending on the legal framework under which the entity was created, the form of ownership is determined once and for all time. To change it requires significant work in terms of communicating with stakeholders (member-owners, governments, etc.) and acquiring their approval. Whatever structural constraints or disadvantages exist at the creation thus remain an integral part of the entity. Common in for instance New York City, Hamburg and Berlin in Germany is a form of real estate ownership known as a cooperative (also co-operative or co-op, in German Wohnungsgenossenschaft-apartment co-operative) which relies heavily on internal rules of operation instead of the legal framework governing condominium associations. These "co-ops", owning the building for the mutual benefit of its members, can ultimately perform most of the functions of a legally constituted condominium, i.e. restricting use appropriately and containing financial liabilities to within tolerable levels. To change their structure now that they are up and operating would require significant effort to achieve acceptance among members and various levels of government.

Sharing Use

The owning entity makes rules governing use of property; each property may comprise areas that are made available to any and every member of the group to use. When the group is the entire nation, the same principle is in effect whether the property is small (e.g. picnic rest stops along highways) or large such as national parks, highways, ports, and publicly owned buildings. Smaller examples of shared use include common areas such as lobbies, entrance hallways and passages to adjacent buildings.

One disadvantage of communal ownership, known as the Tragedy of the Commons, occurs where unlimited unrestricted and unregulated access to a resource (e.g. pasture land) destroys the resource because of over-exploitation. The benefits of exploitation accrue to individuals immediately, while the costs of policing or enforcing appropriate use, and the losses dues to over exploitation, are distributed among many, and are only visible to these gradually.

In an ideal communist nation the means of production of goods would be owned communally by all people of that nation; the original thinkers did not specify rules and regulations.

Ownership Models

State ownership-Assets that a state or certain state agency has jurisdiction over in terms of use.

Government ownership-Assets belonging to a body of government.

Public property-Assets owned by a government or state that are available for public use to all their constituents. Personal ownership-Assets and property belonging to an individual, also known as individual ownership. Common ownership-Assets and property that are held in common by all members of society (or non-ownership).

Communal ownership-Property held in common by a commune.

- Collective ownership-Assets and property that belong to a collective body of people who control their use and collect the proceeds of their operation.
    - Private ownership-A subset of collective property whereby a collective group of owners (such as shareholders) own productive property that is used by employees, usually for the purpose of generating a profit.
    - Cooperative ownership-Property that is owned by those who operate and use it. Also referred to as social ownership.

Types of Property

Personal Property

Personal property is a type of property. In the common law systems personal property may also be called chattels. It is distinguished from real property, or real estate. In the civil law systems personal property is often called movable property or movables-any property that can be moved from one location or another. This term is used to distinguish property that different from immovable property or immovables, such as land and buildings.

Personal property may be classified in a variety of ways, such as goods, money, negotiable instruments, securities, and intangible assets including choses in action.

Land Ownership

Real estate or immovable property is a legal term (in some jurisdictions) that encompasses land along with anything permanently affixed to the land, such as buildings. Real estate (immovable property) is often considered synonymous with real property, in contrast from personal property (also sometimes called *chattel* or *personalty*). However, for technical purposes, some people prefer to distinguish real estate, referring to the land and fixtures themselves, from real property, referring to ownership rights over real estate. The terms *real estate* and *real property* are used primarily in common law, while civil law jurisdictions refer instead to immovable property.

In law, the word *real* means relating to a thing (from Latin *reâlis,* ultimately from *rçs,* 'matter' or 'thing'), as distinguished from a person. Thus the law broadly distinguishes between *real property* (land and anything affixed to it) and *personal property* (everything else, e.g., clothing, furniture, money). The conceptual difference is between immovable property, which would transfer title along with the land, and movable property, which a person would retain title to. (Incidentally, the word *real* in *real estate* is not derived from the notion of land having historically been "royal" property. The word *royal*—and its Spanish cognate, *real*—come from the unrelated Latin word *rçgâlis* 'kingly,' which is a derivative of *rçx,* meaning 'king.')

With the development of private property ownership, real estate has become a major area of business.

Corporations and Legal Entities

An individual or group of individuals can own corporations and other legal entities. A legal entity is a legal construct through which the law allows a group of natural persons to act as if it were an individual for certain purposes. Some companies and entities are owned privately by the individuals who registered them with the government while other companies are owned publicly.

Some duly incorporated entities may not be owned by individuals nor by other entities; they exist without being owned once they are created. Not being owned, they cannot be bought and sold. Mutual life insurance companies, credit unions, and cooperatives are examples of this. No person can purchase the company, as their ownership is not legally available for sale, neither as shares nor as a single whole.

A publicly listed company, known as a public company, is owned by any member of the public who wishes to purchase stock in that company rather than by a relatively few individuals. A company that is owned by stockholders who are members of the general public and trade shares publicly, often through a listing on a stock exchange. Ownership is open to anyone who has the money and inclination to buy shares in the company. Owners, however, are generally classified in three groups. Those with 5% Ownerships of the stock usually hold significant sway over the company. Mutual Funds and regular institutions can also own the stock; if they own enough, can are considered as part of the 5% ownership category. Public companies usually are differentiated from privately held companies where the shares are held by a small group of individuals often members of one or a small group of families or otherwise related individuals (or other companies). For a discussion of the British and Irish variant of this type of company.

Intellectual Property

Intellectual (IP) property refers to a legal entitlement which sometimes attaches to the expressed form of an idea, or to some other intangible subject matter. This legal entitlement generally enables its holder to exercise exclusive rights of use in relation to the subject matter of the IP. The term *intellectual property* reflects the idea that this subject matter is the product of the mind or the intellect, and that IP rights may be protected at law in the same way as any other form of property.

Intellectual property laws confer a bundle of exclusive rights in relation to the particular form or manner in which ideas or information are expressed or manifested, and not in relation to the ideas or concepts themselves. It is therefore important to note that the term "intellectual property" denotes the specific legal rights which authors, inventors and other IP holders may hold and exercise, and not the intellectual work itself.

Intellectual property laws are designed to protect different forms of intangible subject matter, although in some cases there is a degree of overlap.

- copyright may subsist in creative and artistic works (e.g. books, movies, music, paintings, photographs and software), giving a copyright holder the exclusive right to control reproduction or adaptation of such works for a certain period of time.
- A patent may be granted in relation to an invention that is new, useful and not simply an obvious advancement over what existed when the application was filed. A patent gives the holder

an exclusive right to commercially exploit the invention for a certain period of time (typically 20 years from the filing date of a patent application).

- A trademark is a distinctive sign which is used to distinguish the products or services of one business from those of another business.
- An industrial design right protects the form of appearance, style or design of an industrial object (e.g. spare parts, furniture or textiles).
- A trade secret (also known as "confidential information") is an item of confidential information concerning the commercial practices or proprietary knowledge of a business.

Patents, trademarks and designs fall into a particular subset of intellectual property known as industrial property.

Like other forms of property, intellectual property (or rather the exclusive rights which subsist in the IP) can be transferred (with or without consideration) or licensed to third parties. In some jurisdictions it may also be possible to use intellectual property as security for a loan.

The basic public policy rationale for the protection of intellectual property is that IP laws facilitate and encourage disclosure of innovation into the public domain for the common good, by granting authors and inventors exclusive rights to exploit their works and invention for a limited period.

However, various schools of thought are critical of the very concept of intellectual property, and some characterise IP as *intellectual protectionism*. There is ongoing debate as to whether IP laws truly operate to confer the stated public benefits, and whether the protection they are said to provide is appropriate in the context of innovation derived from such things as traditional knowledge and folklore, and patents for software and business methods. Manifestations of this controversy can be seen in the way different jurisdictions decide whether to grant intellectual property protection in relation to subject matter of this kind, and the North-South divide on issues of the role and scope of intellectual property laws.

Ownership laws may vary widely among countries depending on the nature of the property of interest (e.g. firearms, real property, personal property, animals). Persons can own property directly. In most societies legal entities, such as corporations, trusts and nations (or governments) own property.

In the Inca empire, the dead emperors, who were considered gods, still controlled property after death.

Whether and to what Extent the State may Interfere with Property

Under United States law the principal limitations on whether and the extent to which the State may interfere with property rights are set by the Constitution. The "Takings" clause requires that the government (whether state or federal—for the 14th Amendment's due process clause imposes the 5th Amendment's takings clause on state governments) may take private property only for a public purpose, after exercising due process of law, and upon making "just compensation." If an interest is not deemed a "property" right, or the conduct is merely an intentional tort, these limitations do not apply and the doctrine of sovereign immunity precludes relief. Moreover, if the interference does not almost completely make the property valueless, the interference will not be deemed a taking but instead a mere regulation of use. On the other hand, some governmental regulations of property use have been deemed so severe that they have been considered "regulatory takings." Moreover, conduct sometimes deemed only a nuisance or other tort has been held a taking of property where the conduct was sufficiently persistent and severe.

SARA Hospitality (Hotel/Resort/Property Management System)

At one time, a hotel was just a place for temporary stay. Now hotels are also used for entertainment, marketing communication, business development, cultural programs, product launches, wining and dining, socializing, etc. To tap all these opportunities, today's hotels have to use IT to efficiently deliver all the services that a customer requires while simultaneously ensuring customer delight in each and every interaction.

SARA Hospitality covers reservation, check-in and check-out, services and facilities, guest details, kitchen and restaurant management, automatic billing, finance and administration, procurement, inventory control, payroll, employee data, and human resources management. The system is suitable for managing Hotels, Resorts and Properties.

Modules of SARA Hospitality Management System:

- Guest Reservation and Registration
- Guest Care
- Facilities Management and Scheduling
- Guest Record History

- Guest Billing
- Kitchen and Restaurant Management
- Finance and Administration
- Purchase Management
- Payroll
- Human Resources Management.

Asset Management

Asset management, broadly defined, refers to any system whereby things that are of value to an entity or group are monitored and maintained. It may apply to both tangible assets and to intangible concepts such as intellectual property and goodwill.

Asset Management is a systematic process of operating, maintaining, and upgrading assets cost-effectively, (American Associate of State Highway and Transportation Officials).

Alternative views of Asset Management in the engineering environment are:

- The practice of managing assets so that the greatest return is achieved (this concept is particularly useful for productive assets such as plant and equipment)
- the process by which built systems of facilities are monitored and maintained, with the objective of providing the best possible service to users (appropriate for public infrastructure assets).

Historical Background of Asset Management

Civilisation has always relied on its technological assets to support key functions like transport, public health, business and commerce.

There is a clear link between the provision and sophistication of technological assets and our modern lifestyle. Romans built a strong empire through their construction of roads, aqueducts and other assets. Similar storys are found when examining Asia, Africa, Europe and America.

Financial Asset Management:

- Investment management-the sector of the financial services industry that manages collective investment schemes and segregated client accounts.
- Global assets under management
- List of asset management firms.

Enterprise Asset Management: Enterprise asset management is the business processes and enabling information systems that support management of an organization's assets, both physical (such as buildings, equipment, infrastructure etc.) and non-physical such as:

- Physical asset management-the practice of managing the whole life cycle (design, construction, commissioning, operating, maintaining, repairing, modifying, replacing and decommissioning/disposal) of physical and infrastructure assets such as structures, production and service plant, power, water and waste treatment facilities, distribution networks, transport systems, buildings and other physical assets. Infrastructure asset management expands on this theme in relation primarily to public sector, utilities, property and transport systems.
- Fixed assets management-an accounting process that seeks to track fixed assets for the purposes of financial accounting.
- IT asset management-the set of business practices that join financial, contractual and inventory functions to support life cycle management and strategic decision making for the IT environment. This is also one of the processes defined within IT service management.
- Digital asset management – a form of electronic media content management that includes digital assets.

Public Asset Management: Public asset management expands the definition of Enterprise Asset Management (EAM) by incorporating the management of all things which are of value to a municipal jurisdiction and its citizens' expectations.

An EAM requires an asset registry (inventory of assets and their attributes) combined with a computerized maintenance management system. All public assets are interconnected and share proximity, and this connectivity is possible through the use of GIS.

GIS-centric public asset management standardizes data and allows interoperability, providing users the capability to reuse, coordinate, and share information in an efficient and effective manner by making the GIS geo-database the asset registry. A GIS-centric public asset management which standardizes data and allows interoperability, providing users the capability to reuse, coordinate, and share information in an efficient and effective manner.

In the United States the defacto GIS standard is the Esri GIS for utilities and municipalities. An Esri GIS platform combined with the overall public asset management umbrella of both physical "hard" assets and "soft" assets helps remove the traditional silos of structured municipal functions. While the hard assets are the typical physical assets or infrastructure assets, the soft assets of a municipality includes permits, license, code enforcement, right-of-ways and other land-focused work activities.

This definition of "public asset management" was coined and defined by Brian L. Haslam, President and CEO of a leading international GIS-centric Computerized Maintenance Management System (CMMS) company which software is certified by the National Association of GIS-Centric Solutions (NAGCS). GIS-centric public asset management is a system design approach for managing public assets that leverages the investment local governments continue to make in GIS and provides a common framework for sharing useful data from disparate systems. Permits, licenses, code enforcement, right-of-way, and other land-focused work activities are examples of land-focused public assets managed by local government. These public assets occupy location just as in-the-ground or above-ground public assets do.

Land-use development and planning is another area which is interconnected to other local government assets and work activities. Public Asset Management is the term that encompasses this subset of land-focused asset management, considering the importance that public assets affect other public assets and work activities and are important sources of revenue and are various points of citizen interaction.

Enterprise Asset Management

Enterprise asset management (EAM) means the whole life optimal management of the physical assets of an organization to maximize value. It covers such things as the design, construction, commissioning, operations, maintenance and decommissioning/replacement of plant, equipment and facilities. "Enterprise" refers to the management of the assets across departments, locations, facilities and, in some cases, business units. By managing assets across the facility, organizations can improve utilization and performance, reduce capital costs, reduce asset-related operating costs, extend asset life and subsequently improve ROA (return on assets).

The functions of asset management are taking a fundamental turn where organizations are moving from historical reactive (run-to-failure) models and beginning to embrace whole life planning, life cycle costing, planned and proactive maintenance and other industry best practices.

Some companies still regard physical asset management as just a more business-focused term for maintenance management-until they begin to realize the organization-wide impact and interdependencies with operations, design, asset performance, personnel productivity and lifecycle costs. This shift in focus exemplifies the progression from maintenance management to Enterprise Asset Management and is embodied in the British Standards specification PAS 55 (Requirements specification for the optimal management of physical infrastructure assets).

What is Enterprise Asset Management?

In capital-intensive industries such as utilities, process/discrete manufacturing, healthcare as well as real estate, physical assets (buildings, infrastructure and equipment) form a significant proportion of the total assets of the organization. These industries face the harsh realities of operating in highly competitive markets and dealing with high value assets and equipment where each failure is disruptive and costly. At the same time, they must also adhere to stringent occupational and environmental safety regulations.

It is thus important for organizations to maximize the return on investment from their asset base. Life Cycle Asset Management (LCAM) and EAM are paradigms employed to achieve that goal. Given a physical asset, the objective of LCAM is to extract maximum productivity from the asset and minimize the total costs involved in its acquisition, operations as well as maintenance. Quantitatively, the objective of asset management is to strike an optimal balance between maximizing Overall Asset Productivity (OAP) and minimizing Total Cost of Ownership (TCO). Furthermore, LCAM provides guidance on whether it is more cost-effective to continue to maintain, overhaul or replace a failing asset.

When the entire asset portfolio of the organization is considered, EAM takes over. As business and market requirements are dynamic, the output specifications for the organization's assets change constantly (e.g., increase in output capacity due to new customers). EAM provides the framework for capital and labor allocation decision processes across the competing categories of equipment addition/reduction, replacement, over-hauling, redundancy setup and maintenance budgets in order to meet business needs. Correspondingly, it merges the collective LCAM efforts and re-evaluates decisions based on long and short-term economic considerations at the enterprise level.

Public asset management expands the definition of Enterprise Asset Management (EAM) by incorporating the management of all things which are of value to a municipal jurisdiction and its citizen's expectations. An EAM requires an asset registry (inventory of assets and their attributes) combined with a computerized maintenance management system.

Public Asset Management is the term that considers the importance that public assets affect other public assets and work activities which are important sources of revenue for municipal governments and has various points of citizen interaction. The versatility and functionality of a GIS system allows for the control and management of all assets and land-focused activities.

All public assets are interconnected and share proximity, and this connectivity is possible through the use of GIS. GIS-centric public asset management standardizes data and allows interoperability, providing users the capability to reuse, coordinate, and share information in an efficient and effective manner by making the GIS geo-database the asset registry.

In the United States the defacto GIS standard is the ESRI GIS for utilities and municipalities. An ESRI GIS platform combined with the overall public asset management umbrella of both physical "hard" assets and "soft" assets helps remove the traditional silos of structured municipal functions which serves the citizens. While the hard assets are the typical physical assets or infrastructure assets, the soft assets of a municipality includes permits, license, code enforcement, right-of-ways and other land-focused work activities.

This definition of "public asset management" was coined and defined by Brian L. Haslam, President and CEO of a leading International ESRI GIS-centric Computerized Maintenance Management System (CMMS) company located in Utah whose software is certified by the National Association of GIS-Centric Solutions (NAGCS). GIS-centric public asset management is a system design approach for managing public assets that leverages the investment local governments continue to make in GIS and provides a common framework for sharing useful data from disparate systems.

Permits, licenses, code enforcement, right-of-way, and other land-focused work activities are examples of land-focused public assets managed by municipal governments. These public assets occupy location just as in-the-ground or above-ground public assets do. Land-use development and planning is another area which is interconnected to other local government assets and work activities.

Professional Bodies

Investment Recovery Association;

- Institute of Asset Management
- National Property Management Association (NPMA)
- Asset Management Council
- Plant Engineering and Maintenance Association of Canada
- American Water Works Association AWWA
- National Association of GIS-Centric Solutions NAGS.

Information Technology Enterprise Asset Management

ITEAM differs from EAM only in its focus on IT assets. This focus is important for a number of key reasons:

1. Organizational dependence on these assets
2. High cost, particularly of datacenter assets
3. Rapid pace of change/turn-over for assets.

ITEAM focuses on both hardware and software asset management, ensuring that the organization has the ability to manage these assets throughout their life. In the case of software, there is the added component of ensuring license compliance.

Why is EAM Important?

Competitive pressures force organizations to minimize asset total cost of ownership and streamline their asset management operations (these typically involve myriad activities ranging from inventory, parts and labor management to contracts and vendor management for new works). As downtimes become increasingly expensive, both in terms of lost production capacity and unfavorable publicity, organizations are compelled to maximize their asset productive life cycles via optimal maintenance programs. When EAM is used in collaboration with all other forms of service-based operations to achieve better customer retention, it is called Service Lifecycle Management (SLM).

In the event of asset failure, quick response time is critical. In recent years, stringent industry-specific environmental health and occupational safety regulations are being enforced by government oversight agencies, with industrial owners and operators responsible for compliance. Asset registers, risk registers, work planning and scheduling, life cycle costing and systematic methods for problem identification, root cause analysis and continuous improvement are increasingly seen as prerequesites for a robust asset management system.

By providing a platform for connecting people, processes, assets, industry-based knowledge and decision support capabilities based on quality information,EAM provides a holistic view of an organization's asset base, enabling managers to control and optimize their operations for quality and efficiency.

EAM System Challenges

EAM systems need a lot of high quality data to track and analyze the execution of business processes. Capturing data in the field using traditional paper forms and manually inputting it into the EAM system often turns out to be too expensive to be practical. This often slows adoption and erodes the ROI of many EAM deployments.

EAM systems are often not integrated with the rest of the company's enterprise systems (including purchasing, HR, inventory, etc.), which increases management overhead and prevents the organization from realizing the system's full potential.

Mobility

Role of Mobility Technology in EAM

Enterprises use mobility to improve their EAM system in a number of ways. First, mobility can be leveraged to improve dispatch processes. Traditionally, work order dispatch relies on an antiquated, paper-based system. This process is cumbersome because technicians are required travel back-and-forth between work sites and the dispatch center for new assignments. With mobility, technicians can receive their assignments in the field, spend more time working, and create work orders right on their devices.

Also, companies have been using mobility to allow their technicians to access EAM information while on-site. Mobile technology lets technicians view more EAM relevant data. As a result of this increased access, technicians are better prepared to service assets when they require maintenance, service, or inspection.

Finally, with mobile technology, field technicians have the ability to capture more, and better quality, EAM data. Improved data capturing processes allow for better analysis and evaluation; as a result, companies are quickly embracing mobile solutions. With the many uses for mobility, the EAM solution market has seen steady growth over the last few years. Commonly sought providers have solutions that enterprises deploy based upon factors, such as: ease of configurability, integration with back-end systems, cost, features, availability of support, etc. As companies continue to mobilize their EAM processes, the market is expected to continue expanding.

Healthcare Enterprise Asset Management

Healthcare enterprise asset management (HEAM) presents complexities not found in most other industries. Specifically, healthcare environments have a large number of relatively small, mobile, expensive and sophisticated pieces of equipment. Further, the availability, maintenance and cleanliness of these assets directly impacts the "environment of care" and patient safety, as well as the bottom line. Finally, hospitals are highly regulated and assets must be maintained in a manner that complies with JCAHO and U.S. Food and Drug Administration (FDA) requirements. HEAM can include the following components related to assets:

1. Inventory and depreciation
2. Scheduling of repair and maintenance
3. Location and logistics (RFID or barcode powered)
4. Availability and utilization
5. Safety monitoring and incident tracking
6. Total Lifecycle Cost
7. Performance management
8. Capital planning support.

HEAM provides complete visibility of the asset base across the health system, enabling active control of the planning, acquisition, tracking, maintenance and retirement of capital assets.

Real Estate

Real estate is a legal term (in some jurisdictions, such as the United Kingdom, Canada, Australia, USA, Dubai, Trinidad and Tobago and The Bahamas) that encompasses land along with improvements to the land, such as buildings, fences, wells and other site improvements that are fixed in location—immovable. Real estate law is the body of regulations and legal codes which pertain to such matters under a particular jurisdiction and include things such as commercial and residential real property transactions. Real estate is often considered synonymous with real property (sometimes called *realty*), in contrast with personal property (sometimes called *chattel* or *personalty* under *chattel law* or *personal property law*).

However, in some situations the term "real estate" refers to the land and fixtures together, as distinguished from "real property", referring to ownership of land and appurtenances, including anything of a permanent nature such as structures, trees, minerals, and the interest, benefits, and inherent rights thereof. Real property is typically considered to be immovable property. The terms *real estate* and *real property* are used primarily in common law, while civil law jurisdictions refer instead to immovable property.

Etymology

In law, the word *real* means relating to a thing (*res/rei*, thing, from O.Fr. *reel*, from L.L. *realis* "actual," from Latin. *res*, "matter, thing"), as distinguished from a person. Thus the law broadly distinguishes between "real" property (land and anything affixed to it) and "personal" property (everything else, *e.g.*, clothing, furniture, money). The conceptual difference was between immovable property, which would transfer title along with the land, and movable property, which a person would retain title to. The oldest use of the term "Real Estate" that has been preserved in historical records was in 1666. This use of "real" also reflects the ancient and feudal preference for land, and the ownership (and owners) thereof.

Some people have claimed that the word *real* in this sense is descended (like French *royal* and Spanish *real*) from the Latin word for 'king'. In the feudal system (which has left many traces in the common law) the king was the owner of all land, and everyone who occupied land paid him rent directly or indirectly (through lords who in turn paid the king), in cash, goods or services (including military service). Property tax, paid to the state, can be seen as a relic of that system, as is the term fee simple. However, this derivation of *real* is a misconception.

Real Estate Terminology and Practice Outside the United States (Around the World)

Real Estate as "Real Property" in the U.K.

In British usage, "real property", often shortened to just "property", generally refers to land and fixtures, while the term "real estate" is used mostly in the context of probate law, and means all interests in land held by a deceased person at death, excluding interests in money arising under a trust for sale of or charged on land.

In English Common Law, real property, real estate, realty, or immovable property is any subset of land that has been legally defined and the improvements to it made by human efforts: any buildings, machinery, wells, dams, ponds, mines, canals, roads, various property rights, and so forth. *Real property* and *personal property* are the two main subunits of property in *English Common Law*.

In countries with personal ownership of real property, civil law protects the status of real property in real-estate markets, where licensed agents, realtors, work in the market of buying and selling real estate. Scottish civil law calls real property *"heritable property"*, and in French-based law, it is called *immobilier*.

Identification of Real Property

To be of any value a claim to any property must be accompanied by a verifiable and legal property description. Such a description usually makes use of natural or manmade boundaries such as seacoasts, rivers, streams, the crests of ridges, lakeshores, highways, roads, and railroad tracks, and/or purpose-built artificial markers such as cairns, surveyor's posts, fences, official government surveying marks (such as ones affixed by the U.S. Geodetic Survey (USGS)), and so forth.

Estates and Ownership Interests Defined

The law recognizes different sorts of interests, called estates, in real property. The type of estate is generally determined by the language of the deed, lease, bill of sale, will, land grant, etc., through which the estate was acquired. Estates are distinguished by the varying property rights that vest in each, and that determine the duration and transferability of the various estates. A party enjoying an estate is called a "tenant."

Some important types of estates in land include:

- Fee simple: An estate of indefinite duration, that can be freely transferred. The most common and perhaps most absolute type of estate, under which the tenant enjoys the greatest discretion over the disposition of the property.
- Conditional Fee simple: An estate lasting forever as long as one or more conditions stipulated by the deed's grantor does not occur. If such a condition does occur, the property reverts to the grantor, or a remainder interest is passed on to a third party.
- Fee tail: An estate which, upon the death of the tenant, is transferred to his or her heirs.
- Life estate: An estate lasting for the natural life of the grantee, called a "life tenant." If a life estate can be sold, a sale does not

change its duration, which is limited by the natural life of the original grantee.

- o A life estate *pur autre vie* is held by one person for the natural life of another person. Such an estate may arise if the original life tenant sells her life estate to another, or if the life estate is originally granted *pur autre vie*.

- Leasehold: An estate of limited duration, as set out in a contract, called a lease, between the party granted the leasehold, called the lessee, and another party, called the lessor, having a longer lived estate in the property. For example, an apartment-dweller with a one year lease has a leasehold estate in her apartment. Lessees typically agree to pay a stated rent to the lessor.

A tenant enjoying an undivided estate in some property after the termination of some estate of limited duration, is said to have a "future interest." Two important types of future interests are:

- Reversion: A reversion arises when a tenant grants an estate of lesser maximum duration than his own. Ownership of the land returns to the original tenant when the grantee's estate expires. The original tenant's future interest is a reversion.
- Remainder: A remainder arises when a tenant with a fee simple grants someone a life estate or conditional fee simple, and specifies a third party to whom the land goes when the life estate ends or the condition occurs. The third party is said to have a remainder. The third party may have a legal right to limit the life tenant's use of the land.

Estates may be held jointly as joint tenants with rights of survivorship or as tenants in common. The difference in these two types of joint ownership of an estate in land is basically the inheritability of the estate and the shares of interest that each tenant owns.

In a joint tenancy with rights of survivorship deed, or JTWROS, the death of one tenant means that the surviving tenant(s) become the sole owner(s) of the estate. Nothing passes to the heirs of the deceased tenant. In some jurisdictions, the specific words "with right of survivorship" must be used, or the tenancy will assumed to be tenants in common without rights of survivorship. The co-owners always take a JTWROS deed in equal shares, so each tenant must own an equal share of the property regardless of his/her contribution to purchase price. If the property is someday sold or subdivided, the proceeds must be distributed equally with no credits given for any excess than any one co-owner may have contributed to purchase the property.

The death of a co-owner of a tenants in common (TIC) deed will have a heritable portion of the estate in proportion to his ownership interest which is presumed to be equal among all tenants unless otherwise stated in the transfer deed. However, if TIC property is sold or subdivided, in some States, Provinces, etc., a credit can be automatically made for unequal contributions to the purchase price (unlike a partition of a JTWROS deed). However, do not forget that these considerations

Real property may be owned jointly with several tenants, through devices such as the condominium, housing cooperative, and building cooperative.

Jurisdictional Peculiarities

In the law of almost every country, the state is the ultimate owner of all land under its jurisdiction, because it is the sovereign, or supreme lawmaking authority. Physical and corporate persons do not have allodial title; they do not "own" land but only enjoy estates in the land, also known as "equitable interests."

England and Wales

In the United Kingdom, The Crown is held to be the ultimate owner of all real property in the realm. This fact is material when, for example, property has been disclaimed by its erstwhile owner, in which case the law of escheat applies. In some other jurisdictions (not including the United States), real property is held absolutely.

English law has retained the common law distinction between real property and personal property, whereas the civil law distinguishes between "movable" and "immovable" property. In English law, real property is not confined to the ownership of property and the buildings sited thereon – often referred to as "land." Real property also includes many legal relationships between individuals or owners of land that are purely conceptual. One such relationship is the easement, where the owner of one property may enjoy the right to pass over a neighboring property. Another is the various "incorporeal hereditaments," such as profits a prendre, where an individual may have the right to take crops from land that is part of another's estate.

English law retains a number of forms of property which are largely unknown in other common law jurisdictions such as the advowson, chancel repair liability and lordships of the manor. These are all classified as real property, as they would have been protected by real actions in the early common law.

USA

Each U.S. State except Louisiana has its own laws governing real property and the estates therein, grounded in the common law. In Arizona, real property is generally defined as land and the things permanently attached to the land. Things that are permanently attached to the land, which also can be referred to as improvements, include homes, garages, and buildings. Manufactured homes can obtain an affidavit of affixture.

Economic Aspects of Real Property

Land use, land valuation, and the determination of the incomes of landowners, are among the oldest questions in economic theory. Land is an essential input (factor of production) for agriculture, and agriculture is by far the most important economic activity in preindustrial societies. With the advent of industrialization, important new uses for land emerge, as sites for factories, warehouses, offices, and urban agglomerations. Also, the value of real property taking the form of man-made structures and machinery increases relative to the value of land alone. The concept of real property eventually comes to encompass effectively all forms of tangible fixed capital. with the rise of extractive industries, real property comes to encompass natural capital. With the rise of tourism and leisure, real property comes to include scenic and other amenity values.

. Starting in the 1960s, as part of the emerging field of law and economics, economists and legal scholars began to study the property rights enjoyed by tenants under the various estates, and the economic benefits and costs of the various estates. This resulted in a much improved understanding of the:

- Property rights enjoyed by tenants under the various estates. These include the right to:
    - Decide how a piece of real property is used;
    - Exclude others from enjoying the property;
    - Transfer (alienate) some or all of these rights to others on mutually agreeable terms;
- Nature and consequences of transaction costs when changing and transferring estates.

For an introduction to the economic analysis of property law, Ellickson (1993) broadens the economic analysis of real property with a variety of facts drawn from history and ethnography.

Historical Background

The word "real" ultimately derives from Latin *res* "thing" and was used to Middle English to mean "relating to things, especially real property".

In common law, real property was property that could be protected by some form of real action, in contrast to personal property, where a plaintiff would have to resort to another form of action. As a result of this formalist approach, some things the common law deems to be land would not be classified as such by most modern legal systems, for example an advowson (the right to present to the living of a church) was real property. By contrast the rights of a leaseholder originate in personal actions and so the common law originally treated a leasehold as part of personal property.

The law now broadly distinguishes between real property (land and anything affixed to it) and personal property (everything else, *e.g.*, clothing, furniture, money). The conceptual difference was between immovable property, which would transfer title along with the land, and movable property, which a person would retain title to.

In modern legal systems derived from English common law, classification of property as *real* or *personal* may vary somewhat according to jurisdiction or, even within jurisdictions, according to purpose, as in defining whether and how the property may be taxed.

Bethell (1998) contains much historical information on the historical evolution of real property and property rights.

Real Estate in Mexico and Central America

The real estate businesses in Mexico, Canada, Guam and Central America are different from the way that they are conducted in the United States.

Some similarities include a variety of legal formalities (with professionals such as real estate agents generally employed to assist the buyer); taxes need to be paid (but typically less than those in U.S.); legal paperwork will ensure title; and a neutral party such as a title company will handle documentation and money to make the smooth exchange between the parties. Increasingly, U.S. title companies are doing work for U.S. buyers in Mexico and Central America.

Prices are often much cheaper than most areas of the U.S., but in many locations, prices of houses and lots are as expensive as the U.S., one example being Mexico City. U.S. banks have begun to give home loans for properties in Mexico, but, so far, not for other Latin American countries.

One important difference from the United States is that each country has rules regarding where foreigners can buy. For example, in Mexico, foreigners cannot buy land or homes within 50 km (31 mi) of the coast or 100 km (62 mi) from a border unless they hold title in a Mexican Corporation or a Fideicomiso (a Mexican trust). In Honduras, however, they may buy beach front property directly in their name. There are different rules regarding certain types of property: *ejidal land* – communally held farm property – can only be sold after a lengthy entitlement process, but that does not prevent them from being offered for sale.

In Costa Rica, real estate agents do not need a license to operate, but the transfer of property requires a lawyer. In Mexico, real estate agents do not need a license to operate, but the transfer of property requires a notary public.

Business Sector

With the development of private property ownership, real estate has become a major area of business, commonly referred to as commercial real estate. Purchasing real estate requires a significant investment, and each parcel of land has unique characteristics, so the real estate industry has evolved into several distinct fields. Specialists are often called on to valuate real estate and facilitate transactions. Some kinds of real estate businesses include:

- Appraisal: Professional valuation services
- Brokerages: A mediator who charges a fee to facilitate a real estate transaction between the two parties.
- Development: Improving land for use by adding or replacing buildings
- Net leasing
- Property management: Managing a property for its owner(s)
- Real estate marketing: Managing the sales side of the property business
- Real estate investing: Managing the investment of real estate
- Relocation services: Relocating people or business to a different country
- Corporate Real Estate: Managing the real estate held by a corporation to support its core business—unlike managing the real estate held by an investor to generate income.

Within each field, a business may specialize in a particular type of real estate, such as residential, commercial, or industrial property. In addition, almost all construction business effectively has a connection to real estate.

Professional university-level education in real estate is primarily focused at the graduate level. Focus in towards the commercial real estate sector, primarily real estate development or investment rather than residential real estate sales conducted by a REALTOR.

"Internet real estate" is a term coined by the internet investment community relating to ownership of domain names and the similarities between high quality internet domain names and real-world, prime real estate.

Residential Real Estate

The legal arrangement for the right to occupy a dwelling in some countries is known as the housing tenure. Types of housing tenure include owner occupancy, Tenancy, housing cooperative, condominiums (individually parceled properties in a single building), public housing, squatting, and cohousing. The occupants of a residence constitute a household.

Residences can be classified by, if, and how they are connected to neighboring residences and land. Different types of housing tenure can be used for the same physical type. For example, connected residents might be owned by a single entity and leased out, or owned separately with an agreement covering the relationship between units and common areas and concerns.

- Attached/multi-unit dwellings
    - o Apartment-An individual unit in a multi-unit building. The boundaries of the apartment are generally defined by a perimeter of locked or lockable doors. Often seen in multi-story apartment buildings.
    - o Multi-family house-Often seen in multi-story detached buildings, where each floor is a separate apartment or unit.
    - o Terraced house (a.k.a. *townhouse* or *rowhouse*)-A number of single or multi-unit buildings in a continuous row with shared walls and no intervening space.
    - o Condominium-Building or complex, similar to apartments, owned by individuals. Common grounds and common areas within the complex are owned and shared jointly. There are *townhouse* or *rowhouse* style condominiums as well.
    - o Cooperative (a.k.a. "co-op)-A type of multiple ownership in which the residents of a multi-unit housing complex own

shares in the cooperative corporation that owns the property, giving each resident the right to occupy a specific apartment or unit.

- Semi-detached dwellings
    - o Duplex Two units with one shared wall.
- Single-family detached home
- Portable dwellings
    - o Mobile homes-Potentially a full-time residence which can be (might not in practice be) movable on wheels.
    - o Houseboats-A floating home
    - o Tents-Usually very temporary, with roof and walls consisting only of fabric-like material.

The size of an apartment or house can be described in square feet or meters. In the United States, this includes the area of "living space", excluding the garage and other non-living spaces. The "square meters" figure of a house in Europe may report the total area of the walls enclosing the home, thus including any attached garage and non-living spaces, which makes it important to inquire what kind of surface definition has been used.

It can be described more roughly by the number of rooms. A studio apartment has a single bedroom with no living room (possibly a separate kitchen). A one-bedroom apartment has a living or dining room separate from the bedroom. Two bedroom, three bedroom, and larger units are common. (A bedroom is defined as a room with a closet for clothes storage.)

Major categories in India and the Asian Subcontinent;

- Housing Societies (CGHS)
- Condominiums
- Builder flats
- Chawls
- Havelis
- Lal Dora-Where people carry out commercial and residential activities both.

The size is measured in Gaz (square yards), Quila, Marla, Beegha, and acre.

Market Sector Value

According to *The Economist*, "developed economies'" assets at the end of 2002 were the following:

- Residential property: $48 trillion;
- Commercial property: $14 trillion;
- Equities: $20 trillion;
- Government bonds: $20 trillion;
- Corporate bonds: $13 trillion;
- Total: $115 trillion.

That makes real estate assets 54% and financial assets 46% of total stocks, bonds, and real estate assets. Assets not counted here are bank deposits, insurance "reserve" assets, natural resources, and human assets. It is not clear if all debt and equity investments are counted in the categories equities and bond.

Mortgages in Real Estate

In recent years, many economists have recognized that the lack of effective real estate laws can be a significant barrier to investment in many developing countries. In most societies, rich and poor, a significant fraction of the total wealth is in the form of land and buildings.

In most advanced economies, the main source of capital used by individuals and small companies to purchase and improve land and buildings is mortgage loans (or other instruments). These are loans for which the real property itself constitutes collateral. Banks are willing to make such loans at favorable rates in large part because, if the borrower does not make payments, the lender can foreclose by filing a court action which allows them to take back the property and sell it to get their money back. For investors, profitability can be enhanced by using an off plan or pre-construction strategy to purchase at a lower price which is often the case in the pre-construction phase of development.

But in many developing countries there is no effective means by which a lender could foreclose, so the mortgage loan industry, as such, either does not exist at all or is only available to members of privileged social classes.

Chapter 2

Inventory Management

Inventory means a list compiled for some formal purpose, such as the details of an estate going to probate, or the contents of a house let furnished. This remains the prime meaning in British English. In the USA and Canada the term has developed from a list of goods and materials to the goods and materials themselves, especially those held available in stock by a business; and this has become the primary meaning of the term in North American English, equivalent to the term "stock" in British English. In accounting, inventory or stock is considered an asset.

Inventory management is primarily about specifying the shape and percentage of stocked goods. It is required at different locations within a facility or within many locations of a supply network to proceed the regular and planned course of production and stock of materials.

The scope of inventory management concerns the fine lines between replenishment lead time, carrying costs of inventory, asset management, inventory forecasting, inventory valuation, inventory visibility, future inventory price forecasting, physical inventory, available physical space for inventory, quality management, replenishment, returns and defective goods and demand forecasting. Balancing these competing requirements leads to optimal inventory levels, which is an on-going process as the business needs shift and react to the wider environment.

Inventory management involves a retailer seeking to acquire and maintain a proper merchandise assortment while ordering, shipping, handling, and related costs are kept in check. It also involves systems and processes that identify inventory requirements, set targets, provide replenishment techniques, report actual and projected inventory status and handles all functions related to the tracking and management of material. This would include the monitoring of material moved into and out of stockroom locations and the reconciling of the inventory balances. Also may include ABC analysis, lot tracking, cycle counting support etc. Management of the inventories, with the primary objective of determining/controlling stock levels within the physical distribution function to balance the need for product availability against the need for minimizing stock holding and handling costs.

Business Inventory

The Reasons for Keeping Stock

There are three basic reasons for keeping an inventory:

1. Time-The time lags present in the supply chain, from supplier to user at every stage, requires that you maintain certain amounts of inventory to use in this "lead time."
2. Uncertainty-Inventories are maintained as buffers to meet uncertainties in demand, supply and movements of goods.
3. Economies of scale-Ideal condition of "one unit at a time at a place where a user needs it, when he needs it" principle tends to incur lots of costs in terms of logistics. So bulk buying, movement and storing brings in economies of scale, thus inventory.

All these stock reasons can apply to any owner or product stage.

- Buffer stock is held in individual workstations against the possibility that the upstream workstation may be a little delayed in long setup or change over time. This stock is then used while that changeover is happening. This stock can be eliminated by tools like SMED.

These classifications apply along the whole Supply chain, not just within a facility or plant.

Where these stocks contain the same or similar items, it is often the work practice to hold all these stocks mixed together before or after the sub-process to which they relate. This 'reduces' costs. Because they are mixed up together there is no visual reminder to operators of the adjacent sub-processes or line management of the stock, which is due to a particular cause and should be a particular individual's responsibility with inevitable consequences. Some plants have centralized stock holding across sub-processes, which makes the situation even more acute.

Special Terms used in Dealing with Inventory

- *Stock Keeping Unit* (SKU) is a unique combination of all the components that are assembled into the purchasable item. Therefore, any change in the packaging or product is a new SKU. This level of detailed specification assists in managing inventory.
- *Stockout* means running out of the inventory of an SKU.
- "New old stock" (sometimes abbreviated NOS) is a term used in business to refer to merchandise being offered for sale that was manufactured long ago but that has never been used. Such merchandise may not be produced anymore, and the new old stock may represent the only market source of a particular item at the present time.

Typology

1. Buffer/safety stock
2. Cycle stock (Used in batch processes, it is the available inventory, excluding buffer stock)
3. De-coupling (Buffer stock held between the machines in a single process which serves as a buffer for the next one allowing smooth flow of work instead of waiting the previous or next machine in the same process)
4. Anticipation stock (Building up extra stock for periods of increased demand-e.g. ice cream for summer)
5. Pipeline stock (Goods still in transit or in the process of distribution-have left the factory but not arrived at the customer yet).

Inventory Examples

While accountants often discuss inventory in terms of goods for sale, organizations-manufacturers, service-providers and not-for-profits-also have inventories (fixtures, furniture, supplies,...) that they do not intend to sell. Manufacturers', distributors', and wholesalers' inventory tends to cluster in warehouses. Retailers' inventory may exist in a warehouse or in a shop or store accessible to customers. Inventories not intended for sale to customers or to clients may be held in any premises an organization uses. Stock ties up cash and, if uncontrolled, it will be impossible to know the actual level of stocks and therefore impossible to control them.

While the reasons for holding stock were covered earlier, most manufacturing organizations usually divide their "goods for sale" inventory into:

- Raw materials-materials and components scheduled for use in making a product.
- Work in process, WIP-materials and components that have begun their transformation to finished goods.
- Finished goods-goods ready for sale to customers.
- Goods for resale-returned goods that are salable.

For example:

Manufacturing

A canned food manufacturer's materials inventory includes the ingredients to form the foods to be canned, empty cans and their lids (or coils of steel or aluminum for constructing those components), labels, and anything else (solder, glue,...) that will form part of a finished can. The firm's work in process includes those materials from the time of release to the work floor until they become complete and ready for sale to wholesale or retail customers. This may be vats of prepared food, filled cans not yet labeled or sub-assemblies of food components. It may also include finished cans that are not yet packaged into cartons or pallets. Its finished good inventory consists of all the filled and labeled cans of food in its warehouse that it has manufactured and wishes to sell to food distributors (wholesalers), to grocery stores (retailers), and even perhaps to consumers through arrangements like factory stores and outlet centers.

Examples of case studies are very revealing, and consistently show that the improvement of inventory management has two parts: the capability of the organisation to manage inventory, and the way in which it chooses to do so. For example, a company may wish to install a complex inventory system, but unless there is a good understanding of the role of inventory and its parameters, and an effective business process to support that, the system cannot bring the necessary benefits to the organisation in isolation.

Typical Inventory Management techniques include Pareto Curve ABC Classification and Economic Order Quantity Management. A more sophisticated method takes these two techniques further, combining certain aspects of each to create The K Curve Methodology. A case study of k-curve benefits to one company shows a successful implementation.

Unnecessary inventory adds enormously to the working capital tied up in the business, as well as the complexity of the supply chain. Reduction and elimination of these inventory 'wait' states is a key concept in Lean. Too big an inventory reduction too quickly can cause a business to be anorexic. There are well-proven processes and techniques to assist in inventory planning and strategy, both at the business overview and part number level. Many of the big MRP/and ERP systems do not offer the necessary inventory planning tools within their integrated planning applications.

Principle of Inventory Proportionality

Purpose

Inventory proportionality is the goal of demand-driven inventory management. The primary optimal outcome is to have the same number of days' (or hours', etc.) worth of inventory on hand across all products so that the time of runout of all products would be simultaneous. In such a case, there is no "excess inventory," that is, inventory that would be left over of another product when the first product runs out. Excess inventory is sub-optimal because the money spent to obtain it could have been utilized better elsewhere, i.e. to the product that just ran out.

The secondary goal of inventory proportionality is inventory minimization. By integrating accurate demand forecasting with inventory management, replenishment inventories can be scheduled to arrive just in time to replenish the product destined to run out first, while at the same time balancing out the inventory supply of all products to make their inventories more proportional, and thereby closer to achieving the primary goal. Accurate demand forecasting also allows the desired inventory proportions to be dynamic by determining expected sales out into the future; this allows for inventory to be in proportion to expected short-term sales or consumption rather than to past averages, a much more accurate and optimal outcome.

Integrating demand forecasting into inventory management in this way also allows for the prediction of the "can fit" point when inventory storage is limited on a per-product basis.

Applications

The technique of inventory proportionality is most appropriate for inventories that remain unseen by the consumer. As opposed to "keep full" systems where a retail consumer would like to see full shelves of the product they are buying so as not to think they are buying something old, unwanted or stale; and differentiated from the "trigger point" systems where product is reordered when it hits a certain level; inventory proportionality is used effectively by just-in-time manufacturing processes and retail applications where the product is hidden from view.

One early example of inventory proportionality used in a retail application in the United States is for motor fuel. Motor fuel (e.g. gasoline) is generally stored in underground storage tanks. The motorists do not know whether they are buying gasoline off the top or bottom of the tank, nor need they care. Additionally, these storage tanks have a maximum capacity and cannot be overfilled. Finally, the product is expensive. Inventory proportionality is used to balance the inventories of the different grades of motor fuel, each stored in dedicated tanks, in proportion to the sales of each grade. Excess inventory is not seen or valued by the consumer, so it is simply cash sunk (literally) into the ground. Inventory proportionality minimizes the amount of excess inventory carried in underground storage tanks. This application for motor fuel was first developed and implemented by Petrolsoft Corporation in 1990 for Chevron Products Company. Most major oil companies use such systems today.

Roots

The use of inventory proportionality in the United States is thought to have been inspired by Japanese just-in-time parts inventory management made famous by Toyota Motors in the 1980s.

High-level Inventory Management

It seems that around 1880 there was a change in manufacturing practice from companies with relatively homogeneous lines of products to vertically integrated companies with unprecedented diversity in processes and products. Those companies (especially in metalworking) attempted to achieve success through economies of scope-the gains of jointly producing two or more products in one facility. The managers now needed information on the effect of product-mix decisions on overall profits and therefore needed accurate product-cost information. A variety of attempts to achieve this were unsuccessful due to the huge overhead of the information processing of the time. However, the burgeoning need for financial reporting after 1900 created unavoidable pressure for financial accounting of stock and the management need to cost manage products became overshadowed. In particular, it was the need for audited accounts that sealed the fate of managerial cost accounting. The dominance of financial reporting accounting over management accounting remains to this day with few exceptions, and the financial reporting definitions of 'cost' have distorted effective management 'cost' accounting since that time. This is particularly true of inventory.

Hence, high-level financial inventory has these two basic formulas, which relate to the accounting period:

1. Cost of Beginning Inventory at the start of the period + inventory purchases within the period + cost of production within the period = cost of goods available
2. Cost of goods available " cost of ending inventory at the end of the period = cost of goods sold

The benefit of these formulae is that the first absorbs all overheads of production and raw material costs into a value of inventory for reporting. The second formula then creates the new start point for the next period and gives a figure to be subtracted from the sales price to determine some form of sales-margin figure.

Manufacturing management is more interested in *inventory turnover ratio* or *average days to sell inventory* since it tells them something about relative inventory levels.

Inventory turnover ratio (also known as inventory turns) = cost of goods sold/Average Inventory = Cost of Goods Sold/((Beginning Inventory + Ending Inventory)/2) and its inverse.

Average Days to Sell Inventory = Number of Days a Year/Inventory Turnover Ratio = 365 days a year/Inventory Turnover Ratio.

This ratio estimates how many times the inventory turns over a year. This number tells how much cash/goods are tied up waiting for the process and is a critical measure of process reliability and effectiveness. So a factory with two inventory turns has six months stock on hand, which is generally not a good figure (depending upon the industry), whereas a factory that moves from six turns to twelve turns has probably improved effectiveness by 100%. This improvement will have some negative results in the financial reporting, since the 'value' now stored in the factory as inventory is reduced.

While these accounting measures of inventory are very useful because of their simplicity, they are also fraught with the danger of their own assumptions. There are, in fact, so many things that can vary hidden under this appearance of simplicity that a variety of 'adjusting' assumptions may be used. These include:

- Specific Identification
- Weighted Average Cost

- Moving-Average Cost
- FIFO and LIFO.

Inventory Turn is a financial accounting tool for evaluating inventory and it is not necessarily a management tool. Inventory management should be forward looking. The methodology applied is based on historical cost of goods sold. The ratio may not be able to reflect the usability of future production demand, as well as customer demand.

Business models, including Just in Time (JIT) Inventory, Vendor Managed Inventory (VMI) and Customer Managed Inventory (CMI), attempt to minimize on-hand inventory and increase inventory turns. VMI and CMI have gained considerable attention due to the success of third-party vendors who offer added expertise and knowledge that organizations may not possess.

Accounting for Inventory

Each country has its own rules about accounting for inventory that fit with their financial-reporting rules.

For example, organizations in the U.S. define inventory to suit their needs within US Generally Accepted Accounting Practices (GAAP), the rules defined by the Financial Accounting Standards Board (FASB) (and others) and enforced by the U.S. Securities and Exchange Commission (SEC) and other federal and state agencies. Other countries often have similar arrangements but with their own GAAP and national agencies instead.

It is intentional that financial accounting uses standards that allow the public to compare firms' performance, cost accounting functions internally to an organization and potentially with much greater flexibility. A discussion of inventory from standard and Theory of Constraints-based (throughput) cost accounting perspective follows some examples and a discussion of inventory from a financial accounting perspective.

The internal costing/valuation of inventory can be complex. Whereas in the past most enterprises ran simple, one-process factories, such enterprises are quite probably in the minority in the 21st century. Where 'one process' factories exist, there is a market for the goods created, which establishes an independent market value for the good. Today, with multistage-process companies, there is much inventory that would once have been finished goods which is now held as 'work in process' (WIP). This needs to be valued in the accounts, but the valuation is a management decision since there is no market for the partially finished product. This somewhat arbitrary 'valuation' of WIP combined with the allocation of overheads to it has led to some unintended and undesirable results.

Financial Accounting

An organization's inventory can appear a mixed blessing, since it counts as an asset on the balance sheet, but it also ties up money that could serve for other purposes and requires additional expense for its protection. Inventory may also cause significant tax expenses, depending on particular countries' laws regarding depreciation of inventory, as in Thor Power Tool Company v. Commissioner.

Inventory appears as a current asset on an organization's balance sheet because the organization can, in principle, turn it into cash by selling it. Some organizations hold larger inventories than their operations require in order to inflate their apparent asset value and their perceived profitability.

In addition to the money tied up by acquiring inventory, inventory also brings associated costs for warehouse space, for utilities, and for insurance to cover staff to handle and protect it from fire and other disasters, obsolescence, shrinkage (theft and errors), and others. Such holding costs can mount up: between a third and a half of its acquisition value per year.

Businesses that stock too little inventory cannot take advantage of large orders from customers if they cannot deliver. The conflicting objectives of cost control and customer service often pit an organization's financial and operating managers against its sales and marketing departments. Salespeople, in particular, often receive sales-commission payments, so unavailable goods may reduce their potential personal income. This conflict can be minimised by reducing production time to being near or less than customers' expected delivery time. This effort, known as "Lean production" will significantly reduce working capital tied up in inventory and reduce manufacturing costs.

Role of Inventory Accounting

By helping the organization to make better decisions, the accountants can help the public sector to change in a very positive way that delivers increased value for the taxpayer's investment. It can also help to incentivise progress and to ensure that reforms are sustainable and effective in the long term, by ensuring that success is appropriately recognized in both the formal and informal reward systems of the organization.

To say that they have a key role to play is an understatement. Finance is connected to most, if not all, of the key business processes within the organization. It should be steering the stewardship and accountability systems that ensure that the organization is conducting its business in an appropriate, ethical manner. It is critical that these foundations are firmly laid. So often they are the litmus test by which public confidence in the institution is either won or lost.

Finance should also be providing the information, analysis and advice to enable the organizations' service managers to operate effectively. This goes beyond the traditional preoccupation with budgets – how much have we spent so far, how much do we have left to spend? It is about helping the organization to better understand its own performance. That means making the connections and understanding the relationships between given inputs – the resources brought to bear – and the outputs and outcomes that they achieve. It is also about understanding and actively managing risks within the organization and its activities.

FIFO vs. LIFO Accounting

When a merchant buys goods from inventory, the value of the inventory account is reduced by the cost of goods sold (COGS). This is simple where the CoG has not varied across those held in stock; but where it has, then an agreed method must be derived to evaluate it. For commodity items that one cannot track individually, accountants must choose a method that fits the nature of the sale. Two popular methods that normally exist are: FIFO and LIFO accounting (first in-first out, last in-first out). FIFO regards the first unit that arrived in inventory as the first one sold. LIFO considers the last unit arriving in inventory as the first one sold. Which method an accountant selects can have a significant effect on net income and book value and, in turn, on taxation. Using LIFO accounting for inventory, a company generally reports lower net income and lower book value, due to the effects of inflation. This generally results in lower taxation. Due to LIFO's potential to skew inventory value, UK GAAP and IAS have effectively banned LIFO inventory accounting.

Standard Cost Accounting

Standard cost accounting uses ratios called efficiencies that compare the labour and materials actually used to produce a good with those that the same goods would have required under "standard" conditions. As long as similar actual and standard conditions obtain, few problems arise. Unfortunately, standard cost accounting methods developed about 100 years ago, when labor comprised the most important cost in manufactured goods. Standard methods continue to emphasize labor efficiency even though that resource now constitutes a (very) small part of cost in most cases.

Standard cost accounting can hurt managers, workers, and firms in several ways. For example, a policy decision to increase inventory can harm a manufacturing manager's performance evaluation. Increasing inventory requires increased production, which means that processes must operate at higher rates. When (not if) something goes wrong, the process takes longer and uses more than the standard labor time. The manager appears responsible for the excess, even though s/he has no control over the production requirement or the problem.

In adverse economic times, firms use the same efficiencies to downsize, rightsize, or otherwise reduce their labor force. Workers laid off under those circumstances have even less control over excess inventory and cost efficiencies than their managers.

Many financial and cost accountants have agreed for many years on the desirability of replacing standard cost accounting. They have not, however, found a successor.

Theory of Constraints Cost Accounting

Eliyahu M. Goldratt developed the Theory of Constraints in part to address the cost-accounting problems in what he calls the "cost world." He offers a substitute, called throughput accounting, that uses throughput (money for goods sold to customers) in place of output (goods produced that may sell or may boost inventory) and considers labor as a fixed rather than as a variable cost. He defines inventory simply as everything the organization owns that it plans to sell, including buildings, machinery, and many other things in addition to the categories listed here. Throughput accounting recognizes only one class of variable costs: the truly variable costs, like materials and components, which vary directly with the quantity produced.

Finished goods inventories remain balance-sheet assets, but labor-efficiency ratios no longer evaluate managers and workers. Instead of an incentive to reduce labor cost, throughput accounting focuses attention on the relationships between throughput (revenue or income) on one hand and controllable operating expenses and changes in inventory on the other. Those relationships direct attention to the constraints or bottlenecks that prevent the system from producing more throughput, rather than to people-who have little or no control over their situations.

National Accounts

Inventories also play an important role in national accounts and the analysis of the business cycle. Some short-term macroeconomic fluctuations are attributed to the inventory cycle.

Distressed Inventory

Also known as distressed or expired stock, distressed inventory is inventory whose potential to be sold at a normal cost has passed or will soon pass. In certain industries it could also mean that the stock is or will soon be impossible to sell.

Examples of distressed inventory include products that have reached their expiry date, or have reached a date in advance of expiry at which the planned market will no longer purchase them (e.g. 3 months left to expiry), clothing that is defective or out of fashion, and old newspapers or magazines. It also includes computer or consumer-electronic equipment that is obsolete or discontinued and whose manufacturer is unable to support it. One current example of distressed inventory is the VHS format.

In 2001, Cisco wrote off inventory worth US $2.25 billion due to duplicate orders. This is one of the biggest inventory write-offs in business history.

Inventory Credit

Inventory credit refers to the use of stock, or inventory, as collateral to raise finance. Where banks may be reluctant to accept traditional collateral, for example in developing countries where land title may be lacking, inventory credit is a potentially important way of overcoming financing constraints. This is not a new concept; archaeological evidence suggests that it was practiced in Ancient Rome. Obtaining finance against stocks of a wide range of products held in a bonded warehouse is common in much of the world.

It is, for example, used with Parmesan cheese in Italy. Inventory credit on the basis of stored agricultural produce is widely used in Latin American countries and in some Asian countries. A precondition for such credit is that banks must be confident that the stored product will be available if they need to call on the collateral; this implies the existence of a reliable network of certified warehouses. Banks also face problems in valuing the inventory.

The possibility of sudden falls in commodity prices means that they are usually reluctant to lend more than about 60% of the value of the inventory at the time of the loan.

Depreciation

Depreciation refers to two very different but related concepts:

1. the decline in value of assets (fair value depreciation), and
2. the allocation of the cost of assets to periods in which the assets are used (depreciation with the matching principle).

The former affects values of businesses and entities. The latter affects net income. Generally the cost is allocated, as depreciation expense, among the periods in which the asset is expected to be used. Such expense is recognized by businesses for financial reporting and tax purposes.

Methods of computing depreciation may vary by asset for the same business. Methods and lives may be specified in accounting and/or tax rules in a country. Several standard methods of computing depreciation expense may be used, including fixed percentage, straight line, and declining balance methods. Depreciation expense generally begins when the asset is placed in service. Example: a depreciation expense of 100 per year for 5 years may be recognized for an asset costing 500.

In economics, depreciation is the gradual and permanent decrease in the economic value of the capital stock of a firm, nation or other entity, either through physical depreciation, obsolescence or changes in the demand for the services of the capital in question. If capital stock is C_0 at the beginning of a period, investment is I and depreciation D, the capital stock at the end of the period, C_1, is $C_0 + I\text{-}D$.

Accounting Concept

In determining the profits (net income) from an activity, the receipts from the activity must be reduced by appropriate costs. One such cost is the cost of assets used but not currently consumed in the activity. Such costs must be allocated to the period of use. The cost of an asset so allocated is the difference between the amount paid for the asset and the amount expected to be received upon its disposition. Depreciation is any method of allocating such net cost to those periods expected to benefit from use of the asset. The asset is referred to as a depreciable asset. Depreciation is a method of allocation, not valuation.

Any business or income producing activity using tangible assets may incur costs related to those assets. Where the assets produce benefit in future periods, the costs must be deferred rather than treated as a current expense. The business then records depreciation expense as an allocation of such costs for financial reporting. The costs are allocated in a rational and systematic manner as depreciation expense to each period in which the asset is used, beginning when the asset is placed in service. Generally this involves four criteria:

- cost of the asset,
- expected salvage value, also known as residual value of the asset,
- estimated useful life of the asset, and
- a method of apportioning the cost over such life.

Depreciable Basis

Cost generally is the amount paid for the asset, including all costs related to acquisition. In some countries or for some purposes, salvage value may be ignored. The rules of some countries specify lives and methods to be used for particular types of assets. However, in most countries the life is based on business experience, and the method may be chosen from one of several acceptable methods.

Net Basis

When a depreciable asset is sold, the business recognizes gain or loss based on net basis of the asset. This net basis is cost less depreciation.

Impairment

Accounting rules also require that an impairment charge or expense be recognized if the value of assets declines unexpectedly. Such charges are usually nonrecurring, and may relate to any type of asset.

Depletion and Amortization

Depletion and amortization are similar concepts for mineral assets (including oil) and intangible assets, respectively.

Effect on Cash

Depreciation expense does not require current outlay of cash. However, the cost of acquiring depreciable assets may require such outlay. Thus, depreciation does not affect a statement of cash flows, but cost of acquiring assets does.

Historical Cost

Depreciation is generally recognized under historical cost systems of accounting. Some proposals for fair value accounting have no provision for systematic depreciation expense.

Accumulated Depreciation

While depreciation expense is recorded on the income statement of a business, its impact is generally recorded in a separate account and disclosed on the balance sheet as accumulated depreciation, under fixed assets, according to most accounting principles. Accumulated depreciation is known as a contra account, because it separately shows a negative amount that is directly associated with another account.

Without an accumulated depreciation account on the balance sheet, depreciation expense is usually charged against the relevant asset directly. The values of the fixed assets stated on the balance sheet will decline, even if the business has not invested in or disposed of any assets. The amounts will roughly approximate fair value. Otherwise, depreciation expense is charged against accumulated depreciation. Showing accumulated depreciation separately on the balance sheet has the effect of preserving the historical cost of assets on the balance sheet. If there have been no investments or dispositions in fixed assets for the year, then the values of the assets will be the same on the balance sheet for the current and prior year.

Amortization

Amortization (or amortisation) is the process of decreasing, or accounting for, an amount over a period. The word comes from Middle English *amortisen* to kill, alienate in mortmain, from Anglo-French *amorteser*, alteration of *amortir*, from Vulgar Latin *admortire* to kill, from Latin ad-+ mort-, mors death.

When used in the context of a home purchase, amortization is the process by which your loan principal decreases over the life of your loan. With each mortgage payment that you make, a portion of your payment is applied towards reducing your principal and another portion of your payment is applied towards paying the interest on the loan.

Consumption of Fixed Capital

Consumption of fixed capital (CFC) is a term used in business accounts, tax assessments and national accounts for depreciation of fixed assets. CFC is used in preference to "depreciation" to emphasize that fixed capital is used up in the process of generating new output, and because unlike depreciation it is not valued at historic cost but at current market value (so-called "economic depreciation"); CFC may also include other expenses incurred in using or installing fixed assets beyond actual depreciation charges. Normally the term applies only to *producing* enterprises, but sometimes it applies also to real estate assets.

CFC refers to a depreciation charge (or "write-off") against the gross income of a producing enterprise, which reflects the decline in value of fixed capital being operated with. Fixed assets will decline in value after they are purchased for use in production, due to wear and tear, changed market valuation and possibly market obsolescence. Thus, CFC represents a *compensation* for the loss of value of fixed assets to an enterprise.

According to the 2008 manual of the United Nations System of National Accounts;

> *"Consumption of fixed capital is the decline, during the course of the accounting period, in the current value of the stock of fixed assets owned and used by a producer as a result of physical deterioration, normal obsolescence or normal accidental damage. The term depreciation is often used in place of consumption of fixed capital but it is avoided in the SNA because in commercial accounting the term depreciation is often used in the context of writing off historic costs whereas in the SNA consumption of fixed capital is dependent on the current value of the asset."-UNSNA 2008, section H.)*

CFC tends to increase as the asset gets older, even if the efficiency and rental remain constant to the end. The larger the depreciation write-off, the larger the gross income of a business. Consequently, business owners consider this accounting entry as very important; after all, it affects both their income, and their ability to invest.

Valuation

How much the depreciation charge actually will be, depends mainly on the depreciation rates which enterprises are *officially permitted* to charge for tax purposes (usually fixed by law), and on how fixed assets themselves are *valued* for accounting purposes. This makes the assessment of CFC quite complex, because fixed assets may be valued for instance at:

- historic (acquisition) cost
- operating value (as part of a "going concern")
- accrual value
- current average sale-value in the market

- current replacement cost
- cash value
- economic value
- insured value
- scrap value
- deflated value (allowing for price inflation).

By how much then, do fixed assets used in production truly *decline* in value, within an accounting period? How should they be valued? This can be arguable and very difficult to answer, and in practice, various conventions are adopted by accountants and auditors within the framework of legal rules and economic theory.

In addition, the depreciation schedules imposed by tax departments may *differ* from the *actual* depreciation of business assets at market rates. Often, governments permit depreciation write-offs *higher* than true depreciation, to provide an incentive to enterprises for new investment. But this is not always the case; the tax rate might sometimes be lower than the real market-based rate. Furthermore, businesses might engage in creative accounting and deliberately state their assets and liabilities held at a balance date, or interpret the figures in some other way, to increase the amount of depreciation write-offs, and thus boost their income (how this is done will depend a lot on tax law).

For all these reasons, economists distinguish between different kinds of depreciation rates, arguing that the "true" consumption of fixed capital is really the *economic* depreciation, assessed by relating financial data to mathematical models, to arrive at a figure that "seems credible". The economic depreciation rate is based on observations of the average selling prices of assets at different ages. The economic depreciation rate is therefore a market-based depreciation rate, i.e. it is based on what an asset of a given age would currently sell for in the market.

Consumption of Fixed Capital in National Accounts

In national accounts, CFC is a component of value added or Gross Domestic Product, and regarded as a cost of production. It is defined in general terms as the decline, in an accounting period, of the current value of the stock of fixed assets owned and used by a producer as a result of physical deterioration, normal obsolescence or normal accidental damage.

The UNSNA manual notes that "The consumption of fixed capital is one of the most important elements in the System... It may account for 10 per cent or more of total GDP." CFC is defined "in a way that is theoretically appropriate and relevant *for purposes of economic analysis*". Its value may therefore diverge considerably from depreciation actually recorded in business accounts, or as allowed for taxation purposes, especially if there is price inflation.

In principle, CFC is calculated using the actual or estimated prices and rentals of fixed assets prevailing at the time the production takes place, and not at the times fixed assets were originally acquired. The "historic costs" of fixed assets, i.e., the prices originally paid for them, may become quite irrelevant for the calculation of consumption of fixed capital, if prices change sufficiently over time.

Unlike depreciation as calculated in business accounts, CFC in national accounts is, in principle, *not* a method of allocating the costs of past expenditures on fixed assets over subsequent accounting periods. Rather, fixed assets at a given moment in time are valued according to the remaining benefits derived from their use.

Depreciation charges in business accounts are adjusted in national accounts from historic costs to *current* prices, in conjunction with estimates of the capital stock.

Inclusions in CFC

In UNSNA, included are:

- all tangible and intangible fixed assets owned by producers.
- fixed assets constructed to improve land, such as drainage systems, dykes, or breakwaters or on assets which are constructed on or through land-roads, railway tracks, tunnels, dams, etc.
- Losses of fixed assets due to normal accidental damage, i.e. damage caused to assets used in production resulting from their exposure to the risk of fires, storms, accidents due to human errors, etc.
- interest costs incurred in acquiring fixed assets, which may consist either of actual interest paid on borrowed funds, or the loss of interest incurred as a result of investing own funds in the purchase of the fixed asset, instead of a financial asset. Whether owned or rented, the full cost of using the fixed asset in production is thus measured by the actual or imputed rental

on the asset, and not by depreciation alone. If the fixed asset is actually rented under an operating lease or similar contract, the rental is recorded under Intermediate consumption as the purchase of a service produced by the lessor. If the user and the owner are one and the same unit, CFC is considered to represent only part of the cost of using the asset.

- Certain insurance premiums related to the acquisition or maintenance of fixed assets.

Exclusions from CFC

In UNSNA, excluded are:

- the value of fixed assets destroyed by acts of war, or exceptional events such as major natural disasters, earthquakes, volcanic eruptions, tidal waves, exceptionally severe hurricanes, etc. (e.g. Hurricane Katrina) which occur very infrequently.
- valuables (precious metals, precious stones, etc.)
- the depletion or degradation of non-produced assets such as land, mineral or other deposits, or coal, oil, or natural gas.
- losses due to unexpected technological developments that may significantly shorten the service lives of a group of existing fixed assets.

Gross and Net Capital Stocks

In UNSNA, the value at current prices of the *gross capital stock* is obtained, by using price indices for fixed assets at current replacement cost, irrespective of the age of the assets.

The net, or written-down value of a fixed capital asset is equal to its current replacement cost, less CFC accrued up to that point in time.

Criticism

The main criticism made of the way national accounts value CFC is that in trying to arrive at an "economic" concept and magnitude of depreciation, they arrive at figures which are at variance with the real world; even if the figures are argued to be "more realistic" from an economic point of view, they include and exclude portions of gross business income without making this explicit. The business income cited in the social account is not true business income, but a *theoretical* income which is derived from true business income.

Thus, the criticism centres both on the valuation principles used, and the additional items included in the aggregate, which are not directly related to depreciation charges at all. Yet the whole computation strongly affects the size of the GDP figure and the aggregate profit figures provided. Because of the way CFC is calculated, aggregate profit (or [operating surplus]] the residual item in the product account) is likely to be understated, independently of the actual profit calculation, which is usually derived from tax data.

Ultimately, the distinction drawn between that portion of business operating expenditure included in CFC beyond depreciation, in contrast to that portion of operating expenditure included in Intermediate consumption may appear rather capricious, rather than theoretically justified.

In Marxian economics, the official concept of CFC is also disputed, because it is argued that CFC really should refer to the value transferred by living labor from fixed assets to new output. Consequently, operating expenditures associated with fixed assets other than depreciation should be regarded as either as circulating constant capital, faux frais of production or surplus value, depending on the case. Furthermore, the measured difference between economic depreciation and actual depreciation charges will either add or lower the magnitude of total surplus value.

Deferred Financing Costs

Deferred financing costs or debt issuance costs is an accounting concept meaning costs associated with issuing debt (loans and bonds), such as various fees and commissions paid to investment banks, law firms, auditors, regulators, and so on. Since these payments generate future benefits, they are treated as an asset. The costs are capitalised, reflected in the balance sheet as an asset, and amortised over the finite life of the underlying debt instrument. The unamortized amounts are included in other assets in the accompanying consolidated balance sheets. Early debt repayment results in expensing these costs.

In case of issuing securities without specific maturity, such as perpetual preferred stock, financing costs are not capitalised and expensed immediately.

Tax Treatment For U.S. federal income tax purposes, DFC are...

Expense

In common usage, an expense or expenditure is an outflow of money to another person or group to pay for an item or service, or for a category of costs. For a tenant, rent is an expense. For students or parents, tuition is an expense. Buying food, clothing, furniture or an automobile is often referred to as an expense. An expense is a cost that is "paid" or "remitted", usually in exchange for something of value. Something that seems to cost a great deal is "expensive". Something that seems to cost little is "inexpensive". "Expenses of the table" are expenses of dining, refreshments, a feast, etc.

In accounting, expense has a very specific meaning. It is an outflow of cash or other valuable assets from a person or company to another person or company. This outflow of cash is generally one side of a trade for products or services that have equal or better current or future value to the buyer than to the seller. Technically, an expense is an event in which an asset is used up or a liability is incurred. In terms of the accounting equation, expenses reduce owners' equity. The International Accounting Standards Board defines expenses as;

> *...decreases in economic benefits during the accounting period in the form of outflows or depletions of assets or incurrences of liabilities that result in decreases in equity, other than those relating to distributions to equity participants.*

Bookkeeping for Expenses

In double-entry bookkeeping, expenses are recorded as a debit to an expense account (an income statement account) and a credit to either an asset account or a liability account, which are balance sheet accounts. An expense decreases assets or increases liabilities. Typical business expenses include salaries, utilities, depreciation of capital assets, and interest expense for loans. The purchase of a capital asset such as a building or equipment is not an expense.

Cash Flow

In a cash flow statement, expenditures are divided into operating, investing, and financing expenditures.

- Operational expense (OPEX)—salary for employees
- Capital expenditure (CAPEX)—buying equipment
- Financing expense—interest expense for loans and bonds.

An important issue in accounting is whether a particular expenditure is classified as an expense, which is reported immediately on the business's income statement; or whether it is classified as a capital expenditure or an expenditure subject to depreciation, which is not an expense. These latter types of expenditures are reported as expenses when they are depreciated by businesses that use accrual-basis accounting, which is most large businesses and all C corporations.

The most common interpretation of whether an expense is of capital or income variety depends upon its term. Viewing an expense as a purchase helps alleviate this distinction. If, soon after the "purchase", that which was expensed holds no value then it is usually identified as an expense. If it retains value soon and long after the purchase, it will be viewed as capital with life that should be amortized/depreciated and retained on the Balance Sheet.

Deduction of Business Expenses Under the US Tax Code

For tax purposes, the Internal Revenue Code permits the deduction of business expenses in the taxable year in which those expenses are paid or incurred. This is in contrast to capital expenditures that are paid or incurred to acquire an asset. Expenses are costs that do not acquire, improve, or prolong the life of an asset. For example, a person who buys a new truck for a business would be making a capital expenditure because they have acquired a new business-related asset. This cost could not be deducted in the current taxable year. However, the gas the person buys during that year to fuel that truck would be considered a deductible expense. The cost of purchasing gas does not improve or prolong the life of the truck but simply allows the truck to run.

Even if something qualifies as an expense, it is not necessarily deductible. As a general rule, expenses are deductible if they relate to a taxpayer's trade or business activity or if the expense is paid or incurred in the production or collection of income from an activity that does not rise to the level of a trade or business (investment activity).

Section 162(a) of the Internal Revenue Code is the deduction provision for business or trade expenses. In order to be a trade or business expense and qualify for a deduction, it must satisfy 5 elements in addition to qualifying as an expense. It must be (1) ordinary and (2) necessary (Welch v. Helvering, 290 U.S. 111, defines this as necessary for the development of the business at least in that they were appropriate and helpful). Expenses paid to preserve one's reputation do not appear to qualify (Welch v. Helvering). In addition, it must be (3) paid or incurred during the taxable year. It must be paid (4) in carrying on (meaning not prior to the start of a business or in creating it) (5) a trade or business activity. To qualify as a trade or business activity, it must be continuous and regular, and profit must be the primary motive.

Section 212 of the Internal Revenue Code is the deduction provision for investment expenses. In addition to being an expense and satisfying elements 1-4 above, expenses are deductible as an investment activity under Section 212 of the Internal Revenue Code if they are (1) for the production or collection of income, (2) for the management, conservation, or maintenance of property held for the production of income, or (3) in connection with the determination, collection, or refund of any tax.

In investing, one controversy that mounted throughout 2002 and 2003 was whether companies should report the granting of stock options to employees as an expense on the income statement, or should not report this at all in the income statement, which is what had previously been the norm.

Expense Report

An expense report is a form of document that contains all the expenses that an individual as incurred as a result of the business operation. For example, if the owner of a business travels to another location for a meeting, the cost of travel, the meals, and all other expenses that he/she has incurred may be added to the expense report. Consequently, these expenses will be considered business expenses and are tax deductible.

Revaluation of Fixed Assets

In finance, a revaluation of fixed assets is a technique that may be required to accurately describe the true value of the capital goods a business owns. This should be distinguished from planned depreciation, where the recorded decline in value of an asset is tied to its age.

Fixed assets are held by an enterprise for the purpose of producing goods or rendering services, as opposed to being held for resale in the normal course of business. For example, machines, buildings, patents or licenses can be fixed assets of a business.

The purpose of a revaluation is to bring into the books the fair market value of fixed assets. This may be helpful in order to decide whether to invest in another business. If a company wants to sell one of its assets, it is revalued in preparation for sales negotiations.

Reasons for Revaluation

It is common to see companies revaluing their fixed assets. It is important to make the distinctions between a 'private' revaluation to a 'public' revaluation which is carried out in the financial reports. The purposes are varied:

- To show the true rate of return on capital employed.
- To conserve adequate funds in the business for replacement of fixed assets at the end of their useful lives. Provision for depreciation based on historic cost will show inflated profits and lead to payment of excessive dividends.
- To show the fair market value of assets which have considerably appreciated since their purchase such as land and buildings.
- To negotiate fair price for the assets of the company before merger with or acquisition by another company.
- To enable proper internal reconstruction, and external reconstruction.
- To issue shares to existing shareholders (rights issue) or for an external issue of shares (public issue of shares).
- To get fair market value of assets, in case of sale and leaseback transaction.
- When the company intends to take a loan from banks/financial institutions by mortgaging its fixed assets. Proper revaluation of assets would enable the company to get a higher amount of loan.
- Sale of an individual asset or group of assets.
- In financial firms revaluation reserves are required for regulatory reasons. They are included when calculating a firm's funds to give a fairer view of resources. Only a portion of the firm's total funds (usually about 20%) can be loaned or in the hands of any one counterparty at any one time(Large Exposure Regulations).
- To decrease the 'leverage ratio' (the ratio of debt to equity).

Methods of Revaluation of Fixed Assets

The common methods used in revaluing assets are:

Indexation

Under this method, indices are applied to the cost value of the assets to arrive at the current cost of the assets. The Indices by the departments of Statistical Bureau or Economic Surveys may be used for the revaluation of assets.

Current Market Price (CMP)

- Land values can be estimated by using recent prices for similar plots of land sold in the area. However, certain adjustments will have to be made for the plus and minus points of the land possessed by the company. This may be done with the assistance of brokers and agencies dealing in land, or by a licensed appraiser.
- Buildings values can be estimated by a realtor (real estate dealer) or Chartered Surveyor (in the UK) in a similar manner to land.
- Plant & Machinery): The CMP can be obtained from suppliers of the assets concerned. However, with efflux of time, many earlier brands are not available in the market due to closure of companies manufacturing them. Similarly, there is change in the models manufactured by a company from time to time. Comparison of assets to most similar types available for sale, new or used, can provide an estimate of value.

CMP of an asset 'n' years old = (CMP of new asset/useful life of asset)*(useful life of asset –n).

Appraisal Method

Under this method, technical experts are called in to carry out a detailed examination of the assets with a view to determining their fair market value. Proper appraisal is necessary when the company is taking out an insurance policy for protection of its fixed assets. It ensures that the fixed assets are neither over-insured nor under-insured. The factors which are considered in determining the value of an asset, are as follows-:

- Date of purchase.
- Extent of use i.e. single shift, double shift, triple shift.
- Type of asset. Whether the asset is a general purpose or special purpose asset?
- Repairs & Maintenance policy of the enterprise.
- Availability of spares in the future, mainly in the case of imported machines.
- Future demand for the product manufactured by an asset.
- If the asset is part of a bigger fixed asset, the life of the latter is crucial.
- To have the true value for the assets.

Selective Revaluation and why it should be Avoided

Selective revaluation can be defined as revaluation of specific assets within a class or all assets within a specific location.

A manufacturing company may have its manufacturing facilities spread over different locations. Suppose it decides to undertake a revaluation of its plant & machinery. Selective revaluation will mean revaluing specific assets (such as boiler, heater, central air-conditioning system) at all locations, or revaluing all items of Plant & Machinery at a particular location only.

Such revaluation will lead to unrepresentative amounts being shown in the Fixed Assets Register (FAR). In case of revaluation of specific assets of a class, while some assets will be shown at a revalued amount others will be shown at historic cost. The same will happen in case of revaluation of all assets of plant & machinery at a particular location only.

It does not sound logical and correct to value fixed assets using different bases. Similarly, depreciation on such assets too will be faulty.

Points to be Considered before Revaluation is Undertaken

Before revaluation is undertaken, it is necessary to take into confidence the Production Department (PD), Accounts Department (AD), and the Technical Department (TD) in the company. Similarly, liaison with external appraisers becomes necessary. Generally, a team comprising officials from the PD, AD, and the TD is formed to liaison with appraisers and undertake/supervise the task of revaluation of fixed assets.

- Why is the revaluation necessary?
- What is the most suitable method, taking into account the type of fixed assets, statutory requirements, availability of required information? Should the values arrived at by one method be crosschecked with the values derived from another method?
- What assets are to be revalued?
- What is the period within which the revaluation has to be completed?
- Laying down guidelines for the revaluation.
- What modifications will be required in the FAR to show revalued figures in place of historic figures? Similarly, depreciation will be computed twice. One taking into account the historic cost, and the other as per revalued figures.

Upward Revaluation of Fixed Assets

The FASB in the U.S. does not allow upward revaluation of fixed assets to reflect fair market values although it is compulsory to account for impairment in fixed assets (downward revaluation of fixed assets) as per FASB Statement No. 144, Accounting for the Impairment or Disposal of Long-Lived Assets.

In other countries, upward revaluation is mainly done for fixed assets such as land, and real estate whose value keeps rising from year to year. It seems the concept of upward revaluation of fixed assets such as real estate has not been widely welcomed by a majority of companies in USA on account of fear of paying higher property and capital gains taxes. Further, the provision against upward restatement ensures conservative valuation.

The United Kingdom, Australia, and India allow upward revaluation in the values of fixed assets to bring them in consonance with fair market values. However, the law requires disclosure of the basis of revaluation, amount of revaluation made to each class of assets (for a specified period after the financial year in which revaluation is made), and other information. Similarly, law prohibits payment of dividend out of any reserve created as a result of upward revaluation of fixed assets. The law in Australia has been amended recently to allow for the payment of dividends from the increase in value of non-current assets in certain instances where a company meets other liquidity tests.

Important Points

1. The increase in value of fixed assets because of revaluation of fixed assets is credited to 'Revaluation Reserve', and is not available for distribution as dividend. Revaluation Reserve is treated as a Capital Reserve.
2. The increase in depreciation arising out of revaluation of fixed assets is debited to revaluation reserve and the normal depreciation to Profit and Loss account.
3. Selection of the suitable method of revaluation is extremely important. The most used method is the appraisal method. Methods such as indexation, and reference to current market prices are also used. However, when these methods are used they are crosschecked with the values arrived at by using the appraisal method.
4. When any asset, which is revalued, is sold, the part of loss resulting due to revaluation is debited to the 'Revaluation Reserve'.

5. When assets are revalued, every Balance Sheet shall show for a specified period of years, the amount of increase/decrease made in respect of each class of assets. Similarly, the increased/ decreased value shall be shown in place of the original cost.
6. In case of assets such as land and buildings, revaluation is desirable as their value increases over time and is carried out every 3 to 5 years. In case of plant & machinery, revaluation is carried out only if there is a strong case for it. In case of depreciable assets such as vehicles, furniture & fittings, office equipments etc., revaluation is not carried out.
7. Revaluation should not result in the net book value of an asset exceeding its recoverable value.
8. Revaluation does not mean only an upward revision in the book values of the asset. It can also mean a downward revision (also called impairment) in the book values of the assets. However, any downward revision in the book values of the assets is immediately written off to the Profit & Loss account.
9. On upward revaluation of a fixed asset, which has been previously subject to downward revaluation, the amount of upward revaluation as is equal to the amount expensed previously is credited to the Profit & Loss a/c.

Writing Down Allowance

Businesses in the United Kingdom are entitled to claim capital allowances to reduce the Corporation or Income Tax payable on profits.

Capital allowances are claimed on certain purchases or investments under the Capital Allowances Act 2001.

Capital allowances are available on plant and machinery, certain types of buildings-including converting space above commercial premises to flats for renting-and research and development facilities and equipment.

The plant and machinery is claimed on the second fix (all the work after plastering to the finished building).

Under Revenue & Customs rules, when owners spend money buying or improving a property they can offset some of the expenditure against profits of general income. While most firms are aware they can offset the cost of plants and machinery bought for work, few realise they may be able to claim capital allowances on commercial premises they own. However where a capital allowances claim has been made on a property a new purchaser can only make another claim valuing the palnt and machinery at the same rate as claimed previously. There is a popular misconception amongst people even in the capital allowances claims field that a secondary claim is not possible at all. Also further claims can be made on a property where it is extended or re-developed but only on those new elements of plant and machinery introduced to the building.

The amount of the allowance depends on what you're claiming for. In some cases, the rates are different in the year you make the purchase from those in subsequent years.

You can claim capital allowances on:

- The cost of vans and cars, machines, scaffolding, ladders, tools, equipment, furniture, computers and similar items you use in your business
- Expenditure on plant and machinery
- Items you used privately before using them in your business
- You cannot claim for things you buy or sell as your trade-these are claimed as business expenses. If you buy on hire purchase, you can claim a capital allowance on the original cost of the item but the interest and other charges count as business expenses.

Writing down allowance, in United Kingdom Taxation, is the annual rate at which capital allowances can be claimed. This rate is reduced or extended if the chargeable period is shorter or longer than one year.

The writing down allowance is the rate which applies in the absence of initial or first year allowances. The rate applies on a straight line basis for industrial buildings, hotels, agricultural and forestry buildings and works. A reducing balance basis is used for all other assets.

Total writing down allowances may not exceed the balance of expenditure after deducting initial or first year allowances.

Technical

Capital allowance reliefs can be set against the client's taxable profits reducing the amount payable. Companies pay tax at 21% or 28%, whilst individuals pay tax at 20%, 40% or 50%. Please note as it is an allowance against taxable profit, you have to be a tax payer to benefit, therefore this does not normally apply to property owned in SIPPS or by charities and trusts. Allowances are generated when a business client builds or acquires commercial property. The amount of plant contained within the build or acquired property is the key to maximising the relief.

The claim should be considered as an effective discount and cash contribution to the construction cost or purchase price. The claim provides a tax saving that accrues over time. It is possible to claim allowances on investment properties but plant let in a "dwelling house" is excluded. Blocks of flats, halls of residence etc will therefore qualify.

For property that is being acquired, the specialist can apportion the purchase price under a recognised HMRC formula, and this is where the inherent property skill can maximise the claim with optimal costing of the plant contained within the property.

Chapter 3

Building Services Engineering

Building services engineering is the engineering of the internal environment and environmental impact of a building. It essentially brings buildings and structures to life.

Building services engineers are responsible for the design, installation, operation and monitoring of the mechanical, electrical and public health systems required for the safe, comfortable and environmentally friendly operation of modern buildings. The term "building services engineering" is widely used in the United Kingdom, Canada and Australia, however in the United States of America, it is also known as architectural engineering or building engineering.

Introduction

Building services engineering comprises Mechanical engineering, Electrical engineering and Plumbing or Public health (MEP) engineering, all of which are further sub-divided into the following:

- Communication lines, telephones and IT networks (ICT)
- Energy supply-gas, electricity and renewable sources
- Escalators and lifts
- Fire detection and protection
- Heating, ventilation and air conditioning (HVAC)
- Lightning protection
- Low voltage (LV) systems, distribution boards and switchgear
- Natural lighting and artificial lighting, and building facades
- Security and alarm systems

- Ventilation and refrigeration
- Water, drainage and plumbing.

Building services engineers work closely with other construction professionals; architects, structural engineers and quantity surveyors. They influence the architecture of a building and play a significant role on the sustainability and energy demand of a building. Within building services engineering, new roles are emerging, for example in the areas of renewable energy, sustainability, low carbon technologies and energy management. With buildings accounting for around 50% of all carbon emissions, building services engineers play a significant role in combating climate change. As such, a typical building services engineer has a wide-ranging career path:

- Design: *designing layouts and requirements for building services for residential or commercial developments.*
- Construction: *supervising the construction of the building services, commissioning systems and ongoing maintenance and operation of services.*
- Environmental: *developing new energy saving methods for construction, designing new and improved energy conservation systems for buildings.*
- Heating, ventilation and air conditioning (HVAC): *specialising in the design, development, construction and operation of HVAC systems.*
- Electrical technology: *specialising in the design and development of electrical systems required for safe and energy sustaining operation of buildings.*

In 1976 Chartered Institution of Building Services Engineers (CIBSE) was founded and received a Royal Charter in the United Kingdom, and formally recognising building services engineering as a profession. Its objectives of the Institution are to:

> *'support the Science, Art and Practice of building services engineering, by providing our members and the public with first class information and education services and promoting the spirit of fellowship which guides our work.'*

In recent years there has been increasing emphasis on sustainable and green design by the UK government, including in engineered building systems. Building services engineers increasingly seek BREEAM (BRE Environmental Assessment Method), CIBSE Low

Carbon Consultants (LCC) and Energy Assessors (LCEA) status in addition to their Professional Engineering registration.

Building Services Engineering Software

Many building services firms use computer-aided engineering (CAE) software programs, created either in-house or by external parties, to assist in their system design and analysis. This method has many benefits, including easier and more exhaustive visualization of proposed solutions, the ability to create virtual models for analysis and calculations, and the ease of use in spatial planning.

Central Heating

A central heating system provides warmth to the whole interior of a building (or portion of a building) from one point to multiple rooms. When combined with other systems in order to control the building climate, the whole system may be a HVAC (heating, ventilation and air conditioning) system.

Central heating differs from local heating in that the heat generation occurs in one place, such as a furnace room in a house or a mechanical room in a large building (though not necessarily at the "central" geometric point). The most common method of heat generation involves the combustion of fossil fuel in a furnace or boiler. The resultant heat then gets distributed: typically by forced-air through ductwork, by water circulating through pipes, or by steam fed through pipes. Increasingly, buildings utilize solar-powered heat sources, in which case the distribution system normally uses water circulation.

In much of northern Europe and in urban portions of Russia, where people seldom require air conditioning in homes due to the temperate climate, most new housing comes with central heating installed. Such areas normally use gas heaters, district heating, or oil-fired systems. In the western and southern United States natural-gas-fired central forced-air systems occur most commonly; these systems and central-boiler systems both occur in the far northern regions of the USA. Steam-heating systems, fired by coal, oil or gas, feature in the USA, Russia and Europe: primarily for larger buildings. Electrical heating systems occur less commonly and are only practical with low cost electricity or when geothermal heat pumps are used. Considering the combined system of central generating plant and electric resistance heating, the overall efficiency will be less than for direct use of fossil fuel for space heating.

History

Some buildings in the Roman Empire used central heating systems, conducting air heated by furnaces through empty spaces under the floors and out of pipes in the walls — a system known as a *hypocaust*. A similar system of central heating was used in ancient Korea, where it is known as *ondol*. It is thought that the ondol system dates back to the Koguryo or Three Kingdoms (37 BC-AD 668) period when excess heat from stoves were used to warm homes.

In the early medieval Alpine upland, a simpler central heating system where heat travelled through underfloor channels from the furnace room replaced the Roman hypocaust at some places. In Reichenau Abbey a network of interconnected underfloor channels heated the 300 m^2 large assembly room of the monks during the winter months. The degree of efficiency of the system has been calculated at 90%.

In the 13th century, the Cistercian monks revived central heating in Christian Europe using river diversions combined with indoor wood-fired furnaces. The well-preserved Royal Monastery of Our Lady of the Wheel (founded 1202) on the Ebro River in the Aragon region of Spain provides an excellent example of such an application.

The Roman hypocaust continued to be used on a smaller scale during late Antiquity and by the Umayyad caliphate, while later Muslim builder employed a simpler system of underfloor pipes.

By about 1700 Russian engineers had started designing hydrologically based systems for central heating. The Summer Palace (1710–1714) of Peter the Great in Saint Petersburg provides the best extant example. Slightly later, in 1716, came the first use of water in Sweden to distribute heat in buildings. Martin Triewald, a Swedish engineer, used this method for a greenhouse at Newcastle upon Tyne. Jean Simon Bonnemain (1743–1830), a French architect, introduced the technique to industry on a cooperative, at Château du Pêcq, near Paris.

Angier March Perkins developed and installed some of the earliest steam-heating systems in the 1830s. The first was installed in the home of Governor of the Bank of England John Horley Palmer so that he could grow grapes in England's cold climate.

Franz San Galli, a Polish-born Russian businessman living in St. Petersburg, invented the radiator between 1855-1857, which was a major step in the final shaping of modern central heating.

Water Heating

Common components of a central heating system using water-circulation include:

- Gas supply lines (sometimes including a propane tank), oil tank and supply lines or district heating supply lines
- Boiler (or a heat exchanger for district heating) — heats water in a closed-water system
- Pump — circulates the water in the closed system
- Radiators — wall-mounted panels through which the heated water passes in order to release heat into rooms.

Engineers in the United Kingdom and in other parts of Europe commonly combine the needs of room heating with hot-water heating and storage. These systems occur less commonly in the USA. In this case, the heated water in a sealed system flows through a heat exchanger in a hot-water tank or hot-water cylinder where it heats water from the normal water supply before that water gets fed to hot-water outlets in the house. These outlets may service hot-water taps or appliances such as washing machines or dishwashers.

Sealed Water-circulating System

A sealed system provides a form of central heating in which the water used for heating usually circulates independently of the building's normal water supply. An expansion tank contains compressed gas, separated from the sealed-system water by a diaphragm. This allows for normal variations of pressure in the system. A safety valve allows water to escape from the system when pressure becomes too high, and a valve can open to replenish water from the normal water supply if the pressure drops too low. Sealed systems offer an alternative to open-vent systems, in which steam can escape from the system, and gets replaced from the building's water supply via a feed and central storage system.

Electric and Gas-fired Heaters

Electric heating or resistance heating converts electricity directly to heat. Electric heat is often more expensive than heat produced by combustion appliances like natural gas, propane, and oil. Electric resistance heat can be provided by baseboard heaters, space heaters, radiant heaters, furnaces, wall heaters, or thermal storage systems.

Electric heaters are usually part of a fan coil which is part of a central air conditioner. They circulate heat by blowing air across the heating element which is supplied to the furnace through return air ducts. Blowers in electric furnaces move air over one to five resistance coils or elements which are usually rated at five kilowatts. The heating elements activate one at a time to avoid overloading the electrical system. Overheating is prevented by a safety switch called a limit controller or limit switch. This limit controller may shut the furnace off if the blower fails or if something is blocking the air flow. The heated air is then sent back through the home through supply ducts.

In larger commercial applications, central heating is provided through an air handler which incorporates similar components as a furnace but on a larger scale.

Hydronic and Steam Systems

Hydronic heating systems are systems that circulate a medium for heating. Hydronic radiant floor heating systems use a boiler or district heating to heat water and a pump to circulate the hot water in plastic pipes installed in a concrete slab. The pipes, embedded in the floor, carry heated water that conducts warmth to the surface of the floor where it broadcasts heat energy to the room above.

Hydronic systems circulate hot water for heating. Steam heating systems are similar to heating water systems, except steam is used as the heating medium instead of water.

Hydronic heating systems generally consist of a boiler or district heating heat exchanger, hot water circulating pumps, distribution piping, and a fan coil unit or a radiator located in the room or space. Steam heating systems are similar except no circulating pumps are required.

Hydronic systems are closed loop: the same fluid is heated and then reheated. Hydronic heating systems are also used with antifreeze solutions in ice and snow melt systems for walkways, parking lots and streets. They are more commonly used in commercial and whole house radiant floor heat projects, while electric radiant heat systems are more commonly used in smaller "spot warming" applications.

Heat Pumps

In mild climates a heat pump can be used to air condition the building during hot weather, and to warm the building using heat extracted from outdoor air in cold weather. Air-source heat pumps are generally uneconomic for outdoor temperatures much below freezing. In colder climates, geothermal heat pumps can be used to extract heat from the ground. For economy, these systems are designed for average low winter temperatures and use supplemental heating for extreme low temperature conditions. The advantage of the heat pump is that it reduces the purchased energy required for building heating; often geothermal source systems also supply domestic hot water. Even in places where fossil fuels provide most electricity, a geothermal system may offset greenhouse gas production since most of the energy furnished for heating is supplied from the environment, with only 15–30% purchased.

Environmental Aspects

From an energy-efficiency standpoint considerable heat gets lost or goes to waste if only a single room needs heating, since central heating has distribution losses and (in the case of forced-air systems particularly) may heat some unoccupied rooms without need. In such buildings which require isolated heating, one may wish to consider non-central systems such as individual room heaters, fireplaces or other devices. Alternatively, architects can design new buildings to use low-energy building techniques which can virtually eliminate the need for heating, such as those built to the Passive House standard.

However, if a building does need full heating, combustion central heating offers a more environmentally friendly solution than electric-air central heating or than other direct electric heating devices. This stems from the fact that most electricity originates remotely using fossil fuels, with up to two-thirds of the energy in the fuel lost (unless utilized for district heating) at the power station and in transmission losses. In Sweden proposals exist to phase out direct electric heating for this reason. Nuclear and hydroelectric sources reduce this factor.

In contrast, hot-water central heating systems can use water heated in or close to the building using high-efficiency condensing boilers, biofuels, or district heating. Wet underfloor heating has proven ideal. This offers the option of relatively easy conversion in the future to use developing technologies such as heat pumps and solar combisystems, thereby also providing future-proofing.

Typical efficiencies for central heating are: 85-97% for gas fired heating; 80-89% for oil-fired, and 45-60% for coal-fired heating.

Duct (Industrial Exhaust)

Industrial exhaust ducts are pipe systems that connect hoods to industrial chimneys through other components of exhaust systems like fan, collectors etc. Ducts are low-pressure pneumatic conveyors to convey dust, particles, shavings, fumes or chemical hazardous components from air in vicinity to a shop floor or any other specific locations like tanks, sanding machine, or laboratory hood.

HVAC systems do not include this category of industrial application namely exhaust systems. A distinction from HVAC system duct is that the fluid (air) conveyed through the duct system may not be homogeneous. An industrial exhaust duct system is primarily a pneumatic conveying system and is basically governed by laws of flow of fluids.

Fluid Flow

The conveying fluid that flow through duct system is air. Air transports materials from hood to destination. It is also instrumental in capturing the material in to the flow system. Air is a compressible fluid, but for engineering calculations, air is considered as incompressible as a simplification, without any significant errors.

Design

Process design of exhaust system will include 1) Identification of contaminants, its density and size, 2) Deciding of air flow 3) Sizing of the ductwork, 4) Calculation of resistance, 5) Finalizing the capacity of blower etc. The aim is to keep contaminants out using minimum airflow. It is estimated that increase in an inch wg of static pressure can add a few thousands of dollars to the operation cost per annum

Fire Damper

Fire dampers are passive fire protection products used in heating, ventilation, and air conditioning (HVAC) ducts to prevent the spread of fire inside the ductwork through fire-resistance rated walls and floors. Fire/Smoke dampers Are similar to Fire Dampers in fire resistance rating, and also prevent the spread of smoke inside the ducts. When a rise in temperature occurs, the fire damper closes, usually activated by a thermal element which melts at temperatures higher than ambient but high enough to indicate the presence of a fire, allowing springs to close the damper blades. Fire dampers can also close following receipt of an electrical signal from a fire alarm system utilizing detectors remote from the damper, indicating the sensing of heat or smoke in the building occupied spaces or in the HVAC duct system. Regulations and fire test regimes vary from one country to another, which can result in different designs and applications.

Fire Damper Inspection

The National Fire Protection Association, International Code Council, The Joint Commission, State Fire Marshals and Other Authorities Having Jurisdiction (AHJ's), require Fire and Smoke Dampers to be tested at specified intervals.

In regions which enforce NFPA Standards (e.g., North America), fire dampers and combination fire/smoke dampers require inspection and testing one year after installation, and then every 4 years; except in hospitals, where the frequency shall be every 6 years.. Documentation indicating the location of the damper, date of inspection, name of inspector and deficiencies discovered is also required.

Repairs should begin without delay if a damper is found inoperable.

LonWorks — A Competing Network Protocol used for Building Automation Control

LonWorks is a networking platform specifically created to address the needs of control applications. The platform is built on a protocol created by Echelon Corporation for networking devices over media such as twisted pair, powerlines, fiber optics, and RF. It is used for the automation of various functions within buildings such as lighting and HVAC.

Origins and Uptake

The technology has its origins with chip designs, power line and twisted pair, signaling technology, routers, network management software, and other products from Echelon Corporation. In 1999 the communications protocol (then known as LonTalk) was submitted to ANSI and accepted as a standard for control networking (ANSI/CEA-709.1-B). Echelon's power line and twisted pair signaling technology was also submitted to ANSI for standardization and accepted. Since then, ANSI/CEA-709.1 has been accepted as the basis for IEEE 1473-L (in-train controls), AAR electro-pneumatic braking systems for freight trains, IFSF (European petrol station control), SEMI (semiconductor equipment manufacturing), and in 2005 as EN 14908 (European building automation standard). The protocol is also one of several data link/physical layers of the BACnet ASHRAE/ANSI standard for building automation.

China ratified the technology as a national controls standard, GB/Z 20177.1-2006 and as a building and intelligent community standard, GB/T 20299.4-2006; and in 2007 CECED, the European Committee of

Domestic Equipment Manufacturers, adopted the protocol as part of its Household Appliances Control and Monitoring – Application Interworking Specification (AIS) standards.

During 2008 ISO and IEC have granted the communications protocol, twisted pair signaling technology, power line signaling technology, and Internet Protocol (IP) compatibility standard numbers ISO/IEC 14908-1,-2,-3, and-4.

Usage

By 2010 approximately 90 million devices were installed with LonWorks technology. Manufacturers in a variety of industries including building, home, street lighting, transportation, utility, and industrial automation have adopted the platform as the basis for their product and service offerings. Statistics as to the number of locations using the LonWorks technology are scarce, but it is known that products and applications built on top of the platform include such diverse functions as embedded machine control, municipal and highway/tunnel/ street lighting, heating and air conditioning systems, intelligent electricity metering, subway train control, stadium lighting and speaker control, security systems, fire detection and suppression, and newborn location monitoring and alarming.

Technical Details

Two physical-layer signaling technologies, twisted pair "free topology" and power line carrier, are typically included in each of the standards created around the LonWorks technology. The two-wire layer operates at 78 kbit/s using differential Manchester encoding, while the power line achieves either 5.4 or 3.6 kbit/s, depending on frequency.

Additionally, the LonWorks platform uses an affiliated IP tunneling standard—ISO/IEC 14908-4 (ANSI/CEA-852) — in use by a number of manufacturers to connect the devices on previously deployed and new LonWorks platform-based networks to IP-aware applications or remote network-management tools. Many LonWorks platform-based control applications are being implemented with some sort of IP integration, either at the UI/application level or in the controls infrastructure. This is accomplished with web services or IP-routing products available in the market.

An Echelon Corporation-designed IC consisting of several 8-bit processors, the "Neuron chip" was initially the only way to implement a LonTalk protocol node and is used in the large majority of LonWorks platform-based hardware. Since 1999, the protocol has been available for general-purpose processors: a port of the ANSI/CEA-709.1 standard to IP-based or 32-bit chips.

Applications Using LonWorks

- Semiconductor manufacturing
- Lighting control systems
- Energy management systems
- Heating/ventilation/air-conditioning systems
- Security systems
- Home automation
- Consumer appliance controls
- Public street lighting, monitoring, and control
- Petrol station control
- Rail Electronically Controlled Pneumatic Braking.

SNVTs (Standard Network Variable Types)

One of the keys to the interoperability of the system is the standardisation of the variables used to describe physical things to LonWorks, this standards list is maintained by LonMark International and each standard is known as Standard Network Variable Types (SNVTs, pronounced "sniv-its") so for example a thermostat using the temperature SNVT is expected to produce a number between zero and 65535 that equates to a temperature between-274 and 6279.5 degrees Celsius.

Testing Adjusting Balancing

Testing, Adjusting, Balancing (TAB) are the three major steps used on the job to achieve proper operation of heating, ventilating, and air conditioning (HVAC) systems. These systems are also called "environmental systems".

Testing

Testing is the use of specialized and calibrated instruments to measure temperatures, pressures, rotational speeds, electrical characteristics, velocities and air and water quantities for an evaluation of equipment and system performance.

Adjusting

Adjusting is the final setting of balancing devices such as dampers and valves, adjusting fan speeds and pump impeller sizes, in addition to automatic control devices such as thermostats and pressure controllers to achieve maximum specified system performance and efficiency during normal operation.

Balancing

Balancing is the methodical regulation of system fluid flows (air or water) through the use of acceptable procedures to achieve the desired or specified airflow or water flow.

Balancing will be applied to both Air side and Water side. Balancing of air side is known as Air Balancing and water side is known as Water (Hydronic) Balancing.

Underfloor Heating

Underfloor heating and cooling is a form of central heating and cooling which achieves indoor climate control for thermal comfort using conduction, radiation and convection. The terms *radiant heating* and *radiant cooling* are commonly used to describe this approach because radiation is responsible for a significant portion of the resulting thermal comfort but this usage is technically correct only when radiation composes more than 50% of the heat exchanged between the floor and the rest of the space.

History

Underfloor heating has a long history extending back into the Neoglacial and Neolithic periods. Archeological digs in Asia and the Aleutian islands of Alaska reveal how the inhabitants drafted smoke from fires through stone covered trenches which were excavated in the floors of their subterranean dwellings. The hot smoke heated the floor stones which then radiated into the living spaces. These early forms have evolved into modern systems using fluid filled pipes or electrical cables and mats. Below is a chronological overview of under floor heating from around the world.

Time period, c. BC	*Description*
10,000	From China, the word kang, can be traced back to the 11th century B.C. and originally meant, "to dry" before it became known as a heated bed.
5,000	Evidence of "baked floors" are found foreshadowing early forms of kang and dikang "heated floor" later ondol meaning "warm stone" in China and Korea respectively.

Contd...

Time period, c. BC	***Description***
3,000	Korean fire hearth, was used both as kitchen range and heating stove.
1,000	Ondol type system used in the Aleutian Islands, Alaska and in Unggi, Hamgyeongbuk-do (present-day North Korea).
1,000	More than two hearths were used in one dwelling; one hearth located at the center was used for heating, the others at the perimeter was used for cooking throughout the year. This perimeter hearth is the initial form of the budumak (meaning kitchen range), which composes combustion section of the traditional ondol in Korea.
500	Greeks and later Romans scale up the use of conditioned surfaces (floors and walls) with the hypocausts.
200	Central hearth developed into gudeul (meaning heat releasing section of ondol) and perimeter hearth for cooking became more developed and budumak was almost established in Korea.
50	China, Korea and Roman Empire use kang, dikang/ondol and hypocaust respectively.
500	Asia continues to use conditioned surfaces but the application is lost in Europe where it is replaced by the open fire or rudimentary forms of the modern fireplace. Anecdotal literary reference to radiant cooling system in the Middle East using snow packed wall cavities.
700	More sophisticated and developed gudeul was found in some palaces and living quarters of upper class people in Korea. Countries in the Mediterranean Basin (Iraq, Algeria, Turkey, Afghanistan et al.) use various forms of hypocaust type heating in public baths and homes but also use heat from cooking to heat the floors.
1000	Ondol continues to evolve in Asia. The most advanced true ondol system was established. The fire furnace was moved outside and the room was entirely floored with ondol in Korea. Europe uses various forms of the fireplace with the evolution of drafting combustion products with chimneys.
1400	Hypocaust type systems used to heat Turkish Baths of the Ottoman Empire.

Contd...

Time period, c. BC	*Description*
1500	Attention to comfort and architecture in Europe evolves; China and Korea continue to apply floor heating with wide scale adoption.
1600	In France, heated flues in floors and walls are used in greenhouses.
1700	Benjamin Franklin studies the French and Asian cultures and makes note of their respective heating system leading to the development of the Franklin stove. Steam based radiant pipes are used in France. Hypocaust type system used to heat public bath (Hammam) in the citadel town of Erbil located in modern day Iraq.
1800	Beginnings of the European evolution of the modern water heater/boiler and water based piping systems including studies in thermal conductivities and specific heat of materials and emissivity/reflectivity of surfaces (Watt/ Leslie/Rumford). Reference to the use of small bore pipes used in the John Soane house and museum.
1864	Ondol type system used at Civil War hospital sites in America. Reichstag building in Germany uses the thermal mass of the building for cooling and heating.
1899	The earliest beginnings of polyethylene-based pipes occur when German scientist, Hans von Pechmann, discovered a waxy residue at the bottom of a test tube, colleagues Eugen Bamberger and Friedrich Tschirner called it polymethylene but it was discarded as having no commercial use at the time.
1904	Liverpool Cathedral in England is heated with system based on the hypocaust principles.
1905	Frank Lloyd Wright makes first trip to Japan, later incorporates various early forms of radiant heating in his projects.
1907	England, Prof. Barker granted Patent No. 28477 for panel warming using small pipes. Patents later sold to the Crittal Company who appointed representatives across Europe. A.M. Byers of America promotes radiant heating using small bore water pipes. Asia continues to use traditional ondol and kang—wood is used as the fuel, combustion gases sent under floor.
1930	Oscar Faber in England uses water pipes used to radiant heat and cool several large buildings.

Contd...

Time period, c. BC	***Description***
1933	Explosion at England's Imperial Chemical Industries (ICI) laboratory during a high pressure experiment with ethylene gas results in a wax like substance—later to become polyethylene and the re-beginnings of PEX pipe.
1937	Frank Lloyd Wright designs the radiant heated Herbert Jacobs house, the first Usonian home.
1939	First small scale polyethylene plant built in America.
1945	American developer William Levitt builds large scale developments for returning GI's. Water based (copper pipe) radiant heating used throughout thousands of homes. Poor building envelopes on all continents require excessive surface temperatures leading in some cases to health problems. Thermal comfort and health science research (using hot plates, thermal manikins and comfort laboratories) in Europe and America later establishes lower surface temperature limits and development of comfort standards.
1950	Korean War wipes out wood supplies for ondol, population forced to use coal. Developer Joseph Eichler in California begins the construction of thousands of radiant heated homes.
1951	Dr. J. Bjorksten of Bjorksten Research Laboratories in Madison, WI, announces first results of what is believed to be the first instance of testing three types of plastic tubing for radiant floor heating in America. Polyethylene, vinyl chloride copolymer, and vinylidene chloride were tested over three winters.
1953	The first Canadian polyethylene plant is built near Edmonton, Ab.
1960	NRC researcher from Canada installs underfloor heating in his home and later remarks, "Decades later it would be identified as a passive solar house. It incorporated innovative features such as the radiant heating system supplied with hot water from an automatically stoked anthracite furnace."
1965	Thomas Engel patents method for stabilizing polyethylene by cross linking molecules using peroxide (PEx-A) and in 1967 sells license options to a number of pipe producers.

Contd...

Time period, c. BC	*Description*
1970	Evolution of Korean architecture leads to multistory housings, flue gases from coal based ondol results in many deaths leading to the removal of the home based flue gas system to a central water based heating plants. Oxygen permeation becomes corrosion issue in Europe leading to the development of barriered pipe and oxygen permeation standards.
1980	The first standards for floor heating are developed in Europe. Water-based ondol system is applied to almost all of residential buildings in Korea.
1985	Floor heating becomes a traditional heating systems in residential buildings in Middle Europe and Nordic countries and increasing applications in non-residential buildings.
1995	The application of floor cooling and thermal active building systems (TABS) in residential and commercial buildings are widely introduced into the market.
2000	The use of embedded radiant cooling systems in middle of Europe becomes a standard system with many parts of the world applying radiant based HVAC systems as means of using low temperatures for heating and high temperatures for cooling.
2010	Radiant conditioned Pearl River Tower in Guangzhou, China, topped out at 71-stories.

Description

Modern underfloor heating systems use either electrical resistance elements ("electric systems") or fluid flowing in pipes ("hydronic systems") to heat the floor. Either type can be installed as the primary, whole-building heating system or as localized floor heating for thermal comfort. Electrical resistance can only be used for heating so when space cooling is also required, hydronic systems are used. Other applications for which either electric or hydronic systems are suited include snow/ice melting for walks, driveways and landing pads, turf conditioning of football and soccer fields and frost prevention in freezers and skating rinks.

Electric heating elements or hydronic piping can be cast in a concrete floor slab ("poured floor system" or "wet system"). They can also be placed under the floor covering ("dry system") or attached directly to a wood sub floor ("sub floor system" or "dry system").

Some commercial buildings are designed to take advantage of thermal mass which is heated or cooled during off peak hours when utility rates are lower. With the heating/cooling system turned off during the day, the concrete mass and room temperature drift up or down within the desired comfort range. Such systems are known as thermally activated building systems or TABS.

Hydronic Systems

Hydronic systems use water or a mix of water and anti-freeze such as propylene glycol as the heat transfer fluid in a "closed loop" that is recirculated between the floor and the boiler. Various types of pipes are available specifically for hydronic underfloor heating and cooling systems and are generally made from polyethylene including PEX, PEX-Al-PEX and PERT. Older materials such as Polybutylene (PB) and copper or steel pipe are still used in some locales or for specialized applications. Hydronic systems require skilled designers and tradespeople familiar with boilers, circulators, controls, fluid pressures and temperature. The use of modern factory assembled sub-stations, used primarily in district heating and cooling, can greatly simplify design requirements and reduce the installation and commissioning time of hydronic systems.

Hydronic systems can use a single source or combination of energy sources to help manage energy costs. Hydronic system energy source options are:

- Boilers (heaters) including Combined heat and power plants heated by:
- Natural gas, coal, oil or waste oil
- Electricity
- Solar thermal
- wood or other biomass
- bio-fuels.
- Heat pumps and chillers powered by:
- Electricity
- Natural gas.

Electric Systems

Electric systems are used only for heating and employ non-corrosive, flexible heating elements including cables, pre-formed cable mats, bronze mesh, and carbon films. Due to their low profile they can be installed in a thermal mass or directly under floor finishes. Electric systems can also take advantage of time-of-use electricity metering and are frequently used as carpet heaters, portable under area rug heaters, under laminate floor heaters, under tile heating, under wood floor heating, and floor warming systems, including under shower floor and seat heating.

Large electric systems also require skilled designers and tradespeople but this is less so for small floor warming systems. Electric systems use fewer components and are simpler to install and commission than hydronic systems. Some electric systems use line voltage technology while others use low voltage technology. Power consumption of an electric system is not based on voltage but rather wattage output produced by the heating element.

Features

Thermal Comfort Quality: As defined by ANSI/ASHRAE Standard 55 – Thermal Environmental Conditions for Human Occupancy, thermal comfort is, "that condition of mind which expresses satisfaction with the thermal environment and is assessed by subjective evaluation." Relating specifically to underfloor heating, thermal comfort is influenced by floor surface temperature and associated elements such as radiant asymmetry, mean radiant temperature and operative temperature. Research by Nevins, Rohles, Gagge, P. Ole Fanger et al. show that humans at rest with clothing typical of light office and home wear, exchange over 50% of their sensible heat via radiation.

Underfloor heating influences the radiant exchange by thermally conditioning the interior surfaces with low temperature long wave radiation. The heating of the surfaces suppresses body heat loss resulting in a perception of heating comfort. This general sensation of comfort is further enhanced through conduction (feet on floor) and through convection by the surface's influence on air density. Underfloor cooling works by absorbing both short wave and long wave radiation resulting in cool interior surfaces.

These cool surfaces encourage the loss of body heat resulting in a perception of cooling comfort. Localized discomfort due to cold and warm floors wearing normal foot wear and stocking feet is addressed in the ISO 7730 and ASHRAE 55 standards and ASHRAE Fundamentals Handbooks and can be corrected or regulated with floor heating and cooling systems.

Indoor Air Quality

Underfloor heating can have a positive effect on the quality of indoor air by facilitating the choice of otherwise perceived cold flooring materials such as tile, slate, terrazzo and concrete. These masonry surfaces typically have very low VOC emissions (volatile organic compounds) in comparison to other flooring options. In conjunction with moisture control, floor heating also establishes temperature conditions that are less favorable in supporting mold, bacteria, viruses and dust mites. By removing the sensible heating load from the total HVAC (Heating, Ventilating, and Air Conditioning) load, ventilation, filtration and dehumidification of incoming air can be accomplished with dedicated outdoor air systems having less volumetric turnover to mitigate distribution of airborne contaminates. There is recognition from the medical community relating to the benefits of floor heating especially as it relates to allergens.

Sustainability—Energy

Under floor radiant systems are evaluated for sustainability through the principles of efficiency, entropy, exergy and efficacy. When combined with high performance buildings, under floor systems operate with low temperatures in heating and high temperatures in cooling in the ranges found typically in geothermal and solar thermal systems. When coupled with these non combustible, renewable energy sources the sustainability benefits include reduction or elimination of combustion and green house gases produced by boilers and power generation for heat pumps and chillers, as well as reduced demands for non renewables and greater inventories for future generations. This has been supported through simulation evaluations and though research funded by the U.S. Department of Energy, Canada Mortgage and Housing Corporation, Fraunhofer Institute as well as ASHRAE.

Safety

Low temperature underfloor heating is embedded in the floor or placed under the floor covering. As such it occupies no wall space and creates no burn hazards, nor is it a hazard for physical injuries due to accidental contact leading to tripping and falling. This has been referenced as a positive feature in healthcare facilities including those serving elderly clients and those with dementia. Anecdotally, under similar environmental conditions, heated floors will speed evaporation of wetted floors (showering, cleaning, and spills). Additionally, underfloor heating with fluid filled pipes is useful in heating and cooling explosion proof environments where combustion and electrical equipment can be located remotely from the explosive environment.

Longevity, Maintenance and Repair

Equipment maintenance and repair is the same as for other water or electrical based HVAC systems except when pipes, cables or mats are embedded in the floor. Early trials (for example homes built by Levitt and Eichler, c. 1940-70's) experienced failures in embedded copper and steel piping systems as well as failures assigned by the courts to Shell, Goodyear and others for polybutylene and EPDM materials. There also have been a few publicized claims of failed electric heated gypsum panels from the mid 90's.

Failures associated with most installations are attributable to job site neglect, installation errors and product mishandling such as exposure to ultraviolet radiation. Pre-pour pressure tests required by concrete installation standards and good practice guidelines for the design, construction, operation and repair of radiant heating and cooling systems mitigate problems resulting from improper installation and operation.

Fluid based systems using Cross-linked polyethylene (PE-x) a product developed in the 1930s and its various derivatives such as PE-rt, have demonstrated reliable long term performance in harsh cold-climate applications such as bridge decks, aircraft hangar aprons and landing pads. Since the materials are produced from polyethylene and its bonds are cross-linked, it is highly resistant to corrosion or the temperature and pressure stresses associated with typical fluid based HVAC systems.

Design and Installation Considerations

The engineering of underfloor cooling and heating systems is governed by industry standards and guidelines.

Technical Design

The amount of heat exchanged from or to an underfloor system is based on the combined radiant and convective heat transfer coefficients.

- Radiant heat transfer is constant based on the Stefan–Boltzmann constant.
- Convective heat transfer changes over time depending on
  - o the air's density and thus its buoyancy. Air buoyancy changes according to surface temperatures and

- o forced air movement due to fans and the motion of people and objects in the space.

Convective heat transfer with underfloor systems is much greater when the system is operating in a heating rather than cooling mode. Typically with underfloor heating the convective component is almost 50% of the total heat transfer and in underfloor cooling the convective component is less than 10%.

Heat and Moisture Considerations

When heated and cooled pipes or heating cables share the same spaces as other building components, parasitic heat transfer can occur between refrigeration appliances, cold storage areas, domestic cold water lines, air conditioning and ventilation ducts. To control this, the pipes, cables and other building components must all be well insulated.

With underfloor cooling, condensation may collect on the surface of the floor. To prevent this, air humidity is kept low, below 50%, and floor temperatures are maintained above the dew point, 66°F(19°C).

Building Systems and Materials

- Heat losses to below grade
- The thermal conductivity of soil will influence the conductive heat transfer between the ground and heated or cooled slab-on-grade floors.
- Soils with moisture contents greater than 20% can be as much as 15 times more conductive than soils with less than 4% moisture content.
- Water tables and general soil conditions should be evaluated.
- Suitable underslab insulation such as rigid extruded or expanded polystyrene is required by Model National Energy Codes.
- Heat losses at the exterior floor framing
- The heated or cooled sub-floor increases the temperature difference between the outdoors and the conditioned floor.
- The cavities created by the framing timbers such as headers, trimmers and cantilevered sections must then be insulated with rigid, batt or spray type insulations of suitable value based on climate and building techniques.
- Masonry and other hard flooring considerations
- Concrete floors must accommodate shrinkage and expansion due to curing and changes in temperature.

- Curing times and temperatures for poured floors (concrete, lightweight toppings)must follow industry standards.
- Control and expansion joints and crack suppression techniques are required for all masonry type floors including;
- Tile
- Slate
- Terrazzo
- Stone
- Marble
- Concrete,stained, textured and stamped.
- Wood flooring;
- The dimensional stability of wood is based primary on moisture content, however, other factors can mitigate the changes to wood as it is heated or cooled, including;
- Wood species
- Milling techniques, quarter sawn or plane sawn
- Acclimation period
- Relative humidity within the space.
- Piping standards.

Control System

Underfloor heating and cooling systems can have several control points including the management of:

- Fluid temperatures in the heating and cooling plant (e.g. boilers, chillers, heat pumps).
- Influences the efficiency
- Fluid temperatures in distribution network between the plant and the radiant manifolds.
- Influences the capital and operating costs.
- Fluid temperatures in the PE-x piping systems, which is based on;
- Heating and cooling demands
- Tube spacing
- Upward and downward losses
- Flooring characteristics.
- Operative temperature;

- Incorporates the mean radiant and dry bulb.
- Surface temperatures for;
- Comfort
- Health and safety
- Material integrity
- Dew point (for floor cooling).

Sample-Mechanical Schematic

Illustrated is a simplified mechanical schematic of an underfloor heating and cooling system for thermal comfort quality with a separate air handling system for indoor air quality. In high performance residential homes of moderate size (e.g. under 3000 ft^2 (278 m^2) total conditioned floor area), this system using manufactured hydronic control appliances would take up about the same space as a three or four piece bathroom.

Modelling Piping Patterns with Finite Element Analysis

Modelling radiant piping (also tube or loop) patterns with finite element analysis (FEA) predicts the thermal diffusions and surface temperature quality or efficacy of various loop layouts. The performance of the model (left image above) and image to the right are useful to gain an understanding in relationships between flooring resistances, conductivities of surrounding mass, tube spacing's, depths and fluid temperatures. As with all FEA simulations, they depict a snap shot in time for a specific assembly and may not be representative of all floor assemblies nor for system that have been operative for considerable time in a steady state condition. The practical application of FEA for the engineer is being able to assess each design for fluid temperature, back losses and surface temperature quality. Through several iterations it is possible to optimize the design for the lowest fluid temperature in heating and the highest fluid temperature in cooling which enables combustion and compression equipment to achieve its maximum rated efficiency performance.

Using Thermography to Observe Underfloor Systems

Thermography is a useful tool to see the actual thermal efficacy of an underfloor system from its start up (as shown) to its operating conditions. In a startup it is easy to identify the tube location but less so as the system moves into a steady state condition. It is important to interpret thermographic images correctly. As is the case with finite element analysis (FEA), what is seen, reflects the conditions at the time of the image and may not represent the steady conditions. For example, the surfaces viewed in the images shown, may appear 'hot', but in reality are actually below the nominal temperature of the skin and core temperatures of the human body and the ability to 'see' the pipes does not equate to 'feel' the pipes. Thermography can also point out flaws in the building enclosures (left image, corner intersection detail), thermal bridging (right image, studs) and the heat losses associated with exterior doors (center image).

Economics

There is a wide range of pricing for underfloor systems based on regional differences, application and project complexity. It is widely adopted in the Nordic, Asian and European communities consequently the market is more mature and systems relatively more affordable than North America where market share for fluid based systems remains between 3% to 7% of HVAC systems (ref. Statistics Canada and United States Census Bureau).

In energy efficiency buildings such as Passive House, R-2000 or Net Zero Energy, simple thermostatic radiator valves can be installed along with a single compact circulator and small condensing heater controlled without or with basic hot water reset control. Economical electric resistant based systems also are useful in small zones such as bathrooms and kitchens, but also for entire buildings where heating loads are very low and preferably where photovoltaic's, wind or hydro is the generating source of electricity. Larger structures will need more sophisticated systems to deal with cooling and heating needs, and often requiring building management control systems to regulate the energy use and control the overall indoor environment.

Low temperature radiant heating and high temperature radiant cooling systems lend themselves well to district energy systems (community based systems) due to the temperature differentials between the plant and the buildings which allow small diameter insulated distribution networks and low pumping power requirements. The low return temperatures in heating and high return temperatures in cooling enable the district energy plant to achieve maximum efficiency. The principles behind district energy with underfloor systems can also be applied to stand alone multi story buildings with the same benefits. Additionally, underfloor radiant systems are ideally suited to renewable energy sources including geothermal and solar thermal systems or any system where waste heat is recoverable.

In the global drive for sustainability, long term economics supports the need to eliminate where possible, compression for cooling and combustion for heating. It will then be necessary to use low quality heat sources for which radiant underfloor heating and cooling is well suited.

System Efficiency

System efficiency and energy use analysis takes into account building enclosure performance, efficiency of the heating and cooling plant, system controls and the conductivities, surface characteristics, tube/element spacing and depth of the radiant panel, operating fluid temperatures and wire to water efficiency of the circulators. The efficiency in electric systems is analyzed by similar processes and includes the efficiency of electricity generation. Though the efficiency of radiant systems is under constant debate with no shortage of anecdotal claims and scientific papers presenting both sides, the low return fluid temperatures in heating and high return fluid temperatures in cooling enable condensing boilers, chillers and heat pumps to operate at or near their maximum engineered performance. The greater efficiency of 'wire to water' versus 'wire to air' flow due to water's significantly greater heat capacity favors fluid based systems over air based systems. Both field application and simulation research have demonstrated significant electrical energy savings with radiant cooling and dedicated outdoor air systems based in part on the previous noted principles.

In Passive Houses, R-2000 homes or Net Zero Energy buildings the low temperatures of radiant heating and cooling systems present significant opportunities to exploit exergy.

Efficiency Considerations for Flooring Surface Materials

System efficiency is also affected by the floor covering serving as the radiational boundary layer between the floor mass and occupants and other contents of the conditioned space. For example, carpeting has a greater resistance or lower conductance than tile. Thus carpeted floors need to operate at higher internal temperatures than tile which can create lower efficiencies for boilers and heat pumps. However, when the floor covering is known at the time the system is installed then the internal floor temperature required for a given covering can be achieved through proper tube spacing without sacrificing plant efficiency (though the higher internal floor temperatures may result in increased heat loss from the non-room surfaces of the floor).

The emissivity, reflectivity and absorptivity of a floor surface are critical determinants of its heat exchange with the occupants and room. Unpolished flooring surface materials and treatments have very high emissivity's (0.85 to 0.95) and therefore make good heat radiators.

With underfloor heating and cooling ("reversible floors") flooring surfaces with high absorbance and emissivity and low reflectivity are most desirable.

Global Examples of Large Modern Buildings using Radiant Heating and Cooling

- Manitoba Hydro Place, Canada
- California Academy of Science, United States
- Copenhagen Opera House, Denmark
- Post Tower, Germany
- Ewha Womans University, Korea
- NREL Research Support Facility, United States
- Suvarnabhumi Airport, Bangkok
- la Defence Office, Netherlands
- Pearl River Tower, China
- 41 Cooper Square, United States
- Hearst Tower (New York City), United States
- Akron Art Museum, United States
- BMW Welt, Germany
- David Brower Center, United States.

Lighting Control System

A lighting control system consists of a device that controls electric lighting and devices, alone or as part of a daylight harvesting system, for a public, commercial, or residential building or property, or the theater. Lighting control systems are used for working, aesthetic, and security illumination for interior, exterior, and landscape lighting, and theater stage lighting productions. They are often part of sustainable architecture and lighting design for integrated green building energy conservation programs.

Lighting control systems, with an embedded processor or industrial computer device, usually include one or more portable or mounted keypad or touchscreen console interfaces, and can include mobile phone operation. These control interfaces allow users the ability to remotely toggle (on-off) power to individual or groups of lights (and ceiling fans and other devices), operate dimmers, and pre-program space lighting levels.

Advantages

A major advantage of a lighting control system over conventional individual switching is the ability to control any light, group of lights, or all lights in a building from a single user interface device. Any light or device can be controlled from any location. This ability to control multiple light sources from a user device allows complex "light scenes" to be created. A room may have multiple scenes available, each one created for different activities in the room. A lighting scene can create dramatic changes in atmosphere, for a residence or the stage, by a simple button press. In landscape design, in addition to landscape lighting, fountain pumps, water spa heating, swimming pool covers, motorized gates, and outdoor fireplace ignition; can be remotely or automatically controlled.

Benefits

Other benefits include reduced energy consumption, and power costs through more efficient usage, longer bulb life from dimming, and reduced emission carbon footprints. Newer, wireless lighting control systems provide additional benefits including reduced installation costs and increased flexibility in where switches and sensors can be placed.

Controlling Categories

Lighting control systems provide the ability to automatically power a device based on:

- Chronological time (time of day)
- Astronomical time (sunrise/sunset)
- Room or outdoor space occupancy (motion sensors)
- Presence of daylight (lighting costs and energy conservation, and daylight harvesting)
- Events
- Alarm conditions
- Program logic (any combination of events).

Chronological time is a specific time of day as pre-set timers use. Astronomical times includes sunrise, sunset, a specific day of the week or days in a month or year. Room occupancy might be determined with motion detectors or RFID tags, and is part of security and energy conservation programs. Artificial lighting energy use can be reduced by automatically dimming and/or switching electric lights in response to the level of daylighting, a technology known as daylight harvesting. Mobile phone operated controls can turn on a basic group of circulation—safety fixtures serving exterior—interior locations on approach, or to preheat a "water spa" in advance of returning. Events might include special fixtures for social occasions and holiday lighting, or overall brightness for cleaning. Alarm conditions can include doors opening and motion detected in a protected area, or manual "panic buttons-all lights on" for occupants sensing a possible intrusion. Program logic can tie all of the above elements together using constructs such as if-then-else statements and logical operators.

Theatre

Architectural lighting control systems can integrate with a theater's on-off and dimmer controls, and are often used for house lights and stage lighting, and can include worklights, rehearsal lighting, and lobby lighting. Control stations can be placed in several locations in the building and range in complexity from single buttons that bring up preset options-looks, to in-wall or desktop LCD touchscreen consoles. Much of the technology is related to residential and commercial lighting control systems.

The benefit of architectural lighting control systems in the theater is the ability for theater staff to turn worklights and house lights on and off without having to use a lighting control console. Alternately, the light designer can control these same lights with light cues from the lighting control console so that, for instance, the transition from houselights being up before a show starts and the first light cue of the show is controlled by one system.

Housekeeping

Housekeeping is the act of cleaning the rooms and furnishings of a home. It is one of the many chores included in the term *housework*. Housecleaning includes activities such as disposing of rubbish, cleaning dirty surfaces, dusting and vacuuming. It may also involve some outdoor chores, such as removing leaves from rain gutters, washing windows and sweeping doormats. The term is often used also figuratively in politics and business, for the removal of unwanted personnel, methods or policies in an effort at reform or improvement.

Housecleaning is done to make the home look better and be safer and easier to live in. Without housecleaning limescale builds up on taps, mold grows in wet areas, bacterial action make the garbage disposal and toilet smell and cobwebs accumulate. Tools used in housecleaning include vacuum cleaners, brooms, mops and sponges, together with cleaning products such as detergents, disinfectants and bleach.

Removal of Litter

Disposal of rubbish is an important aspect of house cleaning, the reasons for this are psychological, social and practical. Plastic bags are designed and manufactured specifically for the collection of litter. Many are sized to fit common waste baskets and trash cans. Paper bags are made to carry aluminum cans, glass jars and other things. Recycling is possible with some kinds of litter.

Dusting

Over time dust accumulates on household surfaces. As well as making the surfaces dirty, when dust is disturbed it can become suspended in the air, causing sneezing and breathing trouble. It can also transfer from furniture to clothing, making it unclean. Various tools have been invented for dust removal; Feather and lamb's wool dusters, cotton and polyester dust cloths, furniture spray, disposable paper "dust cloths", dust mops for smooth floors and vacuum cleaners. Vacuum cleaners often have a variety of tools to enable them to remove not just from carpets and rugs, but from hard surfaces and upholstery.

Removal of Dirt

Examples of dirt or "soil" can be dry coffee spills and jelly drips or muddy footprints on carpet. Equipment used with a cleaner might be a bucket and sponge. A modern tool is the spray bottle, but the scientific principle is the same.

Household Chemicals

Various household cleaning products have been developed to facilitate the removal of dust and dirt, for surface maintenance, and for disinfection. Products are available in powder, liquid or spray form. The basic ingredients determine the type of cleaning tasks for which they are suitable. Some are packaged as general purpose cleaning materials whilst others are targeted at specific cleaning tasks such as drain clearing, oven cleaning, lime scale removal and polishing furniture. Household cleaning products provide aesthetic and hygiene benefits but are also associated with health risks for the users, and building occupants. The US Department of Health and Human Services offers the public access to the Household Products Database. This database provides consumer information for over 4,000 products based on information provided by the manufacturer through the material safety data sheet.

Surfactants lower the surface tension of water, making it able to flow into smaller tiny cracks and crevices in soils making removal easier. Alkaline chemicals break down known soils such as grease and mud. Acids break down soils such as lime scale, soap scum, and stains of mustard, coffee, tea, and alcoholic beverages. Some solvent-based products are flammable and some can dissolve paint and varnish. Disinfectants stop smell and stains caused by bacteria.

When multiple chemicals are applied to the same surface without full removal of the earlier substance, the chemicals may interact. This interaction may result in a reduction of the efficiency of the chemicals applied (such as a change in pH value caused by mixing alkalis and acids) and in cases may even emit toxic fumes. An example of this is the mixing of ammonia-based cleaners (or acid-based cleaners) and bleach. This causes the production of chloramines that volatilize (become gaseous) causing acute inflammation of the lungs (toxic pneumonitis), long-term respiratory damage, and potential death.

Residue from cleaning products and cleaning activity (dusting, vacuuming, sweeping) have been shown to impact indoor air quality (IAQ) by redistributing particulate matter (dust, dirt, human skin cells, organic matter, animal dander, particles from combustion, fibers from insulation, pollen, and polycyclic aromatic hydrocarbons) that gaseous or liquid particles become adsorbed to. The particulate matter and chemical residual will of be highest concentrations right after cleaning but will decrease over time depending upon levels of contaminants, air exchange rate, and other sources of chemical residual. Of most concern are the family of chemicals called VOCs such as formaldehyde, toluene, and limonene.

Volatile organic compounds (VOCs) are released from many household cleaning products such as disinfectants, polishes, floor waxes, air-freshening sprays, all purpose cleaning sprays, and glass cleaner. These products have been shown to emit irritating vapors. VOCs are of most concern due to their tendency to evaporate and be inhaled into the lungs or adsorbed to existing dust, which can also be inhaled. It has been found that aerosolized (spray) cleaning products are important risk factors and may aggravate symptoms of adult asthma, respiratory irritation, childhood asthma, wheeze, bronchitis, and allergy.

Other modes of exposure to potentially harmful household cleaning chemicals include absorption through the skin (dermis), accidental ingestion, and accidental splashing into the eyes. Products for the application and safe use of the chemicals are also available, such as nylon scrub sponge and rubber gloves. It is up to the consumer to keep themselves safe while using these chemicals. Reading and comprehending the labels is important.

There is a growing consumer and governmental interest in natural cleaning products and green cleaning methods. The use of nontoxic household chemicals is growing as consumers become more informed of the health effects of many household chemicals, and municipalities are having to deal with the expensive disposal of household hazardous waste (HHW).

Tools

"Modern housecleaning tools" is almost an oxymoron. There are few areas where someone from 50 years ago could step into the same job today, but housecleaning is an area where there has been very little change. Brooms remove debris from floors and dustpans carry dust and debris swept into them, buckets hold cleaning and rinsing solutions, vacuum cleaners and carpet sweepers remove surface dust and debris, chamois leather and squeegees are used for window-cleaning, and mops are used for washing floors.

Yard

A home's yard and exterior are sometimes subject to cleaning. Exterior cleaning also occurs for safety, upkeep and usefulness. It includes removal of paper litter and grass growing in sidewalk cracks. Rain gutters, doormats, pools and the screens and glass of windows are also cleanable. Yard junk-removal might occur and porch clutter removal. The paint of door frames might be washed or an old piñata thrown away.

Chapter 4

HVAC Systems

HVAC (Heating, Ventilation, and Air Conditioning) refers to technology of indoor or automotive environmental comfort. HVAC system design is a major subdiscipline of mechanical engineering, based on the principles of thermodynamics, fluid mechanics, and heat transfer. Refrigeration is sometimes added to the field's abbreviation as HVAC&R or HVACR, or ventilating is dropped as in HACR (such as the designation of HACR-rated circuit breakers). HVAC is important in the design of medium to large industrial and office buildings such as skyscrapers and in marine environments such as aquariums, where safe and healthy building conditions are regulated with temperature and humidity, as well as "fresh air" from outdoors.

Figure: *Rooftop HVAC unit with view of fresh air intake vent.*

Background

Heating, ventilating, and air conditioning is based on inventions and discoveries made by Nikolay Lvov, Michael Faraday, Willis Carrier, Reuben Trane, James Joule, William Rankine, Sadi Carnot, and many others.

The invention of the components of HVAC systems went hand-in-hand with the industrial revolution, and new methods of modernization, higher efficiency, and system control are constantly introduced by companies and inventors all over the world. The three central functions of heating, ventilating, and air-conditioning are interrelated, providing thermal comfort, acceptable indoor air quality, within reasonable installation, operation, and maintenance costs. HVAC systems can provide ventilation, reduce air infiltration, and maintain pressure relationships between spaces. How air is delivered to, and removed from spaces is known as room air distribution.

In modern buildings the design, installation, and control systems of these functions are integrated into one or more HVAC systems. For very small buildings, contractors normally "size" and select HVAC systems and equipment. For larger buildings, building services designers and engineers, such as mechanical, architectural, or building services engineers analyze, design, and specify the HVAC systems, and specialty mechanical contractors build and commission them. Building permits and code-compliance inspections of the installations are normally required for all sizes of buildings.

The HVAC industry is a worldwide enterprise, with career opportunities including operation and maintenance, system design and construction, equipment manufacturing and sales, and in education and research. The HVAC industry had been historically regulated by the manufacturers of HVAC equipment, but Regulating and Standards organizations such as HARDI, ASHRAE, SMACNA, ACCA, Uniform Mechanical Code, International Mechanical Code, and AMCA have been established to support the industry and encourage high standards and achievement.

Design of the HVAC System

The starting point in carrying out a heat estimate both for cooling and heating will depend on the ambient and inside conditions specified. However before taking up the heat load calculation, it is necessary to work out the fresh air requirement for each area in details, as pressurization is an important requirement.

Heating

There are many different types of standard heating systems. Central heating is often used in cold climates to heat private houses and public buildings. Such a system contains a boiler, furnace, or heat pump to heat water, steam, or air, all in a central location such as a furnace room in a home or a mechanical room in a large building. The use of water as the heat transfer medium is known as hydronics.

Figure: *Central heating unit*

The system also contains either ductwork, for forced air systems, or piping to distribute a heated fluid and radiators to transfer this heat to the air. The term *radiator* in this context is misleading since most heat transfer from the heat exchanger is by convection, not radiation. The radiators may be mounted on walls or buried in the floor to give under-floor heat.

In boiler fed or radiant heating systems, all but the simplest systems have a pump to circulate the water and ensure an equal supply of heat to all the radiators. The heated water can also be fed through another (secondary) heat exchanger inside a storage cylinder to provide hot running water.

Forced air systems send heated air through ductwork. During warm weather the same ductwork can be used for air conditioning. The forced air can also be filtered or put through air cleaners.

Heating can also be provided from electric, or resistance heating using a filament that becomes hot when electric current is caused to pass through it. This type of heat can be found in electric baseboard heaters, portable electric heaters, and as backup or supplemental heating for heat pump (or reverse heating) system.

The heating elements (radiators or vents) should be located in the coldest part of the room, typically next to the windows to minimize condensation and offset the convective air current formed in the room due to the air next to the window becoming negatively buoyant due to the cold glass. Devices that direct vents away from windows to prevent "wasted" heat defeat this design intent. Cold air drafts can contribute significantly to subjectively feeling colder than the average room temperature. Therefore, it is important to control the air leaks from outside in addition to proper design of the heating system.

The invention of central heating is often credited to the ancient Romans, who installed a system of air ducts called a hypocaust in the walls and floors of public baths and private villas.

Ventilating

Ventilating is the process of "changing" or replacing air in any space to control temperature or remove moisture, odors, smoke, heat, dust, airborne bacteria, carbon dioxide, and to replenish oxygen. Ventilation includes both the exchange of air to the outside as well as circulation of air within the building. It is one of the most important factors for maintaining acceptable indoor air quality in buildings. Methods for ventilating a building may be divided into *mechanical/ forced* and *natural* types. Ventilation is used to remove unpleasant smells and excessive moisture, introduce outside air, to keep interior building air circulating, and to prevent stagnation of the interior air.

Mechanical or Forced Ventilation

"Mechanical" or "forced" ventilation is provided by an air handler and used to control indoor air quality. Excess humidity, odors, and contaminants can often be controlled via dilution or replacement with outside air. However, in humid climates much energy is required to remove excess moisture from ventilation air.

Figure: *HVAC ventilation exhaust for a 12-story building*

Kitchens and bathrooms typically have mechanical exhaust to control odors and sometimes humidity. Factors in the design of such systems include the flow rate (which is a function of the fan speed and exhaust vent size) and noise level. If ducting for the fans traverse unheated space (e.g., an attic), the ducting should be insulated as well to prevent condensation on the ducting. Direct drive fans are available for many applications, and can reduce maintenance needs.

Ceiling fans and table/floor fans circulate air within a room for the purpose of reducing the perceived temperature because of evaporation of perspiration on the skin of the occupants. Because hot air rises, ceiling fans may be used to keep a room warmer in the winter by circulating the warm stratified air from the ceiling to the floor. Ceiling fans do not provide ventilation as defined as the introduction of outside air.

Natural Ventilation

Natural ventilation is the ventilation of a building with outside air without the use of a fan or other mechanical system. It can be achieved with openable windows or trickle vents when the spaces to ventilate are small and the architecture permits. In more complex systems warm air in the building can be allowed to rise and flow out upper openings to the outside (stack effect) thus forcing cool outside air to be drawn into the building naturally through openings in the lower areas. These systems use very little energy but care must be taken to ensure the occupants' comfort. In warm or humid months, in many climates, maintaining thermal comfort solely via natural ventilation may not be possible so conventional air conditioning systems are used as backups. Air-side economizers perform the same function as natural ventilation, but use mechanical systems' fans, ducts, dampers, and control systems to introduce and distribute cool outdoor air when appropriate.

Air Conditioning

An air conditioning system, or a standalone air conditioner, provides cooling and humidity control for all or part of a building. Air conditioned buildings often have sealed windows, because open windows would work against the system intended to maintain constant indoor air conditions. Outside, fresh air is generally drawn into the system by a vent into the indoor heat exchanger section, creating positive air pressure. The percentage of return air made up of fresh air can usually be manipulated by adjusting the opening of this vent. Typical fresh air intake is about 10%

Air conditioning and refrigeration are provided through the removal of heat. Heat can be removed through radiation, convection, or conduction. Refrigeration conduction media such as water, air, ice, and chemicals are referred to as refrigerants. A refrigerant is employed either in a heat pump system in which a compressor is used to drive thermodynamic refrigeration cycle, or in a free cooling system which uses pumps to circulate a cool refrigerant (typically water or a glycol mix).

Refrigeration Cycle

The refrigeration cycle uses four essential elements to cool.

- The system refrigerant starts its cycle in a gaseous state. The compressor pumps the refrigerant gas up to a high pressure and temperature.
- From there it enters a heat exchanger (sometimes called a condensing coil or condenser) where it loses energy (heat) to the outside, cools, and condenses into its liquid phase.
- An expansion valve (also called metering device) regulates the refrigerant liquid to flow at the proper rate.
- The liquid refrigerant is returned to another heat exchanger where it is allowed to evaporate, hence the heat exchanger is often called an evaporating coil or evaporator. As the liquid refrigerant evaporates it absorbs energy (heat) from the inside air, returns to the compressor, and repeats the cycle. In the process, heat is absorbed from indoors and transferred outdoors, resulting in cooling of the building.

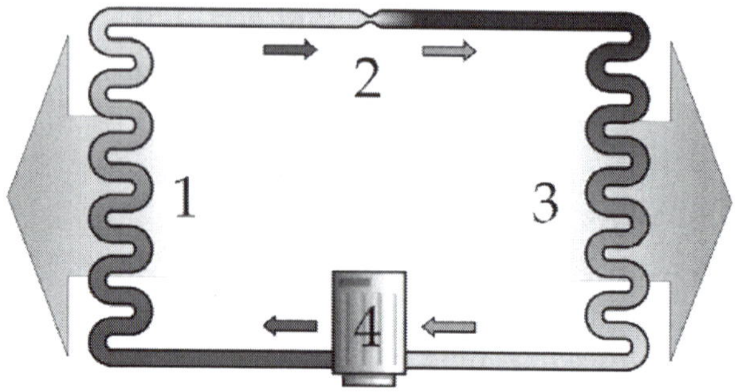

Figure: *A simple stylized diagram of the refrigeration cycle: 1) condensing coil, 2) expansion valve, 3) evaporator coil, 4) compressor*

In variable climates, the system may include a reversing valve that switches from heating in winter to cooling in summer. By reversing the flow of refrigerant, the heat pump refrigeration cycle is changed from cooling to heating or vice versa. This allows a facility to be heated and cooled by a single piece of equipment by the same means, and with the same hardware.

Central vs. Split System

Central, 'all-air' air conditioning systems (or package systems) with a combined outdoor condenser/evaporator unit are often installed in modern residences, offices, and public buildings, but are difficult to retrofit (install in a building that was not designed to receive it) because of the bulky air ducts required to carry the needed air to heat or cool an area. The duct system must be carefully maintained to prevent the growth of pathogenic bacteria such as legionella in the ducts.

An alternative to central systems is the use of separate indoor and outdoor coils in split systems. These systems, although most often seen in residential applications, are gaining popularity in small commercial buildings. The evaporator coil is connected to a remote condenser unit using refrigerant piping between an indoor and outdoor unit instead of ducting air directly from the outdoor unit. Indoor units with directional vents mount onto walls, suspend from ceilings, or fit into the ceiling. Other indoor units mount inside the ceiling cavity, so that short lengths of duct handle air from the indoor unit to vents or diffusers around the room or rooms.

Dehumidification

Dehumidification in an air conditioning system is provided by the evaporator. Since the evaporator operates at a temperature below dew point, moisture in the air condenses on the evaporator coil tubes. This moisture is collected at the bottom of the evaporator in a condensate pan and is removed by piping it to a central drain or onto the ground outside. A dehumidifier is an air-conditioner-like device that controls the humidity of a room or building.

It is often employed in basements which have a higher relative humidity because of their lower temperature (and propensity for damp floors and walls). In food retailing establishments, large open chiller cabinets are highly effective at dehumidifying the internal air. Conversely, a humidifier increases the humidity of a building.

Air-conditioned buildings often have sealed windows, because open windows would disrupt the attempts of the HVAC system to maintain constant indoor air conditions, resulting in the compressor being overworked.

Maintenance

All modern air conditioning systems, down to small "window" package units, are equipped with internal air filters. These are generally of a light weight gauze-type element, and must be replaced as conditions warrant (some models may be washable).

For example, a building in a high-dust environment, or a home with furry pets, will need to have the filters changed more often than buildings without these dirt loads. Failure to replace these filters as needed will contribute to a lower heat-exchange rate, resulting in wasted energy, shortened equipment life, and higher energy bills; also low air flow can result in "iced-up" or "iced-over" evaporator coils, and then there is no air flow at all.

Additionally, very dirty or plugged filters can cause overheating during a heating cycle, and can possibly result in damage to the system or even fire.

It is important to keep in mind that because an air conditioner moves heat between the indoor coil and the outdoor coil, both must be kept just as clean. This means that, in addition to replacing the air filter at the evaporator coil, it is also necessary to regularly clean the condenser coil. Failure to keep the condenser clean will eventually result in harm to the compressor, because the condenser coil is responsible for discharging both the indoor heat (as picked up by the evaporator) plus the heat generated by the electric motor driving the compressor.

Outside, "fresh" air is generally drawn into the system by a vent into the indoor heat exchanger section, creating a positive air pressure. The percentage of return air made up of fresh air can usually be manipulated by adjusting the opening of this vent.

Energy Efficiency

For the last 20 to 30 years, manufacturers of HVAC equipment have been making an effort to make the systems they manufacture more efficient. This was originally driven by rising energy costs, and has more recently been driven by increased awareness of environmental issues. In the USA, the EPA has also imposed tighter restrictions. There are several methods for making HVAC systems more efficient.

Heating Energy

Water heating is more efficient for heating buildings and was the standard many years ago. Today forced air systems can double for air conditioning and are more popular.

A couple of benefits of forced air systems, which are now widely applied in churches, schools and high-end residences,are 1) better air conditioned effect 2) up to 15-20% energy saving, and 3) evenly conditioned effect. A drawback is the installation cost, which might be slightly higher than traditional HVAC system.

Energy efficiency can be improved even more in central heating systems by introducing zoned heating. This allows a more granular application of heat, similar to non-central heating systems. Zones are controlled by multiple thermostats. In water heating systems the thermostats control zone valves, and in forced air systems they control zone dampers inside the vents which selectively block the flow of air. In this case, the control system is very critical to maintain a proper temperature.

Geothermal Heat Pump

Geothermal heat pumps are similar to ordinary heat pumps, but instead of using heat found in outside air, they rely on the stable, even heat of the earth to provide heating, air conditioning and, in most cases, hot water. From Montana's "70 °F ("57 °C) temperature, to the highest temperature ever recorded in the U.S.—134 °F (56.7 °C) in Death Valley, California, in 1913—many parts of the country experience seasonal temperature extremes. A few feet below the earth's surface, however, the ground remains at a relatively constant temperature. Although the temperatures vary according to latitude, at 6 feet (1.83 m) underground, temperatures range from 45 to 75 °F (7.2 to 23.9 °C).

While they may be more costly to install initially than regular heat pumps, they can produce markedly lower energy bills—30 percent to 40 percent lower, according to estimates from the U.S. Environmental Protection Agency.

Ventilation Energy Recovery

Energy recovery systems sometimes utilize heat recovery ventilation or energy recovery ventilation systems that employ heat exchangers or enthalpy wheels to recover sensible or latent heat from exhausted air. This is done by transfer of energy to the incoming outside fresh air.

Air Conditioning Energy

The performance of vapor compression refrigeration cycles is limited by thermodynamics. These air conditioning and heat pump devices *move* heat rather than convert it from one form to another, so *thermal efficiencies* do not appropriately describe the performance of these devices. The Coefficient-of-Performance (COP) measures performance, but this dimensionless measure has not been adopted, but rather the Energy Efficiency Ratio (*EER*). EER is the Energy Efficiency Ratio based on a 35 °C (95 °F) outdoor temperature. To more accurately describe the performance of air conditioning equipment over a typical cooling season a modified version of the EER is used, and is the Seasonal Energy Efficiency Ratio (*SEER*). SEER ratings are based on seasonal temperature averages instead of a constant 35 °C outdoor temperature. The current industry minimum SEER rating is 13 SEER. The SEER article describes it further, and presents some economic comparisons using this useful performance measure.

Engineers have pointed out some areas where efficiency of the existing hardware could be improved. For example, the fan blades used to move the air are usually stamped from sheet metal, an economical method of manufacture, but as a result they are not aerodynamically efficient. A well-designed blade could reduce electrical power required to move the air by a third.

Humidifier/Dehumidifier

A humidifier is a household appliance that increases humidity (moisture) in a single room or in the entire house. There are point-of-use humidifiers, which are commonly used to humidify a single room, and whole-house or furnace humidifiers, which connect to a home's HVAC system to provide humidity to the entire house.

Evaporative Humidifiers

The most common humidifier, an "evaporative", "cool mist", or "wick humidifier", consists of just a few basic parts: a reservoir, wick and fan.

The wick is a filter that absorbs water from the reservoir and provides a larger surface area for it to evaporate from. The fan is adjacent to the wick and blows air onto the wick to aid in the evaporation of the water. Evaporation from the wick is dependent on relative humidity. A room with low humidity will have a higher evaporation rate compared to a room with high humidity. Therefore, this type of humidifier is self-regulating: As the humidity of the room increases, the water vapor output naturally decreases. These wicks become moldy if they are not dried out completely between fillings, and become filled with mineral deposits over time. They regularly need rinsing or replacement—if this does not happen, air cannot pass through them, and the humidifier stops humidifying the area it is in and the water in the tank remains at the same level.

One type of evaporative humidifier makes use of just a reservoir and wick. Sometimes called a natural humidifier, these are usually non-commercial devices that can be assembled at little or no cost. One version of a natural humidifier uses a stainless steel bowl, partially filled with water, covered by a towel. A weight is used to sink the towel in the center of the bowl. There is no need for a fan as the water spreads through the towel by capillary action and the towel surface area is large enough to provide for rapid evaporation. The stainless steel bowl is much easier to clean than typical humidifier water tanks. This, in combination with daily or every other day replacement of the towel, can eliminate the problem with mold and bacteria.

A humidifier for humidifying a fuel cell composed of an anode side humidifier and a cathode side humidifier each possessing a plurality of hollow fiber membrane modules for migrating moisture between a supply gas, which is supplied to a fuel cell, and an exhaust gas, which is exhausted from the fuel cell to thereby humidify the supply gas, the humidifier comprising: a pair of heads which hold both ends of the hollow fiber membrane modules, a connecting member which connects each of heads, and a device for warming the supply gas composed of conduits through which a cooling medium exhausted from the fuel cell is passed. The device for warming the supply gas is configured so that first warms a humidifier at an outlet side of the supply gas, and then warms a humidifier at an inlet side of the supply gas.

A CPAP device includes a humidifier including humidifier tub having a heat conducting base plate; and a cradle to support the humidifier tub in an operative position. The cradle may also support a flow generator in operative relation to the humidifier tub. The cradle includes a heater plate in communication with the heat conducting base plate of the humidifier tub in use. The cradle further includes a retaining mechanism to retain the humidifier tub in the cradle, the retaining mechanism being structured to force the base plate into engagement with the heater plate. The humidifier and/or flow generator may include various features to manage inadvertent back-spill of water from the humidifier to the flow generator.

The present invention relates to ultrasonic humidifier. Previous ultrasonic humidifiers have been very inconvenient to clean so that consumers could not clean them quite often. Therefore serious contamination used to occur due to the proliferation of fungi and bacteria when ultrasonic humidifiers were used for a long time. Though there were several ways to solve the problem such as injection of antibiotics and sanitization by heating water, their effects were limited in that they accrued additional cost while they failed to eliminate the cause of contamination. The main objective of the present invention is to uproot the cause of contamination without additional cost by making it easy to clean ultrasonic humidifiers. To achieve this objective, the ultrasonic humidifier of the present invention comprises a humidifying unit (200) which is formed into a single body and comprises a water tank which stores water for humidification, and a humidifying chamber which humidifies external air; and a base unit (100) which supplies electricity and external air to said humidifying unit when sufficient water is sensed for humidification, wherein said humidifying unit and base unit are separable, humidifying unit has a water feeding hole or a water feeding canal in the lower part of the partition which divides water tank and humidifying chamber, and said water tank has an inlet port in the bottom of it.

A humidifier and a method for producing it can reduce gas leakage through inside the surfaces of humidifying membranes or through interfaces between the humidifying membranes and separators. The humidifier includes water permeable humidifying membranes and gas separators each having one or two channels opened at least one side in a direction of lamination, through which at least one of a dry gas and a wet gas is caused to flow. A humidifying membrane, a gas separator, a humidifying membrane and a gas separator are repeatedly laminated one over another in this order, or a gas separator, a humidifying membrane and a gas separator are repeatedly laminated one over another in this order. Each gas separator has a frame-shaped portion surrounding the one or two channels, and that portion of each humidifying membrane which, when laminated, faces the frame-shaped portion of a corresponding gas separator is filled with a resin.

Other Types of Humidifiers

Other types of humidifiers include:

- Vaporizer (Steam Humidifier) (Warm Mist Humidifier) — Boils water, releasing steam and moisture into the air. A medicated inhalant can also be added to the steam vapor to help reduce coughs. Vaporizers may be more healthful than cool mist types of humidifiers because steam is less likely to convey mineral impurities or microorganisms from the standing water in the reservoir. Boiling water requires significantly more energy than other techniques. The heat source in poorly-designed humidifiers can overheat, causing the product to melt, leak, and start fires.
- Impeller Humidifier (Cool Mist Humidifier) — A rotating disc flings water at a diffuser, which breaks the water into fine droplets that float into the air.
- Ultrasonic Humidifier — A metal diaphragm vibrating at an ultrasonic frequency creates water droplets that silently exit the humidifier in the form of a cool fog. Ultrasonic humidifiers use a piezo-electric transducer to create a high frequency mechanical oscillation in a body of water. The water tries to follow the high frequency oscillation but cannot because of its comparative weight and mass inertia. Thus, a momentary vacuum is created on the negative oscillation, causing the water to cavitate into vapour. The transducer follows this with a positive oscillation that creates high pressure compression waves on the water's surface, releasing tiny vapour molecules of water into the air. This is an extremely fine mist, about one micrometre in diameter, that is quickly absorbed into the air flow. Unlike the humidifiers that boil water, these water droplets contain any impurities that are in the reservoir, including minerals from hard water (which then forms a difficult to remove white dust on nearby objects and furniture), and pathogens growing in the stagnant tank. Ultrasonic Humidifiers should be cleaned regularly to avoid bacterial contamination which may be projected into the air.

Impeller and ultrasonic humidifiers do not selectively put water in the air, they also add any suspended material in the water to the air such as microorganisms and minerals. The amount of minerals and other materials can be greatly reduced by using distilled water, though no water is absolutely pure. Filters may also reduce the amount of material but the EPA warns, "the ability of these devices to remove minerals may vary widely." Depending on the volume, this dust may have negative health effects. Wick humidifiers trap the mineral deposits in the wick; vaporizer types tend to collect minerals on or around the heating element and require regular cleaning with vinegar or citric acid to control buildup.

Forced-Air Humidifiers (Whole-house)

For buildings with a forced-air furnace, a humidifier may be installed into the furnace. They can also protect wooden objects, antiques and other furnishings which may be sensitive to damage from overly dry air. In colder months, they may provide substantial energy savings, since as humidity increases, occupants feel warm at a lower temperature. *Bypass humidifiers* are connected between the heated and cold air return ducts, using the pressure difference between these ducts to cause some heated air to make a bypass through the humidifier and return to the furnace. The humidifier should usually be disabled during the summer months if air conditioning is used; air conditioners partially function by reducing indoor humidity. Common styles:

- Drum style (bypass): A pipe brings water directly to a reservoir (a pan) attached to the furnace. The water level in the pan is controlled by a float valve, similar to a small toilet tank float. The wick is typically a foam pad mounted on a drum and attached to a small motor; hot air enters the drum at one end and is forced to leave through the sides of the drum. When the hygrostat calls for humidity, the motor is turned on causing the drum to rotate slowly through the pan of water and preventing the foam pad from drying out.

Advantages include:

- Low cost
- Inexpensive maintenance (drum-style pads are cheap and readily available).

Disadvantages include:

- Requirement for frequent (approximately monthly) inspections of cleanliness and pad condition
- Water evaporation even when humidification is not required (due to the pan of water which remains exposed to a high velocity air stream)
- Mold growth in the pan full of water (this problem is exacerbated by the large quantity of air, inevitably carrying mold spores, passing through the humidifier whether in use or not).

For the latter reason especially, drum-style humidifiers should always be turned off at the water supply during summer (air conditioning) months, and should always be used with high quality furnace air filters (MERV ratings as high as possible to ensure small numbers of mold spores reaching the humidifier's pan) when the water supply is turned on.

- Disc Wheel Style (bypass): Very similar in design to the drum style humidifiers, this type of furnace humidifier replaces the foam drum with a number of plastic discs with small grooves on both sides. This allows for a very large evaporative surface area, without requiring a great deal of space. Unlike the drum style humidifiers, the disc wheel does not need replacing.

Advantages include:

- Very low maintenance (basin of humidifier should be cleaned out periodically, unless automatic flushing device is installed)
- No regular replacement of parts necessary
- Higher output due to large evaporative surface area
- Can be installed in hard water situations
- Maintains efficiency throughout lifespan.

Disadvantages include:

- Higher price
- Water evaporation even when humidification is not required (due to the pan of water which remains exposed to a high velocity air stream).
- Bypass Flow-Through Style (bypass-also known as "biscuit style" or many other, similar variant names): A pipe brings water directly to an electrically-controlled valve at the top of the humidifier. Air passes through an aluminum "biscuit" (often called a pad; using the term "biscuit" to emphasize the solid rather than foamy form) which is similar to a piece of extremely coarse steel wool. The biscuit has a coating of a matte ceramic, resulting in an extremely large surface area within a small space. When the hygrostat calls for humidity, the valve is opened and causes a spray of water onto the biscuit. Hot air is passed through the biscuit, causing the water to evaporate from the pad and be carried into the building.

Advantages include:

- Reduced maintenance (new biscuit only when clogged with dust or mineral deposits, typically once per year)

- Lack of a pan of potentially stagnant water to serve as a breeding ground for mold as with a drum-style humidifier
- No incidental humidification caused by a constantly-replenished pan of water in a high velocity air stream
- Reduced requirement for expensive air filters
- Uses little electricity.

Disadvantages include:

- A somewhat higher purchase price
- Manufacturer and model-specific replacement biscuits versus the relatively generic drum-style pads
- A portion of the water supplied to the unit is not evaporated. This can generate a considerable amount of waste water, and does require connection to a drain.
- Spray Mist Type: A pipe, usually a small plastic tube, brings water directly to an electrically-controlled valve in the humidifier. Water mist is sprayed directly into the supply air, and the mist is carried into the premises by the air flow.

Advantages include:

- Low cost.
- Simpler than bypass types to install-single cut hole for installation, no additional ducting.
- Uses little electricity.
- Small, compact unit-fits where other types cannot. (Approx 6 inches square.)
- Because it does not require bypass ducting it does not undermine the pressure separation (and therefore, blower efficiency) of the return and supply ducts.
- Does not require use of moisture pads (on-going expense).
- Highly efficient usage of water. Does not generate waste water and does not require separate connection to a drain.
- Requires little maintenance. Periodic cleaning of nozzle may be required in hard water environments.
- Lack of a pan of potentially stagnant water to serve as a breeding ground for mold as with a drum-style humidifier.

Disadvantages include:

- Spray nozzle can become clogged in hard water situations, necessitating the use of water filter, periodic cleaning of nozzle, or nozzle replacement.

- Additional types: 'Non-Bypass Flow-Through' (fan augmented), 'Steam', 'Impeller or Centrifugal Atomizer' and 'Under Duct'.

Disadvantages and Risks

Unnecessary or overuse of a humidifier can raise the relative humidity to high levels, promoting the growth of dust mites and mold. A relative humidity of 30% to 50% is recommended for most homes. Can also cause Hypersensitivity pneumonitis (humidifier lung).

The EPA provides detailed information of the risks as well as recommended maintenance procedures. If the tap water contains a lot of minerals, also known as hard water, then the ultrasonic or impeller humidifiers will produce a "white dust" (calcium is the most common mineral in tap water), which usually spreads over furniture, and is attracted to static electricity generating devices such as CRT monitors. The white dust can usually be prevented by using distilled water and a demineralization cartridge in ultrasonic humidifiers.

Deeming the design to be unsafe, the Supreme Court of Minnesota held the manufacturer of a humidifier strictly liable in products liability in the 1960s when a three-year-old knocked it over, severely burning herself.

Piping and Plumbing Fittings

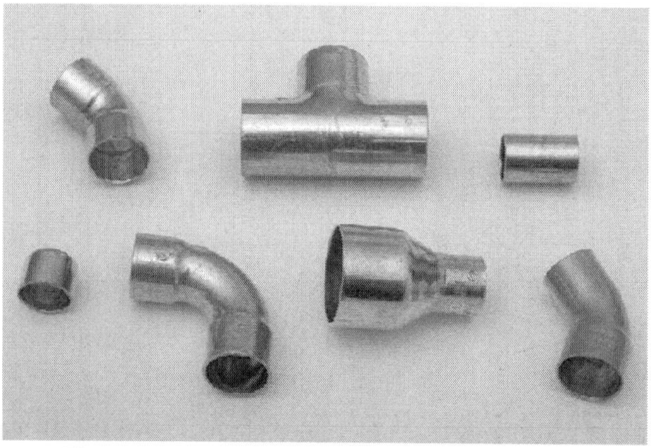

Figure: *Copper fittings for soldered joints*

Fittings are used in pipe and plumbing systems to connect straight pipe or tubing sections, to adapt to different sizes or shapes, and for other purposes, such as regulating or measuring fluid flow. The term *plumbing* is generally used to describe conveyance of water, gas, or liquid waste in ordinary domestic or commercial environments, whereas *piping* is often used to describe high-performance (e.g. high pressure, high flow, high temperature, hazardous materials) conveyance of fluids in specialized applications. The term *tubing* is sometimes used for lighter-weight piping, especially types that are flexible enough to be supplied in coiled form.

Fittings (especially uncommon types) require money, time, materials, and tools to install, so they are a non-trivial part of piping and plumbing systems. Valves are technically fittings, but are usually discussed separately.

Materials

The bodies of fittings for pipe and tubing are most often of the same base material as the pipe or tubing being connected, for example, copper, steel, polyvinyl chloride (PVC), chlorinated polyvinyl chloride (CPVC), or acrylonitrile butadiene styrene (ABS). However, any material that is allowed by the plumbing, health, or building code (as applicable) may be used, but must be compatible with the other materials in the system, the fluids being transported, and the temperatures and pressures inside and outside of the system. For example, brass-or bronze-bodied fittings are common in otherwise copper piping and plumbing systems. Fire hazards, earthquake resistance, and other factors also influence choice of fitting materials.

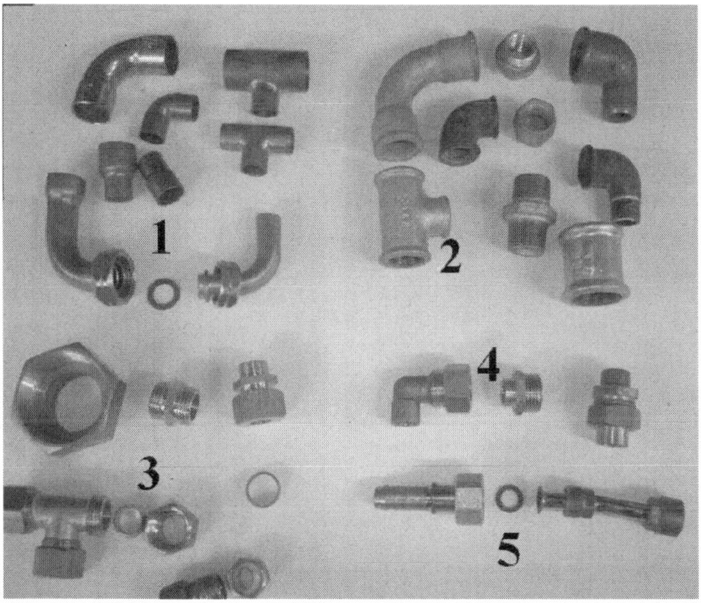

Figure: *Assorted pipe fittings: 1.Copper, solder; 2.Iron or brass, threaded; 3.Brass, compression; 4.Brass, transition from compression to solder; 5.Brass, special adaptors*

Gender of Fittings

Piping or tubing are usually (but not always) inserted *into* fittings to make connections. To avoid confusion, connections are conventionally assigned a gender of male or female, respectively abbreviated as "M" or "F".

Common Fittings for Both Piping and Plumbing

While there are hundreds of specialized fittings manufactured, some common types of fittings are used widely in piping and plumbing systems.

Elbow

An elbow is a pipe fitting installed between two lengths of pipe or tubing to allow a change of direction, usually a 90° or 45° angle, though 22.5° elbows are also made. The ends may be machined for butt welding, threaded (usually female), or socketed, etc. When the two ends differ in size, the fitting is called a reducing elbow or reducer elbow.

Most elbows are available in short radius or long radius types. The short radius elbows have a center-to-end distance equal to the Nominal Pipe Size (NPS) in inches, while the long radius is 1.5 times the NPS in inches. Short elbows are widely available; long elbows are readily available in acrylonitrile butadiene styrene (ABS plastic), polyvinyl chloride (PVC) for DWV, sewage and central vacuums, chlorinated polyvinyl chloride (CPVC) and copper for 1950s to 1960s houses with copper drains.

Coupling

A coupling connects two pipes to each other. If the size of the pipe is not the same, the fitting may be called a reducing coupling or reducer, or an adapter. By convention, the term "expander" is not generally used for a coupler that increases pipe size; instead the term "reducer" is used.

Union

A union is similar to a coupling, except it is designed to allow quick and convenient disconnection of pipes for maintenance or fixture replacement. While a coupling would require either solvent welding, soldering or being able to rotate with all the pipes adjacent as with a threaded coupling, a union provides a simple transition, allowing easy connection or disconnection at any future time. Pipe unions are essentially a type of flange connector, as discussed further below.

In addition to a standard union, there exist dielectric unions which are used to separate dissimilar metals (such as copper and galvanized steel) to avoid the damaging effects of galvanic corrosion. When two dissimilar metals are placed in an electrically conductive solution (even tap water is conductive), they will form a battery and generate a voltage by electrolysis.

When the two metals are in contact with each other the current from one metal to the other will cause a movement of ions from one to the other, dissolving one metal and depositing it on the other. A dielectric union breaks the electric current path with a plastic liner between two halves of the union, thus limiting galvanic corrosion.

Reducer

A reducer allows for a change in pipe size to meet hydraulic flow requirements of the system, or to adapt to existing piping of a different size. Reducers are usually concentric but eccentric reducers are used when required to maintain the same top-or bottom-of-pipe level.

Tee

A tee is used to either combine or split a fluid flow. Most common are tees with the same inlet and outlet sizes, but reducing tees are available as well.

Cross

A cross has one inlet and three outlets, or vice versa. Crosses are common in fire sprinkler systems, but not in plumbing due to their extra cost as compared to using two tees. The three outlet sizes should be named in order (e.g. left, middle, right; measuring 15-22-15).

Cap

A type of pipe fitting, usually liquid or gas tight, which covers the end of a pipe. A cap has a similar function to a plug. In plumbing systems that use threads, the cap has female threads.

Plug

A plug closes off the end of a pipe. It is similar to a cap but it fits inside the fitting it is mated to. In a threaded iron pipe plumbing system, plugs have male threads.

Nipple

A short stub of pipe, usually threaded iron, brass, chlorinated polyvinyl chloride (CPVC) or copper; occasionally just bare copper. A nipple is defined as being a short stub of pipe which has two male ends. Nipples are commonly used for plumbing and hoses, and second as valves for funnels and pipes.

Barb

A barb is used to connect flexible hoses to pipes. The barbed end has a tapered stub with ridges which is inserted into the flexible hose to secure it.

Drain-waste-vent (DWV) and Related Fittings

Because they operate at low pressure and rely on gravity to move fluids (and often entrained solids), drain-waste-vent systems use fittings designed to be as smooth as possible on their interior surfaces. The fittings may be "belled" or expanded slightly in diameter, or otherwise shaped to accommodate insertion of pipe or tubing, without forming a sharp interior ridge that might catch debris or accumulate buildup of material and cause clogging. The absence of interior snags also makes it much easier to "snake out" or "rod out" a clogged pipe using long flexible tools made for this purpose.

Underground piping systems for landscaping drainage, or disposal of stormwater or groundwater, similarly use gravity flow at low pressure, often with entrained solids. Piping fittings used for these systems bear a strong resemblance to DWV fittings, though often at a larger scale. When high peak flow volumes are involved, the design and construction of these systems are closely inter-related to sewer design.

Fittings for central vacuum systems are very similar to DWV fittings, though usually of thinner and lighter construction, since the weight of the materials conveyed through the system is much less. Vacuum system designs share with DWV designs a concern about eliminating internal ridges, burrs, sharp turns, or other obstructions to smooth flow that might cause build-up of material into pipe blockages.

Sweep Elbow

DWV elbows are usually long radius or sweep types, to reduce flow resistance and solids deposition when the direction of flow is changed. A well-designed system will often employ multiple 45° elbows in preference over 90° elbows (even sweep elbows), to reduce flow disruption as much as possible.

Central vacuum system inlet fittings are intentionally designed with a tighter radius of curvature than any other bends in the system. This is done to insure that if any vacuumed debris becomes stuck, it will jam right at the inlet, where it is easiest to discover and to remove.

Closet Flange

The closet flange is the drain pipe flange to which a water closet (toilet) is attached. It is a specialized type of flange connection designed to sit flush with the floor, allowing a standard toilet to be installed above it.

Clean-outs

Clean-outs are fittings with removable elements that allow access to drains without requiring removal of plumbing fixtures. They are used for allowing an auger or plumber's snake to clean out a plugged drain. Clean-outs should be placed in accessible locations at regular intervals throughout a drainage system, often including outside the building, because clean-out augers have limited length. The minimum requirement is typically at the end of each branch in piping, just ahead of each water closet, at the base of each vertical stack, and both inside and outside the building in the building main drain/sewer. Clean-outs normally have screw-on caps or screw-in plugs. Clean-outs are also known as rodding eyes from the eye-shaped cover plates often used on external versions.

Trap Primers

Trap primers regularly inject water into traps so that "water seals" are maintained, as necessary to keep sewer gases out of buildings. The trap primer must be installed in a readily available place for easy access for adjustments, replacement, and repair. Strictly speaking, a trap primer is a specialized valve, and it is usually connected to a clean water supply, in addition to a DWV system. Because of this dual connection, the design usually must be certified to resist accidental backflow of contaminated water.

Combo-Tee

A combination tee (combo tee) is a tee with a gradually curving center connecting joint. It is used in drain systems to provide a smooth, gradually curving path to reduce the likelihood of clogs, and to ease pushing a plumber's snake through a drain system. The "combo" is a combination of a wye and a 1/8 bend or 45° elbow.

Sanitary Tee

A sanitary tee is a tee with a curved center section designed to minimize the possibility of siphon action that could draw water out of a trap. The center connection is generally connected to the pipe which leads to a trap (the trap arm).

Double Sanitary Tee (Sanitary Cross)

Similar to a cross. This fitting differs from a standard cross in that two of the ports have curved inlets. The fitting has been used in the past for connecting the drains of back-to-back fixtures (such as back-to-back bathroom sinks). Some current codes (including the 2006 UPC) prohibit the use of this fitting for that purpose, instead requiring a special "double fixture fitting".

Wye Fitting

A type of waste fitting tee which has the side inlet pipe entering at a 45° angle.

Double-tapped Bushing

A double-tapped bushing is a fitting that has opposing threads on the inside diameter of the bushing.

Hydraulic Fittings

Hydraulic systems use extremely high fluid pressures to create useful work, such as in the hydraulic actuators for powered machinery such as bulldozers and backhoes. Therefore, hydraulic fittings are designed and rated for much greater pressures than those experienced in general piping systems, and they are generally not compatible for use in general plumbing. Fittings are designed and constructed to resist leakage and sudden explosive failure. More information on hydraulics and their specialized fittings can be found in the hydraulic machinery article.

Connection Types

Much of the work of installing a piping or plumbing system involves making leakproof, reliable connections. Depending on the technology used, basic skills may be required, or specialized skills and professional licensure may be required.

Threaded Pipe

A threaded pipe is a pipe with a screw thread at one or both ends for assembly. Steel pipe is often joined using threaded connections, where tapered threads are cut into the end of the tubing segment, sealant is applied in the form of thread sealing compound or thread seal tape (also known as PTFE or Teflon tape), and it is then threaded into a corresponding threaded fitting using a pipe wrench.

Threaded steel pipe is still widely used in many homes and businesses to convey natural gas or propane fuel, and is a popular choice in fire sprinkler systems due to its high heat resistance. Threaded brass pipe was once used in a similar fashion, and was considered superior to steel for carrying drinking water, but is now effectively obsolete.

Assembling threaded steel pipe takes some skill, plus careful planning to allow lengths of pipe to be screwed together in proper sequence. Most threaded pipe systems require occasional use of pipe union fittings to allow final assembly.

Solvent Welding

A solvent is applied to PVC, CPVC, ABS, or other plastic piping, to partially dissolve and fuse the adjacent surfaces of piping and fitting. Solvent welding is usually used with a sleeve-type joint, to connect pipe and fittings made of the same (or closely compatible) material.

Unlike regular welding of metals, solvent welding is relatively easy to perform, although care is still needed to produce reliable joints. Solvents typically used for plastics are usually toxic, may be carcinogenic, and may also be flammable, requiring adequate ventilation.

Soldering

To make a solder connection, a chemical flux is applied to the inner sleeve of a sleeve type joint, and the pipe is inserted. The joint is then heated using a propane torch or MAPP gas torch, solder is applied to the heated joint, and the melted solder is drawn into the joint by capillary action as the flux vaporizes. Sweating is an alternate term sometimes used to describe soldering of pipe joints.

In situations where many connections must be made in a short period of time (such as plumbing of a new building), solder offers much quicker and much less expensive joinery than compression or flare fittings. A degree of skill is needed to rapidly make large numbers of reliable soldered joints. If flux residues are thoroughly cleaned, soldering can produce a long-lasting connection at low cost. However, the use of open flames for heating joints can present fire and health hazards to occupants of a building being worked on, and requires adequate ventilation.

Brazing

Brazing is closely related to soldering, but uses harder materials and higher temperatures.

Welding

Welding of metals differs from soldering and brazing, in that the connection is made without adding a special low-melting-point material (e.g. solder) to complete a joint. Instead, the material of the pipe or tubing is itself partially melted in a carefully controlled manner, and the fitting and piping are directly fused together. Generally this requires that the piping and the fitting be made of the same (or closely compatible) material. Pipe welding is a specialized skill, and is often performed by specially licensed workers who are tested periodically for the quality of their work. For ultra-critical applications, every joint is tested using non-destructive testing methods. Properly welded and inspected joints are considered to be very reliable, robust, and long-lasting. Proper ventilation is essential to remove dangerous metallic fumes from welding operations. Because of the expensive skilled labor required, welded pipe joints are usually restricted to high-performance applications, such as in shipbuilding, chemical reactors, and nuclear reactors.

Compression Fittings

Compression fittings consist of a tapered concave conical seat, a hollow barrel-shaped compression ring, and a compression nut which is threaded onto the body of the fitting and tightened to make a leakproof connection. Fittings are typically made of brass or plastic, but stainless steel or other materials may be used. Compression connections do not typically have the long life that sweat connections offer, but are advantageous in many cases because they are easy to make using basic tools. A disadvantage of compression connections is that they take longer to make than sweated joints, and sometimes require retightening over time to stop leaks.

Flare Fittings

Flared connectors should not be confused with compression connectors, with which they are generally not interchangeable. Flared connectors lack a compression ring, but do use a threaded nut. A special flaring tool is used to enlarge tubing into a tapered "bellmouth" shape that matches the tapered projecting conical shape of the flare fitting. The flare nut, which has previously been installed over the tubing, is then tightened onto the fitting. Fittings are typically made of brass or plastic, but stainless steel or other materials may be used.

Flare connections are a labor intensive method of making connections, but are quite reliable over the course of many years. Flared fittings are sometimes thought to be more secure against leaks and sudden failures, and are often preferred for safety-critical connections, such as in hydraulic brake systems.

Flange Fittings

Flange fittings generally involve pressing two surfaces to be joined tightly together, by means of threaded bolts, wedges, clamps, or other means of applying high compressive forces. Often, a gasket, packing, or an O-ring is installed between the flanges to prevent leakage, but it is sometimes possible to use only a special grease, or nothing at all, if the mating surfaces are precisely formed. Flanged connections tend to be more bulky than other connections, but can perform well in demanding applications, such as large water mains and hydroelectric power systems.

Mechanical Fittings

Manufacturers such as Victaulic or Grinnell produce special sleeve clamp fittings that are increasingly replacing classic flanged connections. They typically attach to the end of a pipe segment by using circumferential grooves pressed (or cut, in older designs) around the end of the pipe to be joined. Mechanical connectors are widely used on larger steel pipes, but can also be used with other materials.

The chief advantage of these newer connectors is that they can be installed in the field after cutting the pipe to length, which is much faster than traditional flanged connections, which must be factory-welded or field-welded to pipe segments.

Crimped or Pressed Fittings

Crimped or pressed connections use special fittings which are permanently attached to tubing with a powered crimper. The special fittings, manufactured with sealant already inside, slide over the tubing to be connected. High pressure is used to deform the fitting and compress the sealant against the inner tubing, creating a leakproof seal.

The advantages of this method are that it should last as long as the tubing, it takes less time to complete than other methods, it is cleaner in both appearance and the materials used to make the connection, and no open flame is used during the connection process. The disadvantages are that the fittings used are harder to find and cost significantly more than sweat type fittings.

Underfloor Air Distribution

Underfloor air distribution (UFAD) is an air distribution strategy for providing ventilation and space conditioning in buildings as part of the design of an HVAC system. UFAD systems use the air plenum beneath a raised floor to provide conditioned air through diffusers directly to the occupied zone.

Applications

Underfloor air distribution is frequently used in office buildings, particularly highly-reconfigurable and open plan offices where raised floors are desirable for cable management. UFAD is also common in command centers, IT data centers and computer rooms which have large cooling loads from electronic equipment and requirements for routing power and data cables. The ASHRAE Underfloor Air Distribution Design Guide suggests that any building considering a raised floor for cable distribution should consider UFAD.

Figure: *Diagram of air movement in an underfloor air distribution system*

System Description

Like other HVAC systems, UFAD systems rely on air handling units to filter and condition air to the appropriate supply conditions so it can be delivered to the occupied zone. While overhead systems typically use ducts to distribute the air, UFAD systems use the plenum formed by installation of a raised floor. The plenum generally sits 0.3-0.48 m (12-18 in) above the structural concrete slab, although lower heights are possible. Specially designed floor diffusers are used as the supply outlets. The most common UFAD configuration consists of a central air handling unit delivering air through a pressurized plenum and into the space through floor diffusers. Other approaches may incorporate fan powered thermal units at the outlets, underfloor ducts, desktop vents or connections to Personal Environmental Control Systems.

UFAD Air Distribution and Stratification

UFAD systems rely on the natural stratification that occurs when warm air rises due to thermal buoyancy. In a UFAD design, cold, fresh air stays in the lower, occupied part of the room, while heat sources such as occupants and equipment generate thermal plumes, which carry the warm air and pollutants towards the ceiling where they are exhausted through the return air ducts. The optimal ventilation strategy controls the supply outlets to limit the mixing of supply air with room air to just below the breathing height of the space. Above this height, stratified and more polluted air is allowed to occur. The air that the occupant breathes will have a lower concentration of contaminants compared to conventional uniformly mixed systems.

Many factors, including the ceiling height, diffuser characteristics, number of diffusers, supply air temperature, total flow rate, cooling load and conditioning mode affect the efficacy of the UFAD system. Swirl diffusers and perforated-floor-panel diffusers have been shown to create a low air velocity in the occupied zone, while linear diffusers created the highest velocity in the occupied zone, disturbing thermal stratification and posing a potential draft risk.

UFAD and Energy

The energy efficiency of UFAD systems is a not fully solved issue, currently generating numerous research projects within the building science and mechanical engineering community. Proponents of UFAD point to the lower fan pressures required to deliver air in a building via the plenum as compared to through ducts. Typical plenum pressures are 0.1 in. H2O (25 Pa) or less. The improvements in cooling-system efficiency inherent in operation at higher temperatures save energy, and relatively higher supply air temperatures allow longer periods of economizer operation. However, an economizer strategy is highly climate-dependent and necessitate careful control of humidity to avoid condensation. Critics, on the other hand, cite the shortage of rigorous research and testing to account for variations in climate, system design, thermal comfort and air quality to question whether UFAD is able to deliver improved energy efficiency in practice. Limited simulation tools, the shortage of design standards and relatively scarcity of exemplar projects compound these problems.

Thermal Decay

Thermal decay is the temperature increase of the conditioned air due to convective heat gain as it travels through the underfloor supply plenum from the plenum inlet to the floor diffusers. This is caused by cool supply air coming into contact with the concrete slab and raised floor warmed by heat gains, for example from the story below. Modelling studies have shown that for a range of typical operating conditions the total supply plenum heat gain can amount to 30-40% of the total system heat gain.

UFAD Compared to other Distribution Systems

Overhead (Mixing): Conventional *overhead mixing systems* usually locate both the supply and return air ducts at the ceiling level. Supply air is supplied at velocities higher than typically acceptable for human comfort and the air temperature may be lower, higher or the same as desired room temperature depending on the cooling/heating load. High speed turbulent air jets mix incoming supply air with the room air.

Displacement Ventilation: *Displacement Ventilation* systems (DV) work on similar principals as UFAD systems. DV systems deliver cool air into the conditioned space at or near the floor level and return air at the ceiling level. This works by utilizing the natural buoyancy of warm air and the thermal plumes generated by heat sources as cooler air is delivered from lower elevations. While similar, UFAD tends to encourage more mixing within the occupied zone. The major practical differences are that in UFAD, air is supplied at a higher velocity through smaller sized supply outlets than in DV, and the supply outlets are usually controlled by the occupants.

HVAC Industry and Standards

International

ISO16813:2006 is one of the ISO building environment standards. It establishes the general principles of building environment design taking into account healthy indoor environment for the occupants, and protecting the environment for future generations, and promoting collaboration among the various parties involved in building environmental design to provide a sustainable building environment. ISO16813 is applicable for new construction and the retrofit of existing buildings.

The building environmental design standard aims to:

Provide the constraints concerning sustainability issues from the initial stage of the design process, including building and plant life cycle together with owning and operating costs to be considered at all stages in the design process;

Assess the proposed design with rational criteria for indoor air quality, thermal comfort, acoustical comfort, visual comfort, energy efficiency and HVAC system controls at every stage of the design process; make iterations between decisions and evaluations of the design throughout the design process.

North America

USA: In the United States, HVAC engineers generally are members of the American Society of Heating, Refrigerating, and Air-Conditioning Engineers (ASHRAE). ASHRAE is an international technical society for all individuals and organizations interested in HVAC. The Society, organized into Regions, Chapters, and Student Branches, allows exchange of HVAC knowledge and experiences for the benefit of the field's practitioners and the public. ASHRAE provides many opportunities to participate in the development of new knowledge via, for example, research and its many Technical Committees. These committees meet typically twice per year at the ASHRAE Annual and Winter Meetings. A popular product show, the AHR Expo, is held in conjunction with each Winter Meeting. The Society has approximately 50,000 members and has headquarters at Atlanta, Georgia, USA.

The most recognized standards for HVAC design is based on ASHRAE data. ASHRAE is the American Society of Heating, Refrigerating and Air-Conditioning Engineers. The ASHRAE Handbook's most general volume, of four, is Fundamentals; it includes heating and cooling calculations. Each volume of the ASHRAE Handbook is updated every four years. The design professional must consult ASHRAE data for the standards of design and care as the typical building codes provides little to no information on HVAC design practices; such codes, such as the UMC and IMC, do include much details on installation requirements, however. Other useful reference materials include items from SMACNA, ACCA, and technical trade journals.

American design standards are legislated in the Uniform Mechanical Code or International Mechanical Code. In certain states, counties, or cities, either of these codes may be adopted and amended via various legislative processes. These codes are updated and published by the International Association of Plumbing and Mechanical Officials (IAPMO) or the International Code Council (ICC) respectively, on a 3-year code development cycle. Typically, local Building Permit Departments are charged with enforcement of these standards on private and certain public properties.

In the United States, as well as throughout the world, HVAC contractors and companies are members of NADCA, the National Air Duct Cleaners Association. NADCA was formed in 1989 as a non-profit association of companies engaged in the cleaning of HVAC systems. Its mission was to promote source removal as the only acceptable method of cleaning and to establish industry standards for the association. NADCA has expanded its mission to include the representation of qualified companies engaged in the assessment, cleaning, and restoration of HVAC systems, and to assist its members in providing high quality service to their customers. The goal of the association is to be the number one source for the HVAC cleaning and restoration services: first time, every time. NADCA has experienced phenomenal membership growth and has been extremely successful with the training and certification of air systems cleaning specialists, mold remediators, and HVAC inspectors. The association has also published important standards and guidelines, educational materials, and other useful information for the consumer and members of NADCA. Their headquarters are located in Washington, D.C.

Europe

United Kingdom: The Chartered Institute of Building Services Engineers is a body that covers the essential Service (systems architecture) that allow buildings to operate. It includes the electrotechnical, heating, ventilating, air conditioning, refrigeration and plumbing industries. To train as a building services engineer, the academic requirement are GCSEs (A-C)/Standard Grades (1-3) in Maths and Science, which are important in measurements, planning and theory. Employers will often want a degree in a branch of engineering, such as building environment engineering, electrical engineering or mechanical engineering. To become a full member of CIBSE, and so also to be registered by the Engineering Council UK as a chartered engineer, one must also attain an Honours Degree and a Masters Degree in a relevant engineering subject.

CIBSE publishes several guides to HVAC design relevant to the UK market, and also the Republic of Ireland, Australia, New Zealand and Hong Kong. These guides include for various recommended design criteria and standards, some of which are cited within the UK building regulations, and therefore form a legislative requirement for major building services works. The main guides are:

Guide A: Environmental Design

Guide B: Heating, Ventilating, Air Conditioning and Refrigeration

Guide C: Reference Data

Guide D: Transportation systems in Buildings

Guide E: Fire Safety Engineering

Guide F: Energy Efficiency in Buildings

Guide G: Public Health Engineering

Guide H: Building Control Systems

Guide J: Weather, Solar and Illuminance Data

Guide K: Electricity in Buildings

Guide L: Sustainability

Guide M: Maintenance ENgineering and Management.

Within the construction sector, it is the job of the building services engineer to design and oversee the installation and maintenance of the essential services such as gas, electricity, water, heating and lighting, as well as many others. These all help to make buildings comfortable and healthy places to live and work in. Building Services is part of a sector that has over 51,000 businesses and employs represents 2%-3% of the GDP.

Australia

Air Conditioning and Mechanical Contractors Association of Australia (AMCA), Australian Institute of Refrigeration, Air Conditioning and Heating (AIRAH), CIBSE.

Asia

India: The Indian Society of Heating, Refrigerating and Air Conditioning Engineers (ISHRAE) was established to promote the HVAC industry in India. ISHRAE is an associate of ASHRAE. ISHRAE was started at Delhi in 1981 and a chapter was started in Bangalore in 1989. Between 1989 & 1993, ISHRAE chapters were formed in all major cities in India and also in the Middle East.

Pakistan: Air-conditioning technology has been in use in Pakistan since 1947, the time of its independence. At that point local expertise was dependent on the supply and installation of imported equipment in accordance with the system designs from abroad. Once Pakistani engineers recognized the importance of the field they became active in developing expertise in design, manufacture, installation, operation, and maintenance. In 1995 the Pakistan HVACR Society was formed, and has organized the various disciplines of the field under its umbrella, and has regularly holds an Annual Expo & Conference, which rotates yearly between the cities of Karachi, Lahore & Islamabad, and is the premium industry event in Pakistan, and also attended by many international manufacturers and visitors. In 2003 the ASHRAE Pakistan Chapter was formed, followed by ASHRAE Northern Pakistan Chapter in 2005, and also subsequently ASHRAE Central Pakistan Chapter in 2011.

Building Automation

Building automation describes the functionality provided by the control system of a building. A building automation system (BAS) is an example of a distributed control system. The control system is a computerized, intelligent network of electronic devices, designed to monitor and control the mechanical and lighting systems in a building.

BAS core functionality keeps the building climate within a specified range, provides lighting based on an occupancy schedule, and monitors system performance and device failures and provides email and/or text notifications to building engineering staff. The BAS functionality reduces building energy and maintenance costs when compared to a non-controlled building. A building controlled by a BAS is often referred to as an intelligent building system.

Topology

Most building automation networks consist of a *primary* and *secondary* bus which connect high-level controllers (generally specialized for building automation, but may be generic programmable logic controllers) with lower-level controllers, input/output devices and a user interface (also known as a human interface device).

The primary and secondary bus can be BACnet, optical fiber, ethernet, ARCNET, RS-232, RS-485 or a wireless network.Most controllers are proprietary. Each company has its own controllers for specific applications. Some are designed with limited controls: for example, a simple Packaged Roof Top Unit. Others are designed to be flexible. Most have proprietary software that will work with ASHRAE's open protocol BACnet or the open protocol LonTalk.

Some newer building automation and lighting control solutions use wireless mesh open standards (such as ZigBee). These systems can provide interoperability, allowing users to mix-and-match devices from different manufacturers, and to provide integration with other compatible building control systems. Inputs and outputs are either analog or digital (some companies say binary).

Analog inputs are used to read a variable measurement. Examples are temperature, humidity and pressure sensor which could be thermistor, 4-20 mA, 0-10 volt or platinum resistance thermometer (resistance temperature detector), or wireless sensors.

A digital input indicates if a device is turned on or not. Some examples of an digital input would be a 24VDC/AC signal, an air flow switch, or a volta-free relay contact (Dry Contact).

Analog outputs control the speed or position of a device, such as a variable frequency drive, a I-P (current to pneumatics) transducer, or a valve or damper actuator. An example is a hot water valve opening up 25% to maintain a setpoint.

Digital outputs are used to open and close relays and switches. An example would be to turn on the parking lot lights when a photocell indicate it is dark outside.

Infrastructure

Controller: Controllers are essentially small, purpose-built computers with input and output capabilities. These controllers come in a range of sizes and capabilities to control devices commonly found in buildings, and to control sub-networks of controllers.

KMC Digital Controls (BACnet and Proprietary)

KMC Electronic Controls, Actuators, and Valves

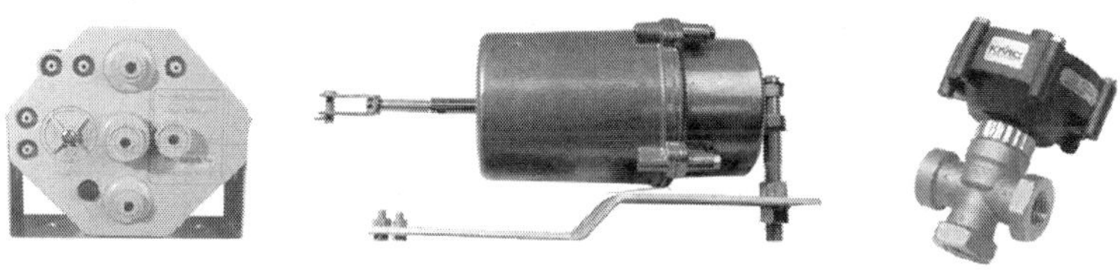

KMC Pneumatic Controls, Actuators, and Valves

Figure: *Various components that make up a building automation system*

Inputs allow a controller to read temperatures, humidity, pressure, current flow, air flow, and other essential factors. The outputs allow the controller to send command and control signals to slave devices, and to other parts of the system. Inputs and outputs can be either digital or analog. Digital outputs are also sometimes called discrete depending on manufacturer.

Controllers used for building automation can be grouped in 3 categories. Programmable Logic Controllers (PLCs), System/Network controllers, and Terminal Unit controllers. However an additional device can also exist in order to integrate 3rd party systems (i.e. a stand-alone AC system) into a central Building automation system).

PLC's provide the most responsiveness and processing power, but at a unit cost typically 2 to 3 times that of a System/Network controller intended for BAS applications. Terminal Unit controllers are usually the least expensive and least powerful. PLC's may be used to automate high-end applications such as clean rooms or hospitals where the cost of the controllers is less of a concern.

In office buildings, supermarkets, malls, and other common automated buildings the systems will use System/Network controllers rather than PLC's. Most System controllers provide general purpose feedback loops, as well as digital circuits, but lack the millisecond response time that PLC's provide.

System/Network controllers may be applied to control one or more mechanical systems such as an Air Handler Unit (AHU), boiler, chiller, etc., or they may supervise a sub-network of controllers. In the diagram above, System/Network controllers are often used in place of PLCs.

Terminal Unit controllers usually are suited for control of lighting and/or simpler devices such as a package rooftop unit, heat pump, VAV box, or fan coil, etc. The installer typically selects 1 of the available pre-programmed personalities best suited to the device to be controlled, and does not have to create new control logic.

Occupancy: Occupancy is one of 2 or more operating modes for a building automation system. Unoccupied, Morning Warmup, and Night-time Setback are other common modes.

Occupancy is usually based on time of day schedules. In Occupancy mode, the BAS aims to provides a comfortable climate and adequate lighting, often with zone-based control so that users on one side of a building have a different thermostat (or a different system, or sub system) than users on the opposite side. A temperature sensor in the zone provides feedback to the controller, so it can deliver heating or cooling as needed.

If enabled, Morning Warmup (MWU) mode occurs prior to Occupancy. During Morning Warmup the BAS tries to bring the building to setpoint just in time for Occupancy. The BAS often factors in outdoor conditions and historical experience to optimize MWU. This is also referred to as Optimised Start.

An override is a manually-initiated command to the BAS. For example, many wall-mounted temperature sensors will have a push-button that forces the system into Occupancy mode for a set number of minutes. Where present, web interfaces allow users to remotely initiate an override on the BAS.

Some buildings rely on occupancy sensors to activate lighting and/or climate conditioning. Given the potential for long lead times before a space becomes sufficiently cool or warm, climate conditioning is not often initiated directly by an occupancy sensor.

Lighting: Lighting can be turned on, off, or dimmed with a building automation or lighting control system based on time of day, or on occupancy sensors, photosensors and timers. One typical example is to turn the lights in a space on for a half hour since the last motion was sensed. A photocell placed outside a building can sense darkness, and the time of day, and modulate lights in outer offices and the parking lot.

Lighting is also a good candidate for Demand response, with many control systems providing the ability to dim (or turn off) lights to take advantage of DR incentives and savings. if occupancy sensors are present they can also be used as burglar alarms

Air Handlers: Most air handlers mix return and outside air so less temperature change is needed. This can save money by using less chilled or heated water (not all AHUs use chilled/hot water circuits). Some external air is needed to keep the building's air healthy.

Analog or digital temperature sensors may be placed in the space or room, the return and supply air ducts, and sometimes the external air. Actuators are placed on the hot and chilled water valves, the outside air and return air dampers. The supply fan (and return if applicable) is started and stopped based on either time of day, temperatures, building pressures or a combination.

Constant Volume Air-handling Units: The less efficient type of air-handler is a "constant volume air handling unit," or CAV. The fans in CAVs do not have variable-speed controls. Instead, CAVs open and close dampers and water-supply valves to maintain temperatures in the building's spaces. They heat or cool the spaces by opening or closing chilled or hot water valves that feed their internal heat exchangers. Generally one CAV serves several spaces

Variable Volume Air-handling Units: A more efficient unit is a "variable air volume (VAV) air-handling unit," or VAV. VAVs supply pressurized air to VAV boxes, usually one box per room or area. A VAV air handler can change the pressure to the VAV boxes by changing the speed of a fan or blower with a variable frequency drive or (less efficiently) by moving inlet guide vanes to a fixed-speed fan. The amount of air is determined by the needs of the spaces served by the VAV boxes.

Each VAV box supply air to a small space, like an office. Each box has a damper that is opened or closed based on how much heating or cooling is required in its space. The more boxes are open, the more air is required, and a greater amount of air is supplied by the VAV air-handling unit.

Some VAV boxes also have hot water valves and an internal heat exchanger. The valves for hot and cold water are opened or closed based on the heat demand for the spaces it is supplying. These heated VAV boxes are sometimes used on the perimeter only and the interior zones are cooling only.

A minimum and maximum CFM must be set on VAV boxes to assure adequate ventilation and proper air balance.

VAV Hybrid Systems: Another variation is a hybrid between VAV and CAV systems. In this system, the interior zones operate as in a VAV system. The outer zones differ in that the heating is supplied by a heating fan in a central location usually with a heating coil fed by the building boiler. The heated air is ducted to the exterior dual duct mixing boxes and dampers controlled by the zone thermostat calling for either cooled or heated air as needed.

Central Plant: A central plant is needed to supply the air-handling units with water. It may supply a chilled water system, hot water system and a condenser water system, as well as transformers and auxiliary power unit for emergency power. If well managed, these can often help each other. For example, some plants generate electric power at periods with peak demand, using a gas turbine, and then use the turbine's hot exhaust to heat water or power an absorptive chiller.

Chilled Water System: Chilled water is often used to cool a building's air and equipment. The chilled water system will have chiller(s) and pumps. Analog temperature sensors measure the chilled water supply and return lines. The chiller(s) are sequenced on and off to chill the chilled water supply.

Condenser Water System: Cooling tower(s) and pumps are used to supply cool condenser water to the chillers. Because the condenser water supply to the chillers has to be constant, variable speed drives are commonly used on the cooling tower fans to control temperature. Proper cooling tower temperature assures the proper refrigerant head pressure in the chiller. The cooling tower set point used depends upon the refrigerant being used. Analog temperature sensors measure the condenser water supply and return lines.

Hot Water System: The hot water system supplies heat to the building's air-handling unit or VAV box heating coils, along with the domestic hot water heating coils (Calorifier). The hot water system will have a boiler(s) and pumps. Analog temperature sensors are placed in the hot water supply and return lines. Some type of mixing valve is usually used to control the heating water loop temperature. The boiler(s) and pumps are sequenced on and off to maintain supply.

Alarms and Security: Many building automation systems have alarm capabilities. If an alarm is detected, it can be programmed to notify someone. Notification can be through a computer, pager, cellular phone, or audible alarm.

- Common temperature alarms are: space, supply air, chilled water supply and hot water supply.
- Differential pressure switches can be placed on the filter to determine if it is dirty.
- Status alarms are common. If a mechanical device like a pump is requested to start, and the status input indicates it is off. This can indicate a mechanical failure.
- Some valve actuators have end switches to indicate if the valve has opened or not.
- Carbon monoxide and carbon dioxide sensors can be used to alarm if levels are too high.
- Refrigerant sensors can be used to indicate a possible refrigerant leak.
- Current sensors can be used to detect low current conditions caused by slipping fan belts, or clogging strainers at pumps.

At sites with several buildings, momentary power failures can cause hundreds or thousands of alarms from equipment that has shut down. Some sites are programmed so that critical alarms are automatically re-sent at varying intervals. For example, a repeating critical alarm (of an [uninterruptible power supply] in 'by pass') might resound at 10 minutes, 30 minutes, and every 2 to 4 hours there after until the alarms are resolved.

Security systems can be interlocked to a building automation system. If occupancy sensors are present, they can also be used as burglar alarms.

Fire and smoke alarm systems can be hard-wired to override building automation. For example: if the smoke alarm is activated, all the outside air dampers close to prevent air coming into the building, and an exhaust system can isolate

Room Automation

Room automation is a subset of building automation and with a similar purpose, it is the consolidation of one or more systems under centralised control, though in this case in one room.

The most common example of *room automation* is corporate boardroom, presentation suites, and lecture halls, where the operation of the large number of devices that define the room function (such as videoconferencing equipment, video projectors, lighting control systems, public address systems etc.) would make manual operation of the room very complex. It is common for room automation systems to employ a touchscreen as the primary way of controlling each operation.

Building Indoor Environment

Building science is the collection of scientific knowledge that focuses on the analysis and control of the physical phenomena affecting buildings. It traditionally includes the detailed analysis of building materials and building envelope systems. In Europe, building physics is a term used for the knowledge domain that overlaps heavily with building science, and includes fire protection, sound control, and daylighting as well as the heat and moisture concerns that tend to dominate North American building science. The practical purpose of building science is to provide predictive capability to optimize building performance and understand or prevent building failures.

This is the architectural-engineering-construction technology discipline that concerns itself with the 'mainly detail-design' of buildings in response to naturally occurring physical phenomenon such as:

- the weather (sun, wind, rain, temperature, humidity), and related issues:e.g. freeze/thaw cycles, dew point/frost point, snow load & drift prediction, lightning patterns etc.
- subterranean conditions including (potential for seismic or other soil + ground-water activity, frost penetration etc.).
- characteristics of materials,(e.g. Galvanic corrosion between dissimilar metals, permeability of materials to water and water

vapour, construct-ability, compatibility, material-adjacency and longevity issues).

- characteristics of physics, chemistry and biology such as capillary-action, absorption, condensation ("will the dew point occur at a good or bad place within the wall?"), gravity, thermal migration/transfer (conductivity, radiation and convection), vapour pressure dynamics, chemical reactions (incl. combustion process), adhesion/cohesion, friction, ductility, elasticity, and also the physiology of fungus/mold.
- human physiology (comfort, sensory reaction e.g.radiance perception, sweat function, chemical sensitivity etc.).
- energy consumption, environmental control-ability, building maintenance considerations, longevity/sustainability, and occupant (physical) comfort/health.

The building science of a project refers to strategies implemented in the general and specific arrangement of building materials and component-assemblies.

Building Envelope

The building envelope is the physical separator between the interior and the exterior environments of a building. Another emerging term is "Building Enclosure". It serves as the outer shell to help maintain the indoor environment (together with the mechanical conditioning systems) and facilitate its climate control. Building envelope design is a specialized area of architectural and [[engineering practice that draws from all areas of building science and indoor climate control.

The many functions of the building envelope can be separated into three categories :

- Support (to resist and transfer mechanical loads)
- Control (the flow of matter and energy of all types)
- Finish (to meet human desires on the inside and outside).

The control function is at the core of good performance, and in practise focuses, in order of importance, on rain control, air control, heat control, and vapour control.

Control of rain is most fundamental, and there are numerous strategies to this end, namely, perfect barriers, drained screens, and mass/storage systems.

Control of air flow is important to ensure indoor air quality, control energy consumption, avoid condensation (and thus help ensure durability), and to provide comfort. Control of air movement includes flow through the enclosure (the assembly of materials that perform this function is termed the air barrier system) or through components of the building envelope (interstitial) itself, as well as into and out of the interior space, (which can affect building insulation performance greatly). Hence, air control includes the control of windwashing and convective loops.

The physical components of the envelope include the foundation, roof, walls, doors and windows. The dimensions, performance and compatibility of materials, fabrication process and details, their connections and interactions are the main factors that determine the effectiveness and durability of the building enclosure system.

Common measures of the effectiveness of a building envelope include physical protection from weather and climate (comfort), indoor air quality (hygiene and public health), durability and energy efficiency. In order to achieve these objectives, all building enclosure systems must include a solid structure, a drainage plane, an air barrier, a thermal barrier, and may include a vapour barrier. Moisture control is essential in all climates, but cold climates and hot-humid climates are especially demanding.

The thermal envelope (or heat flow control layer) is usually different than the building envelope. The difference can be illustrated by understanding that an insulated attic floor is the primary thermal control layer between the inside of the house and the exterior while the entire roof (from the surface of the shingles to the interior paint finish on the ceiling) comprises the building envelope.

Building Envelope Thermography involves using an infrared camera to view temperature anomalies on the interior and exterior surfaces of the structure. Analysis of infrared images can be useful in identifying moisture issues from water intrusion, or internal condensation. Shown below is an example of an image within the scope of a residential infrared inspection in which an uninsulated HVAC plenum was located in a confined attic space. The humidity from the warm attic air condensed on the plenum and was damaging the ceiling and walls.

In a city planning and zoning context, the "building envelope" can be 'the *three dimensional space created by the designated setbacks and height restrictions in place for a zoning district*'.

The practical outcome of building science knowledge is reflected in the design of the architectural details of the building enclosure and ultimately in the long-term performance of the building's 'skin'. The scope can be, and is, much wider than this on most projects; after all,engineering is applied science mixed with experience and judgement. When architects talk of "building science", they usually mean the 'science' issues that traditional engineering disciplines traditionally avoided, albeit there are emerging disciplines of 'building scientists', 'envelope consultants', and 'building engineers'.

Many aspects of building science are the responsibility of the architect (in Canada, many architectural firms employ a architectural technologist for this purpose), often in collaboration with the engineering disciplines that have evolved to handle 'non-building envelope' building science concerns: Civil engineering, Structural engineering, Earthquake engineering, Geotechnical engineering, Mechanical engineering, Electrical engineering, Acoustic engineering, & fire code engineering. Even the interior designer will inevitably generate a few building sciencc issues.

Building Design

Earthquake/Seismic Design

All kinds of structures are projected according to two strain conditions: static and dynamic. The static ones are tied to the structure's dead loads added to the so-called live loads (of people, furniture, etc.), the dynamic ones are tied to the natural, abnormal, and artificial movements (earthquake and loads wind) the structure can sustain during its life cycle. The parameters which characterize structure dynamics are tied to the geometry of the building and to the physical and mechanic properties of its composition. The parameters are:

- The fundamental frequency of vibration (f) and the respective oscillation period (T=1/f)-The equivalent dumping coefficient (neq);
- The mode shape (the way in which the structure buckles);

The first parameter varies according to the structure stiffness; very tall and then very flexible buildings as skyscrapers (low oscillation frequencies) oscillate slowly with respect to lower and squat buildings, and according to the building mass. The second parameter takes into account all the dissipation phenomena tied to the viscosity of materials and to friction phenomena. The mode shape describes the way of deformation which the structure is subjected to during the seismic event, and highlights whether or not the structures presents a good seismic behavior.

Reducing the Effect of Earthquakes on Buildings

By monitoring the response of structures subject to earthquakes and by applying new knowledge and technologies, scientists and engineers continuously develop design and repair techniques on buildings, so that their ability to control the earthquake effects will grow. In order to reduce the destructive effects of earthquakes both on new-built buildings and especially on older ones, there exist some seismic adjustment techniques, with the aim of reducing the strain effects that earthquake causes. These techniques can be divided into two different categories:

Base isolation: it is aimed to untie the ground-foundation system, so that the structure can be seen as it is "floating" on the ground during the seismic event, thus reducing the strains.

Dissipation systems: there exist various types of dissipation systems, but they all have in common the effect of increasing the previously seen viscous dissipation coefficient of the structure. The better known base isolation technique consists of inserting some special equipment (isolator (building design)) in the proximity of foundations. This equipment offers a high stiffness for vertical loads so that the structure is not subject to sinking, while offering a low stiffness for horizontal ones, which are peculiar of seismic events. This way all seismic effects are absorbed by the equipment, whereas the structure is subject to low oscillations and consequently to low strains.

The dissipation systems (dissipator (building design)) are made by a series of devices inserted on the inside of the building frame using different techniques, with the aim of slowing down the structure oscillation and dispelling seismic energy.

Energy Efficiency In the US contractors certified by the independent organization Building Performance Institute advertise that they operate businesses as Building Scientists. This is questionable due to their lack of scientific background and credentials.

Indoor Environment

Building indoor environment covers the environmental aspects in the design, analysis, and operation of energy-efficient, healthy, and comfortable buildings. Fields of specialization include architecture, HVAC design, thermal comfort, indoor air quality (IAQ), lighting, acoustics, and control systems.

Chapter 5

Building Transportation Systems

Elevator

An elevator (or lift in British English) is a vertical transport equipment that efficiently moves people or goods between floors (levels, decks) of a building, vessel or other structure. Elevators are generally powered by electric motors that either drive traction cables or counterweight systems like a hoist, or pump hydraulic fluid to raise a cylindrical piston like a jack.

Figure: *A set of elevators in the lower level of the Borough station on the London Underground. The "up" and "down" arrows indicate each elevator's position and direction of travel.*

Design

Some people argue that lifts began as simple rope or chain hoists. A lift is essentially a platform that is either pulled or pushed up by a mechanical means. A modern day lift consists of a cab (also called a "cage" or "car") mounted on a platform within an enclosed space called a shaft or sometimes a "hoistway". In the past, lift drive mechanisms were powered by steam and water hydraulic pistons or by hand. In a "traction" lift, cars are pulled up by means of rolling steel ropes over a deeply grooved pulley, commonly called a sheave in the industry. The weight of the car is balanced by a counterweight. Sometimes two lifts always move synchronously in opposite directions, and they are each other's counterweight.

The friction between the ropes and the pulley furnishes the traction which gives this type of lift its name.

Hydraulic lifts use the principles of hydraulics (in the sense of hydraulic power) to pressurize an above ground or in-ground piston to raise and lower the car. Roped hydraulics use a combination of both ropes and hydraulic power to raise and lower cars. Recent innovations include permanent magnet motors, machine room-less rail mounted gearless machines, and microprocessor controls.

The technology used in new installations depends on a variety of factors. Hydraulic lifts are cheaper, but installing cylinders greater than a certain length becomes impractical for very high lift hoistways. For buildings of much over seven storeys, traction lifts must be employed instead. Hydraulic lifts are usually slower than traction lifts.

Lifts are a candidate for mass customization. There are economies to be made from mass production of the components, but each building comes with its own requirements like different number of floors, dimensions of the well and usage patterns.

Elevator Doors: Elevator doors protect riders from falling into the shaft. The most common configuration is to have two panels that meet in the middle, and slide open laterally. In a cascading configuration (potentially allowing wider entryways within limited space), the doors run on independent tracks so that while open, they are tucked behind one another, and while closed, they form cascading layers on one side. This can be configured so that two sets of such cascading doors operate like the center opening doors described above, allowing for a very wide elevator cab. In less expensive installations the elevator can also use one large "slab" door: a single panel door the width of the doorway that opens to the left or right laterally.

Some buildings have elevators with the single door on the shaft way, and double cascading doors on the cab.

Machine Room-less (MRL) Elevators

Machine room-less elevators are designed so that most of the components fit within the shaft containing the elevator car; and a small cabinet houses the elevator controller. Other than the machinery being in the hoistway, the equipment is similar to a normal traction elevator.

Figure: *Kone EcoDisc. The entire drive system is in the hoistway.*

This new design was first developed by Kone in 1996.

Benefits:

- creates more usable space
- use less energy (70-80% less than hydraulic elevators)
- uses no oil
- all components are above ground similar to roped hydraulic type elevators (this takes away the environmental concern that was created by the hydraulic cylinder on direct hydraulic type elevators being stored underground)
- slightly lower cost than other elevators
- can operate at faster speeds than hydraulics but not normal traction units.

Detriments:

- Equipment can be harder to service and maintain.
- No code has been approved for the installation of Residential elevator Equipment.

Facts:

- Noise level is at 50-55 dBA (A-weighted decibels), which can be lower than some but not all types of elevators
- Usually used for low-rise to mid-rise buildings
- The motor mechanism is placed in the hoistway itself
- The US was slow to accept the commercial MRL Elevator because of codes.

National and local building codes did not address elevators without machine rooms. Residential MRL Elevators are still not allowed by the ASME A17 code in the US.

Elevator Traffic Calculations

Round Trip Time Calculations: The majority of elevator designs are developed from Up Peak Round Trip Time calculations as described in the following publications:-CIBSE Guide D: Transportation Systems in Building Elevator Traffic Handbook, Theory and Practice. Gina Barney The Vertical Transportation Handbook. George Strakosch.

Traditionally these calculations have formed the basis of establishing the Handling Capacity of an elevator system.

Modern Installations with more complex elevator arrangements have led to the development of more specific formulae such as the General Analysis calculation.

Subsequently this has been extended for Double Deck elevators.

Simulation: Elevator traffic simulation software can be used to model complex traffic patterns and elevator arrangements that cannot necessarily be analysed by RTT calculations.

Lift Traffic Patterns: There are four main types of elevator traffic patterns that can be observed in most modern office installations. They are up peak traffic, down peak traffic, lunch time (two way) traffic and interfloor traffic.

Elevator Modernization

Most elevators are built to provide about 20 years of service, as long as service intervals specified and periodic maintenance/inspections by the manufacturer are followed. As the elevator ages and equipment become increasingly difficult to find or replace, along with code changes and deteriorating ride performance, a complete overhaul of the elevator may be suggested to the building owners.

A typical modernization consists of controller equipment, electrical wiring and buttons, position indicators and direction arrows, hoist machines and motors (including door operators), and sometimes door hanger tracks. Rarely are car slings, rails, or other heavy structures changed. The cost of an elevator modernization can range greatly depending on which type of equipment is to be installed.

Modernization can greatly improve operational reliability by replacing mechanical relays and contacts with solid-state electronics. Ride quality can be improved by replacing motor-generator-based drive designs with Variable-Voltage, Variable Frequency (V3F) drives, providing near-seamless acceleration and deceleration. Passenger safety is also improved by updating systems and equipment to conform to current code.

History: The first reference to an elevator is in the works of the Roman architect Vitruvius, who reported that Archimedes (c. 287 BC – c. 212 BC) built his first elevator probably in 236 BC. In some literary sources of later historical periods, elevators were mentioned as cabs on a hemp rope and powered by hand or by animals. It is supposed that elevators of this type were installed in the Sinai monastery of Egypt.

In 1000, the *Book of Secrets* by Ibn Khalaf al-Muradi in Islamic Spain described the use of an elevator-like lifting device, in order to raise a large battering ram to destroy a fortress. In the 17th century the prototypes of elevators were located in the palace buildings of England and France.

Ancient and medieval elevators used drive systems based on hoists or winders. The invention of a system based on the screw drive was perhaps the most important step in elevator technology since ancient times, leading to the creation of modern passenger elevators. The first screw drive elevator was built by Ivan Kulibin and installed in Winter Palace in 1793. Several years later another of Kulibin's elevators was installed in Arkhangelskoye near Moscow. In 1823, an "ascending room" made its debut in London.

In the middle 1800s, there were many types of crude elevators that carried freight. Most of them ran hydraulically. The first hydraulic elevators used a plunger below the car to raise or lower the elevator. A pump applied water pressure to a steel column inside a vertical cylinder. Increasing the pressure caused the elevator to ascend. The elevator also used a system of counter-balancing so that the plunger did not have to lift the entire weight of the elevator and its load. The plunger, however, was not practical for tall buildings, because it required a pit as deep below the building as the building was tall. Later, a rope-geared elevator with multiple pulleys was developed. Henry Waterman of New York is credited with inventing the "standing rope control" for an elevator in 1850.

In 1852, Elisha Otis introduced the safety elevator, which prevented the fall of the cab if the cable broke. The design of the Otis safety elevator is somewhat similar to one type still used today. A governor device engages knurled roller(s), locking the elevator to its guides should the elevator descend at excessive speed. He demonstrated it at the New York exposition in the Crystal Palace in a dramatic, death-defying presentation in 1854.

On March 23, 1857 the first Otis passenger elevator was installed at 488 Broadway in New York City.

The first elevator shaft preceded the first elevator by four years. Construction for Peter Cooper's Cooper Union Foundation building in New York began in 1853. An elevator shaft was included in the design, because Cooper was confident that a safe passenger elevator would soon be invented. The shaft was cylindrical because Cooper felt it was the most efficient design. Later, Otis designed a special elevator for the building. Today the Otis Elevator Company, now a subsidiary of United Technologies Corporation, is the world's largest manufacturer of vertical transport systems.

The first electric elevator was built by Werner von Siemens in 1880. The safety and speed of electric elevators were significantly enhanced by Frank Sprague. The inventor Anton Freissler developed the ideas of von Siemens and built up a successful enterprise in Austria-Hungary. The development of elevators was led by the need for movement of raw materials including coal and lumber from hillsides. The technology developed by these industries and the introduction of steel beam construction worked together to provide the passenger and freight elevators in use today.

In 1874, J.W. Meaker patented a method which permitted elevator doors to open and close safely. U.S. Patent 147,853

In 1882, when hydraulic power was a well established technology, a company later named the London Hydraulic Power Company was formed. It constructed a network of high pressure mains on both sides of the Thames which, ultimately, extended to 184 miles and powered some 8,000 machines, predominantly lifts (elevators) and cranes.

In 1887, American Inventor Alexander Miles of Duluth, Minnesota patented an elevator with automatic doors that would close off the elevator shaft.

Elevator Safety

Pneumatic Vacuum Elevators: Pneumatic Vacuum Elevators operate without cables or pistons and can be installed more easily and quickly than their alternatives since their housing is composed of prefabricated sections which are considerably narrower than conventional lift shafts. These sections are transparent and afford the passenger a near 360° view. Other notable features of the vacuum elevator are as follows:

- No pit excavation, hoist way, or machine room needed.
- Installation within one to two days
- Two to four stops for residential, marine, and stage use (35ft. total rise)
- Ideal for new and existing homes due to the minimal space needed to fit the elevator
- Self-supporting structure: the elevator can rest on any existing ground floor
- "Green Elevator" : minimal energy consumption used during ascent and no energy used during descent
- Minimal maintenance: no oils or lubrication required for the elevator
- Absolute safety in case of a power failure since the moving car automatically descends to the lowest level and the electro-mechanical door will open to let the passenger out
- Elevator runs on 220Volts and cabin electric circuits are 24 volts, eliminating the risk of shock.

Cable-borne Elevators: Statistically speaking, elevators are extremely safe. Their safety record is unsurpassed by any other vehicle system. In 1998, it was estimated that approximately eight millionths of one percent (1 in 12 million) of elevator rides result in an anomaly, and the vast majority of these were minor things such as the doors failing to open. For all practical purposes, there are no cases of elevators simply free-falling and killing the passengers inside; of the 20 to 30 elevator-related deaths each year, most of them are maintenance-related-for example, technicians leaning too far into the shaft or getting caught between moving parts, and most of the rest are attributed to easily avoidable accidents, such as people stepping blindly through doors that open into empty shafts or being strangled by scarves caught in the doors. In fact, prior to the September 11th terrorist attacks, the only known free-fall incident in a modern cable-borne elevator happened in 1945 when a B-25 bomber struck the Empire State Building in fog, severing the cables of an elevator cab, which fell from the 75th floor all the way to the bottom of the building, seriously injuring (though not killing) the sole occupant-the female elevator operator. However, there was an incident in 2007 at a Seattle children's hospital, where a ThyssenKrupp ISIS machine room-less elevator free-fell until the safety brakes were engaged. This was due to a flaw in the design where the cables were connected at one common point, and the kevlar ropes had a tendency to overheat and cause slipping (or, in this case, a free-fall). While it is possible (though extraordinarily unlikely) for an elevator's cable to snap, all elevators in the modern era have been fitted with several safety devices which prevent the elevator from simply free-falling and crashing. An elevator cab is typically borne by six or eight hoist cables, each of which is capable on its own of supporting the full load of the elevator plus twenty-five percent more weight. In addition, there is a device which detects whether the elevator is descending faster than its maximum designed speed; if this happens, the device causes copper brake shoes to clamp down along the vertical rails in the shaft, stopping the elevator quickly, but not so abruptly as to cause injury. This device is called the governor, and was invented by Elisha Graves Otis. In addition, a hydraulic buffer is installed at the bottom of the shaft to somewhat cushion any impact.

Hydraulic Elevators

Past problems with early hydraulic elevators meant those built prior to a code change in 1972 were subject to possible catastrophic failure. The code had previously required only single-bottom hydraulic cylinders. In the event of a cylinder breach, an uncontrolled fall of the elevator might result. Because it is impossible to verify the system completely without a pressurized casing (as described below), it is necessary to remove the piston to inspect it. The cost of removing the piston is such that it makes no economic sense to re-install the old cylinder; therefore it is necessary to replace the cylinder and install a new piston. Another solution to protect against a cylinder blowout is to install a "life jacket." This is a device which, in the event of an excessive downward speed, clamps onto the cylinder and stops the car. A device known as a rupture valve is often attached to the hydraulic inlet/outlet of the piston and can be adjusted for a maximum flow rate. If a pipe or hose were to break (rupture), the flow rate of the rupture valve will surpass a set limit and mechanically stop the outlet flow of hydraulic fluid, thus stopping the piston and the car in the down direction.

In addition to the safety concerns for older hydraulic elevators, there is risk of leaking hydraulic oil into the aquifer and causing potential environmental contamination. This has led to the introduction of PVC liners (casings) around hydraulic cylinders which can be monitored for integrity.

In the past decade, recent innovations in inverted hydraulic jacks have eliminated the costly process of drilling the ground to install a borehole jack. This also eliminates the threat of corrosion to the system and increases safety.

Mine-shaft Elevators

Safety testing of mine shaft elevator rails is routinely undertaken. The method involves destructive testing of a segment of the cable. The ends of the segment are frayed, then set in conical zinc molds. Each end of the segment is then secured in a large, hydraulic stretching machine. The segment is then placed under increasing load to the point of failure. Data about elasticity, load, and other factors is compiled and a report is produced. The report is then analyzed to determine whether or not the entire rail is safe to use.

Uses of Elevators

Passenger Service: A passenger elevator is designed to move people between a building's floors.

Passenger elevators capacity is related to the available floor space. Generally passenger elevators are available in capacities from 1,000 to 6,000 pounds (450–2,700 kg) in 500 lb (230 kg) increments. Generally passenger elevators in buildings eight floors or less are hydraulic or electric, which can reach speeds up to 200 ft/min (1.0 m/s) hydraulic and up to 500 ft/min electric. In buildings up to ten floors, electric and gearless elevators are likely to have speeds up to 500 ft/min (2.5 m/s), and above ten floors speeds begin at 500 ft/min (2.5 m/s) up to 2000 ft/min (10 m/s).

Sometimes passenger elevators are used as a city transport along with funiculars. For example, there is a 3-station underground public elevator in Yalta, Ukraine, which takes passengers from the top of a hill above the Black Sea on which hotels are perched, to a tunnel located on the beach below. At Casco Viejo station in the Bilbao Metro, the elevator that provides access to the station from a hilltop neighbourhood doubles as city transportation: the station's ticket barriers are set up in such a way that passengers can pay to reach the elevator from the entrance in the lower city, or vice versa.

The Equitable Building completed in 1870 in New York City was the first office building to have passenger elevators.

Types of Passenger Elevators

Passenger elevators may be specialized for the service they perform, including: hospital emergency (Code blue), front and rear entrances, a television in high rise buildings, double decker, and other uses. Cars may be ornate in their interior appearance, may have audio visual advertising, and may be provided with specialized recorded voice instructions.

An express elevator does not serve all floors. For example, it moves between the ground floor and a skylobby, or it moves from the ground floor or a skylobby to a range of floors, skipping floors in between. These are especially popular in eastern Asia.

Capacity

Residential elevators may be small enough to only accommodate one person while some are large enough for more than a dozen. Wheelchair, or platform lifts, a specialized type of elevator designed to move a wheelchair 6 ft (1.8 m) or less, often can accommodate just one person in a wheelchair at a time with a load of 1000 lb (450 kg).

Freight Elevators

A freight elevator, or goods lift, is an elevator designed to carry goods, rather than passengers. Freight elevators are generally required to display a written notice in the car that the use by passengers is prohibited (though not necessarily illegal), though certain freight elevators allow dual use through the use of an inconspicuous riser. Freight elevators are typically larger and capable of carrying heavier loads than a passenger elevator, generally from 2,300 to 4,500 kg. Freight elevators may have manually operated doors, and often have rugged interior finishes to prevent damage while loading and unloading. Although hydraulic freight elevators exist, electric elevators are more energy efficient for the work of freight lifting.

Stage Lifts

Stage and orchestra lifts are specialized lifts, typically powered by hydraulics, that are used to lift entire sections of a theatre stage. For example, Radio City Music Hall has four such lifts: an "orchestra lift" that covers a large area of the stage, and three smaller lifts near the rear of the stage. In this case, the orchestra lift is powerful enough to raise an entire orchestra, or an entire cast of performers (including live elephants) up to stage level from below.

Vehicle Elevators

Vehicular elevators are used within buildings or areas with limited space (in lieu of ramps), typically to move cars into the parking garage or manufacturer's storage. Geared hydraulic chains (not unlike bicycle chains) generate lift for the platform and there are no counterweights. To accommodate building designs and improve accessibility, the platform may rotate so that the driver only has to drive forward. Most vehicle elevators have a weight capacity of 2 tons.

Rare examples of extra-heavy elevators for 20-ton lorries, and even for railcars (like one that was used at Dnipro Station of the Kiev Metro) also occur.

Boat Elevators

In some smaller canals, boats and small ships can pass between different levels of a canal with a boat lift rather than through a canal lock.

Aircraft Elevators

On aircraft carriers, elevators carry aircraft between the flight deck and the hangar deck for operations or repairs. These elevators are designed for much greater capacity than other elevators, up to 200,000 pounds (90 tonnes) of aircraft and equipment. Smaller elevators lift munitions to the flight deck from magazines deep inside the ship.

On some passenger double-deck aircraft such as the Boeing 747, Lockheed L-1011 or other widebody aircraft, lifts transport flight attendants and food and beverage trolleys from lower deck galleys to upper passenger carrying decks.

Residential Elevator

The residential elevator is often permitted to be of lower cost and complexity than full commercial elevators. They may have unique design characteristics suited for home furnishings, such as hinged wooden shaft-access doors rather than the typical metal sliding doors of commercial elevators. Construction may be less robust than in commercial designs with shorter maintenance periods, but safety systems such as locks on shaft access doors, fall arrestors, and emergency phones must still be present in the event of malfunction.

Limited Use/Limited Application

The limited-use, limited-application (LU/LA) elevator is a special purpose passenger elevator used infrequently, and which is exempt from many commercial regulations and accommodations. For example, a LU/LA is primarily meant to be handicapped accessible, and there might only be room for a single wheelchair and a standing passenger.

Dumbwaiter

Dumbwaiters are small freight elevators that are intended to carry food rather than passengers. They often link kitchens with rooms on other floors.

Paternoster

A special type of elevator is the paternoster, a constantly moving chain of boxes. A similar concept, called the manlift or humanlift, moves only a small platform, which the rider mounts while using a handhold and was once seen in multi-story industrial plants.

Scissor Lift

The scissor lift is yet another type of lift. As most of these lifts are self-contained, these lifts can be easily moved to where they are needed.

Rack-and-pinion Lift

The rack-and-pinion lift is another type of lift. This lifts are simpler in construction, but noisy and slow. They are nonetheless the most used type of lift for buildings under construction (to move materials and tools up and down).

Material Handling Belts and Belt Elevators

A different kind of elevator is used to transport material. It generally consists of an inclined plane on which a conveyor belt runs. The conveyor often includes partitions to prevent the material from sliding backwards. These elevators are often used in industrial and agricultural applications. When such mechanisms (or spiral screws or pneumatic transport) are used to elevate grain for storage in large vertical silos, the entire structure is called a grain elevator.

There have occasionally been lift belts for humans; these typically have steps about every seven feet along the length of the belt, which moves vertically, so that the passenger can stand on one step and hold on to the one above. These belts are sometimes used, for example, to carry the employees of parking garages, but are considered too dangerous for public use.

Traction Elevators

Geared and Gearless Traction Elevators

Geared traction machines are driven by AC or DC electric motors. Geared machines use worm gears to control mechanical movement of elevator cars by "rolling" steel hoist ropes over a drive sheave which is attached to a gearbox driven by a high speed motor. These machines are generally the best option for basement or overhead traction use for speeds up to 500 ft/min (2.5 m/s).

Gearless traction machines are low speed (low RPM), high torque electric motors powered either by AC or DC. In this case, the drive sheave is directly attached to the end of the motor. Gearless traction elevators can reach speeds of up to 2,000 ft/min (10 m/s), or even higher. A brake is mounted between the motor and drive sheave (or gearbox) to hold the elevator stationary at a floor. This brake is usually an external drum type and is actuated by spring force and held open electrically; a power failure will cause the brake to engage and prevent the elevator from falling.

In each case, cables are attached to a hitch plate on top of the cab or may be "underslung" below a cab, and then looped over the drive sheave to a counterweight attached to the opposite end of the cables which reduces the amount of power needed to move the cab. The counterweight is located in the hoist-way and rides a separate railway system; as the car goes up, the counterweight goes down, and vice versa. This action is powered by the traction machine which is directed by the controller, typically a relay logic or computerized device that directs starting, acceleration, deceleration and stopping of the elevator cab. The weight of the counterweight is typically equal to the weight of the elevator cab plus 40-50% of the capacity of the elevator. The grooves in the drive sheave are specially designed to prevent the cables from slipping. "Traction" is provided to the ropes by the grip of the grooves in the sheave, thereby the name. As the ropes age and the traction grooves wear, some traction is lost and the ropes must be replaced and the sheave repaired or replaced. Sheave and rope wear may be significantly reduced by ensuring that all ropes have equal tension, thus sharing the load evenly. Rope tension equalisation may be achieved using a rope tension gauge, and is a simple way to extend the lifetime of the sheaves and ropes.

Elevators with more than 100' (30 m) of travel have a system called compensation. This is a separate set of cables or a chain attached to the bottom of the counterweight and the bottom of the elevator cab. This makes it easier to control the elevator, as it compensates for the differing weight of cable between the hoist and the cab. If the elevator cab is at the top of the hoist-way, there is a short length of hoist cable above the car and a long length of compensating cable below the car and vice versa for the counterweight. If the compensation system uses cables, there will be an additional sheave in the pit below the elevator, to guide the cables. If the compensation system uses chains, the chain is guided by a bar mounted between the counterweight railway lines.

Hydraulic Elevators

- *Conventional hydraulic elevators.* They use an underground cylinder, are quite common for low level buildings with 2-5 floors (sometimes but seldom up to 6-8 floors), and have speeds of up to 200 feet/minute (1 meter/second).
- *Holeless hydraulic elevators* were developed in the 1970s, and use a pair of above ground cylinders, which makes it practical for environmentally or cost sensitive buildings with 2, 3, or 4 floors.
- *Roped hydraulic elevators* use both above ground cylinders and a rope system, which combines the reliability of inground hydraulic with the versatility of holeless hydraulic, even though they can serve up to 8-10 floors.

Climbing Elevator

A climbing elevator is a self-ascending elevator with its own propulsion. The propulsion can be done by an electric or a combustion engine. Climbing elevators are used in guyed masts or towers, in order to make easy access to parts of these constructions, such as flight safety lamps for maintenance. An example would be the Moonlight towers in Austin, Texas, where the elevator holds only one person and equipment for maintenance. The Glasgow Tower-an observation tower in Glasgow, Scotland also makes use of two climbing elevators.

Elevator Air Conditioning

Concept

Elevator air conditioning is fast becoming a popular concept around the world. The primary reason for installing an elevator air conditioner is the comfort that it provides while travelling in the elevator. It stabilizes the condition of the air inside the lift car. Some elevator air conditioners can be used in countries with cold climates if a thermostat is used to reverse the refrigeration cycle to warm the lift car.

Health

One of the benefits of installing an elevator air conditioner is the clean air it provides. Air was typically drawn from the elevator shaft or hoistway into the car using a motorized fan. This air could contain dust mites, germs and bacteria. With an elevator air conditioner, the air is much cleaner because it is recirculated within the car itself and is usually filtered to remove contaminants. A poorly maintained air-conditioning system may promote the growth and spread of microorganisms, but as long as the air conditioner is kept clean, these health hazards can be avoided.

Drawbacks

Heat generated from the cooling process is rejected into the hoistway. The elevator cab (or car) is not air-tight, and some of this heat will reenter the car and reduce the overall cooling effect, which may be less than ideal.

Energy

The air from the lobby constantly leaks into the elevator shaft due to elevator movements as well as elevator shaft ventilation requirements. Using this conditioned air in the elevator does not increase energy costs. However, by using an independent elevator air conditioner to achieve better temperature control inside the car, more energy will be used.

Condensation

Air conditioning poses a problem to elevators because of the condensation that occurs. The condensed water produced has to be disposed of; otherwise, it would create flooding in the elevator car and hoistway.

Ways to Remove Condensed Water

There are at least four ways to remove condensed water from the air conditioner. However, each solution has its pros and cons.

Atomizing

Atomizing, also known as misting the condensed water, is another way to dispose of the condensed water. Spraying ultra-fine water droplets onto the hot coils of the air conditioner ensures that the condensed water evaporates quickly.

Though this is one of the best methods to dispose of the condensed water, it is also one of the costliest because the nozzle that atomizes the water easily gets choked. The majority of the cost goes to maintaining the entire atomizing system.

Boiling

Disposing of condensed water works by firstly collecting the condensed water and then heating it to above boiling point. The condensed water is eventually evaporated, thereby disposing of it. Consumers are reluctant to employ this system because of the high rate of energy used just to dispose of this water.

Cascading

The cascading method works by flowing the condensed water directly onto the hot coils of the air conditioner. This eventually evaporates the condensed water. The downside of this technology is that the coils have to be at extremely high temperature for the condensed water to be evaporated. There is a chance that the water might not evaporate entirely and that would cause water to overflow onto the exterior of the car.

Drainage System

Drainage system works by creating a sump to collect the condensed water and using a pump to dispose it through a drainage system.

It is an efficient method, but it comes at a heavy price because the cost of building the sump. Moreover, maintaining the pump to make sure it operates is very expensive. Furthermore, the pipes used for drainage would look ugly on the exterior. This system also cannot be implemented on a built project.

Controlling Elevators

General Controls

A typical modern passenger elevator will have:

- Space to stand in, guardrails, seating cushion (luxury)
- Overload sensor—prevents the elevator from moving until excess load has been removed. It may trigger a voice prompt or buzzer alarm. This may also trigger a "full car" indicator, indicating the car's inability to accept more passengers until some are unloaded.
- Electric fans or air conditioning units to enhance circulation and comfort.
- Call buttons to choose a floor. Some of these may be key switches (to control access). In some elevators, certain floors are inaccessible unless one swipes a security card or enters a passcode (or both). In the United States and other countries, call button text and icons are raised to allow blind users to operate the elevator; many have Braille text besides.
- A set of doors kept locked on each floor to prevent unintentional access into the elevator shaft by the unsuspecting individual.

The door is unlocked and opened by a machine sitting on the roof of the car, which also drives the doors that travel with the car. Door controls are provided to close immediately or reopen the doors. Objects in the path of the moving doors will either be detected by sensors or physically activate a switch that reopens the doors. Otherwise, the doors will close after a preset time.

- A stop switch (not allowed under British regulations) to halt the elevator while in motion and often used to hold an elevator open while freight is loaded. Keeping an elevator stopped for too long may trigger an alarm. Unless local codes require otherwise, this will most likely be a key switch.
- An alarm button or switch, which passengers can use to signal that they have been trapped in the elevator.

Some elevators may have one or more of the following:

- An elevator telephone, which can be used (in addition to the alarm) by a trapped passenger to call for help.
- Hold button: This button delays the door closing timer, useful for loading freight and hospital beds.
- Call cancellation: A destination floor may be deselected by double clicking.
- Access restriction by key switches, RFID reader, code keypad, hotel room card, etc..
- One or more additional sets of doors that can serve different floor plans. For example, in an elevated crosswalk setup, the front doors may open on the street level, and the rear doors open on the crosswalk level.
- Security camera
- Plain walls or mirrored walls giving the illusion of larger area
- Glass windowpane providing a view of the building interior or onto the streets.

Other controls, which are generally inaccessible to the public (either because they are key switches, or because they are kept behind a locked panel), include:

- Fireman's service, phase II key switch
- Switch to enable or disable the elevator.
- An *inspector's* switch, which places the elevator in inspection mode (this may be situated on top of the elevator)
- Manual up/down controls for elevator technicians, to be used in inspection mode, for example.

- An *independent service/exclusive mode* will prevent the car from answering to hall calls and only arrive at floors selected via the panel. The door should stay open while parked on a floor. This mode may be used for temporarily transporting goods.
- Attendant service mode.

Controls in Early Elevators

- Some older freight elevators are controlled by switches operated by pulling on adjacent ropes. Safety interlocks ensure that the inner and outer doors are closed before the elevator is allowed to move.
- Early elevators had no automatic landing positioning. Elevators were operated by elevator operators using a motor controller. The controller was contained within a cylindrical container about the size and shape of a cake container and this was operated via a projecting handle. This allowed some control over the energy supplied to the motor (located at the top of the elevator shaft or beside the bottom of the elevator shaft) and so enabled the elevator to be accurately positioned — if the operator was sufficiently skilled. More typically the operator would have to "jog" the control to get the elevator reasonably close to the landing point and then direct the outgoing and incoming passengers to "watch the step". After stopping at the landing the operator would open the door/doors. Some slightly later lifts though, had door(s) that could be operated by the same control (so when the lever is moved in the desired direction, between the idle and motion points there is a trigger to close the doors. When the handle is moved to idle, the doors open again.) This sort of arrangement was used sometimes in subway stations. Manually operated elevators were generally refitted or the cabs replaced by automatic equipment by the 1950s. The major exception is freight elevators which today are just as commonly operated manually as automatically, and even when equipped with automatic controls, are often operated by an attendant to ensure efficiency.
- Early automatic elevators used relays as logic gates to control them, which began to be replaced by microprocessors in the late 1980s.
- Large buildings with multiple elevators of this type also had an *elevator dispatcher* stationed in the lobby to direct passengers and to signal the operator to leave with the use of a mechanical "cricket" noisemaker.

- Some elevators still in operation have pushbutton manual controls.

External Controls

Elevators are typically controlled from the outside by up and down buttons at each stop. When pressed at a certain floor, the elevator arrives to pick up more passengers. If the particular elevator is currently serving traffic in a certain direction, it will only answer hall calls in the same direction unless there are no more calls beyond that floor.

In a group of two or more elevators, the call buttons may be linked to a central dispatch computer, such that they illuminate and cancel together. This is done to ensure that only one car is called at one time.

Key switches may be installed on the ground floor so that the elevator can be remotely switched on or off from the outside.

In sky lobby elevator systems, one selects the intended destination floor (in lieu of pressing "up") and is then notified which elevator will serve their request.

Floor Numbering

The Elevator Algorithm: The elevator algorithm, a simple algorithm by which a single elevator can decide where to stop, is summarized as follows:

- Continue travelling in the same direction while there are remaining requests in that same direction.
- If there are no further requests in that direction, then stop and become idle, or change direction if there are requests in the opposite direction.

The elevator algorithm has found an application in computer operating systems as an algorithm for scheduling hard disk requests. Modern elevators use more complex heuristic algorithms to decide which request to service next. An introduction to these algorithms can be found in the "Elevator traffic handbook: theory and practice" given in the references below.

Destination Control System

Some skyscraper buildings and other types of installation feature a destination operating panel where a passenger registers their floor calls before entering the car. The system lets them know which car to wait for, instead of everyone boarding the next car. In this way, travel time is reduced as the elevator makes fewer stops for individual passengers, and the computer distributes adjacent stops to different cars in the bank. Although travel time is reduced passenger waiting times may be longer as they will not necessarily be allocated the next car to depart. During the down peak period the benefit of destination control will be limited as passengers have a common destination.

It can also improve accessibility, as a mobility-impaired passenger can move to his or her designated car in advance. Inside the elevator there is no call button to push, or the buttons are there but they cannot be pushed-except door opening and alarm button – they only indicate stopping floors.

The idea of destination control was originally conceived by Leo Port from Sydney in 1961 but at that time lift controllers were implemented in relays and were unable to optimise the performance of destination control allocations. The system was first pioneered by Schindler Elevator in 1992 as the Miconic 10. Manufacturers of such systems claim that average travelling time can be reduced by up to 30%.

However, performance enhancements cannot be generalized as the benefits and limitations of the system are dependent on many factors. One problem is that the system is subject to gaming. Sometimes, one person enters the destination for a large group of people going to the same floor. The dispatching algorithm is usually unable to completely cater for the variation, and latecomers may find the elevator they are assigned to is already full. Also, occasionally, one person may press the floor multiple times. This is common with up/down buttons when people believe this to be an effective way to hurry elevators. However, this will make the computer think multiple people are waiting and will allocate empty cars to serve this one person.

To prevent this problem, in one implementation of destination control, every user gets an RFID card to identify himself so the system knows every user call and can cancel the first call if the passenger decides to travel to another destination to prevent empty calls. The newest invention knows even where people are located and how many on which floor because of their identification, either for the purposes of evacuating the building or for security reasons.

The same destination scheduling concept can also be applied to public transit such as in group rapid transit.

Special Operating Modes

Anti-Crime Protection (ACP)

Anti-Crime Protection will force each car to stop at a pre-defined landing and open its doors. This allows a security guard or a receptionist at the landing to visually inspect the passengers. The car stops at this landing as it passes to serve further demand.

Up Peak (MIT)

During Up Peak mode (also called Moderate Incoming Traffic), elevator cars in a group are recalled to the lobby to provide expeditious service to passengers arriving at the building, most typically in the morning as people arrive for work or at the conclusion of a lunch-time period. Elevators are dispatched one-by-one when they reach a pre-determined passenger load, or when they have had their doors opened for a certain period of time. The next elevator to be dispatched usually has its hall lantern or a "this car leaving next" sign illuminated to encourage passengers to make maximum use of the available elevator system capacity.

The commencement of Up Peak may be triggered by a time clock, by the departure of a certain number of fully loaded cars leaving the lobby within a given time period, or by a switch manually operated by a building attendant.

Down Peak

During Down Peak mode, elevator cars in a group are sent away from the lobby towards the highest floor served, after which they commence running down the floors in response to hall calls placed by passengers wishing to leave the building. This allows the elevator system to provide maximum passenger handling capacity for people leaving the building.

The commencement of Down Peak may be triggered by a time clock, by the arrival of a certain number of fully loaded cars at the lobby within a given time period, or by a switch manually operated by a building attendant.

Sabbath Service (SHO)

In areas with large populations of observant Jews or in facilities catering to Jews, one may find a "Sabbath elevator". In this mode, an elevator will stop automatically at every floor, allowing people to step on and off without having to press any buttons. This prevents violation of the Sabbath prohibition against operating electrical devices when Sabbath is in effect for those who observe this ritual.

However, Sabbath mode has the side effect of wasting considerable amounts of energy, running the elevator car sequentially up and down every floor of a building, repeatedly servicing floors where it is not needed. For a tall building with many floors, the car must move on a frequent enough basis so as to not cause undue delay for potential users that will not touch the controls as it opens the doors on every floor up the building.

Independent Service (ISC)

Independent service is a special service mode found on most elevators. It is activated by a key switch either inside the elevator itself or on a centralized control panel in the lobby. When an elevator is placed on independent service, it will no longer respond to hall calls. (In a bank of elevators, traffic is rerouted to the other elevators, while in a single elevator, the hall buttons are disabled). The elevator will remain parked on a floor with its doors open until a floor is selected and the door close button is held until the elevator starts to travel. Independent service is useful when transporting large goods or moving groups of people between certain floors.

Inspection Service (INS)

Inspection service is designed to provide access to the hoistway and car top for inspection and maintenance purposes by qualified elevator mechanics. It is first activated by a key switch on the car operating panel usually labeled 'Inspection', 'Car Top', 'Access Enable' or 'HWENAB'. When this switch is activated the elevator will come to a stop if moving, car calls will be cancelled (and the buttons disabled), and hall calls will be assigned to other elevator cars in the group (or cancelled in a single elevator configuration).

The elevator can now only be moved by the corresponding 'Access' key switches, usually located at the top-most (to access the top of the car) and bottom-most (to access the elevator pit) landings. The access key switches will bypass the door lock circuit for the floor it is located on and allow the car to move at reduced inspection speed with the hoistway door open. This speed can range from anywhere up to 60% of normal operating speed on most controllers, and is usually defined by local safety codes.

Elevators have a car top inspection station that allows the car to be operated by a mechanic in order to move it through the hoistway. Generally, there are three buttons-UP, RUN, and DOWN. Both the RUN and a direction button must be held to move the car in that direction, and the elevator will stop moving as soon as the buttons are released. Most other elevators have an up/down toggle switch and a RUN button. The inspection panel also has standard power outlets for work lamps and powered tools.

Fire Service Mode (EFS)

Depending on the location of the elevator, fire service code will vary state to state and country to country. Fire service is usually split up into two modes: Phase One and Phase Two. These are separate modes that the elevator can go into.

Phase one mode is activated by a corresponding smoke sensor or heat sensor in the building. Once an alarm has been activated, the elevator will automatically go into phase one. The elevator will wait an amount of time, then proceed to go into nudging mode to tell everyone the elevator is leaving the floor. Once the elevator has left the floor, depending on where the alarm was set off, the elevator will go to the Fire Recall Floor. However, if the alarm was activated on the fire recall floor the elevator will have an alternate floor to recall to. When the elevator is recalled, it proceeds to the recall floor and stops with its doors open. The elevator will no longer respond to calls or move in any direction. Located on the fire recall floor is a fire service key switch. The fire service key switch has the ability to turn fire service off, turn fire service on or to bypass fire service. The only way to return the elevator to normal service is to switch it to bypass after the alarms have reset.

Phase two mode can only be activated by a key switch located inside the elevator on the centralized control panel. This mode was created for firefighters so that they may rescue people from a burning building. The phase two key switch located on the COP has three positions: off, on, and hold. By turning phase two on, the firefighter enables the car to move. However, like independent service mode, the car will not respond to a car call unless the firefighter manually pushes and holds the door close button. Once the elevator gets to the desired floor it will not open its doors unless the firefighter holds the door open button. This is in case the floor is burning and the firefighter can feel the heat and knows not to open the door. The firefighter must hold door open until the door is completely opened. If for any reason the firefighter wishes to leave the elevator, they will use the hold position on the key switch to make sure the elevator remains at that floor. If the firefighter wishes to return to the recall floor, they simply turn the key off and close the doors.

Fire Service is for emergency use only, although fire service keys can be purchased on eBay, and other websites. Only trained responders should use this feature, and it is by no means a safe way to escape from a burning building.

Medical Emergency/'Code Blue' Service (EHS)

Commonly found in hospitals, Code Blue service allows an elevator to be summoned to any floor for use in an emergency situation. Each floor will have a 'Code Blue' recall key switch, and when activated, the elevator system will immediately select the elevator car that can respond the fastest, regardless of direction of travel and passenger load. Passengers inside the elevator will be notified with an alarm and indicator light to exit the elevator when the doors open.

Once the elevator arrives at the floor, it will park with its doors open and the car buttons will be disabled to prevent a passenger from taking control of the elevator. Medical personnel must then activate the Code Blue key switch inside the car, select their floor and close the doors with the door close button. The elevator will then travel non-stop to the selected floor, and will remain in Code Blue service until switched off in the car. Some hospital elevators will feature a 'hold' position on the Code Blue key switch (similar to fire service) which allows the elevator to remain at a floor locked out of service until Code Blue is deactivated.

Emergency Power Operation (EPR)

Many elevator installations now feature emergency power systems which allow elevator use in blackout situations and prevent people from becoming trapped in elevators.

Traction Elevators

When power is lost in a traction elevator system, all elevators will initially come to a halt. One by one, each car in the group will return to the lobby floor, open its doors and shut down. People in the remaining elevators may see an indicator light or hear a voice announcement informing them that the elevator will return to the lobby shortly. Once all cars have successfully returned, the system will then automatically select one or more cars to be used for normal operations and these cars will return to service. The car(s) selected to run under emergency power can be manually overridden by a key or strip switch in the lobby. In order to help prevent entrapment, when the system detects that it is running low on power, it will bring the running cars to the lobby or nearest floor, open the doors and shut down.

Hydraulic Elevators

In hydraulic elevator systems, emergency power will lower the elevators to the lowest landing and open the doors to allow passengers to exit. The doors then close after an adjustable time period and the car remains unusable until reset, usually by cycling the elevator main power switch. Typically, due to the high current draw when starting the pump motor, hydraulic elevators aren't run using standard emergency power systems. Buildings like hospitals and nursing homes usually size their emergency generators to accommodate this draw. However, the increasing use of current limiting motor starters, commonly known as "Soft-Start" contactors, avoid much of this problem and the current draw of the pump motor is less of a limiting concern.

Elevator Convenience Features

Elevators may feature talking devices as an accessibility aid for the blind. In addition to floor arrival notifications, the computer announces the direction of travel, and notifies the passengers before the doors are to close.

In addition to the call buttons, elevators usually have floor indicators (often illuminated by LED) and direction lanterns. The former are almost universal in cab interiors with more than two stops and may be found outside the elevators as well on one or more of the floors. Floor indicators can consist of a dial with a rotating needle, but the most common types are those with successively illuminated floor indications or LCDs. Likewise, a change of floors or an arrival at a floor is indicated by a sound, depending on the elevator.

Direction lanterns are also found both inside and outside elevator cars, but they should always be visible from outside because their primary purpose is to help people decide whether or not to get on the elevator. If somebody waiting for the elevator wants to go up, but a car comes first that indicates that it is going down, then the person may decide not to get on the elevator. If the person waits, then one will still stop going up. Direction indicators are sometimes etched with arrows or shaped like arrows and/or use the convention that one that lights up red means "down" and green means "up". Since the colour convention is often undermined or overridden by systems that do not invoke it, it is usually used only in conjunction with other differentiating factors. An example of a place whose elevators use only the colour convention to differentiate between directions is the Museum of Contemporary Art in Chicago, where a single circle can be made to light up green for "up" and red for "down". Sometimes directions must be inferred by the position of the indicators relative to one another.

In addition to lanterns, most elevators have a chime to indicate if the elevator is going up or down either before or after the doors open, usually in conjunction with the lanterns lighting up. Universally, one chime is for up, two is for down, and none indicates an elevator that is 'free'.

Observatory service elevators often convey other facts of interest, including elevator speed, stopwatch, and current position (altitude), as with the case for Taipei 101's service elevators.

Standards

The mechanical and electrical design of elevators is dictated according to various standards (aka elevator codes), which may be international, national, state, regional or city based. Whereas once many standards were prescriptive, specifying exact criteria which must be complied with, there has recently been a shift towards more performance-based standards where the onus falls on the designer to ensure that the elevator meets or exceeds the standard.

Some of the national elevator standards include:

- Australia – AS1735
- Canada – CAN/CSA B44
- Europe – EN 81 series (EN 81-1, EN 81-2, EN 81-28, EN 81-70, EN 12015, EN 12016, EN 13015, etc.)
- USA – ASME A17.

Because an elevator is part of a building, it must also comply with standards relating to earthquake resilience, fire standards, electrical wiring rules and so forth.

The American National Elevator Standards Group (ANESG) sets an elevator weight standard to be 2200 lbs.

Additional requirements relating to access by disabled persons, may be mandated by laws or regulations such as the Americans with Disabilities Act.

US and Canadian Elevator Standard Specifics

In most US and Canadian jurisdictions, passenger elevators are required to conform to the American Society of Mechanical Engineers' Standard A17.1, Safety Code for Elevators and Escalators. In Canada the document is the CAN/CSA B44 Safety Standard, which was harmonized with the US version in the 2000 edition. In addition, passenger elevators may be required to conform to the requirements of A17.3 for existing elevators where referenced by the local jurisdiction. Passenger elevators are tested using the ASME A17.2 Standard. The frequency of these tests is mandated by the local jurisdiction, which may be a town, city, state or provincial standard.

Passenger elevators must also conform to many ancillary building codes including the Local or State building code, National Fire Protection Association standards for Electrical, Fire Sprinklers and Fire Alarms, Plumbing codes, and HVAC codes. Also, passenger elevators are required to conform to the Americans with Disabilities Act and other State and Federal civil rights legislation regarding accessibility.

Residential elevators are required to conform to ASME A17.1. Platform and Wheelchair lifts are required to comply with ASME A18.1 in most US jurisdictions.

Most elevators have a location in which the permit for the building owner to operate the elevator is displayed. While some jurisdictions require the permit to be displayed in the elevator cab, other jurisdictions allow for the operating permit to be kept on file elsewhere – such as the maintenance office – and to be made available for inspection on demand. In such cases instead of the permit being displayed in the elevator cab, often a notice is posted in its place informing riders of where the actual permits are kept.

Unique Elevator Installations

World statistics

Country	*Number of elevators installed*
Italy	900,000
United States	700,000
People's Republic of China	610,000

As of January 2008, Italy is the nation with the most elevators installed in the world, with 850,000 elevators installed that run more than one hundred million lifts every day, followed by United States with 700,000 elevators installed and People's Republic of China with 610,000 elevators installed since 1949. In Brazil, it is estimated that there are approximately 300,000 elevators currently in operation. The world's largest market for elevators is Italy with more than 1,629 million euros of sales and 1,224 million euros of internal market.

Eiffel Tower

The Eiffel Tower has Otis double-deck elevators built into the legs of the tower, serving the ground level to the first and second levels. Even though the shaft runs diagonally upwards with the contour of the tower, both the upper and lower cars remain horizontally level. The offset distance of the two cars changes throughout the journey.

There are four elevator cars of the traditional design that run from the second level to the third level. The cars are connected to their opposite pairs (opposite in the elevator landing/hall) and use each other as the counterweight. As one car ascends from level 2, the other descends from level 3. The operations of these elevators are synchronized by a light signal in the car.

Taipei 101

Double deck elevators are used in the Taipei 101 office tower. Tenants of even-numbered floors first take an escalator (or an elevator from the parking garage) to the 2nd level, where they will enter the upper deck and arrive at their floors. The lower deck is turned off during low-volume hours, and the upper deck can act as a single-level elevator stopping at all adjacent floors. For example, the 85th floor restaurants can be accessed from the 60th floor sky-lobby. Restaurant customers must clear their reservations at the reception counter on the 2nd floor. A bank of express elevators stop only on the sky lobby levels (36 and 60, upper deck car), where tenants can transfer to "local" elevators.

The high speed observation deck elevators accelerate to a world-record certified speed of 1010 meters per minute (60.6 km/h) in 16 seconds, and then it slows down for arrival with subtle air pressure sensations. The door opens after 37 seconds from the 5th floor. Special features include aerodynamic car and counterweights, and cabin pressure control to help passengers adapt smoothly to pressure changes. The downwards journey is completed at a reduced speed of 600 meters per minute, with the doors opening at the 52nd second.

The Gateway Arch

The Gateway Arch in St. Louis, Missouri has a unique elevator system which carries passengers from the visitors' center underneath the Arch to the observation deck at the top of the structure.

Called a *tram* or *tramway*, people enter this unique tramway much as one would enter an ordinary elevator, through double doors. Passing through the doors the passengers in small groups enter a horizontal cylindrical compartment containing seats on each side and a flat floor. A number of these compartments are linked to form a train. These compartments each individually retain an appropriate level orientation by tilting while the entire train follows curved tracks up one leg of the arch.

There are two tramways within the Arch, one at the north end, and the other at the south end. The entry doors have windows, so people travelling within the Arch are able to see the interior structure of the

Arch during the ride to and from the observation deck. At the beginning of the trip the cars hang from the drive cables, but as the angle of the shaft changes, they end up beside and then on top of the cables.

New City Hall, Hanover, Germany

The elevator in the New City Hall in Hanover, Germany is a technical rarity, and unique in Europe, as the elevator starts straight up but then changes its angle by 15 degrees to follow the contour of the dome of the hall. The cabin therefore tilts 15 degrees during the ride. The elevator travels a height of 43 meters. The new city hall was built in 1913. The elevator was destroyed in 1943 and rebuilt in 1954.

Luxor Inclinator Elevator

In Las Vegas, Nevada, at the Luxor Hotel, is the Inclinator. The shape of this casino is a pyramid. Therefore, the elevator travels up the side of the pyramid at a 39 degree angle. Although people refer to this "inclined elevator" as an inclinator, this is incorrect.

Twilight Zone Tower of Terror

The Twilight Zone Tower of Terror is the common name for a series of elevator attractions at the Disney's Hollywood Studios park in Orlando, the Disney's California Adventure park in Anaheim, the Walt Disney Studios Park in Paris and the Tokyo DisneySea park in Tokyo. The central element of this attraction is a simulated free-fall achieved through the use of a high-speed elevator system. For safety reasons, passengers are seated and secured in their seats rather than standing. Unlike most traction elevators, the elevator car and counterweight are joined using a rail system in a continuous loop running through both the top and the bottom of the drop shaft. This allows the drive motor to pull down on the elevator car from underneath, resulting in downward acceleration greater than that of normal gravity. The high-speed drive motor is used to rapidly lift the elevator as well.

The passenger cabs are mechanically separated from the lift mechanism, thus allowing the elevator shafts to be used continuously while passengers board and embark from the cabs. Multiple elevator shafts are used to further improve passenger throughput. The doorways of the top few "floors" of the attraction are open to the outdoor environment, thus allowing passengers to look out from the top of the structure.

"Top of the Rock" elevators

Guests ascending to the 67th, 69th, and 70th level observation decks (dubbed "Top of the Rock") atop the GE Building at Rockefeller

Center in New York City ride a high-speed glass-top elevator. When entering the cab, it appears to be any normal elevator ride. However, once the cab begins moving, the interior lights turn off and a special blue light above the cab turns on. This lights the entire shaft, so riders can see the moving cab through its glass ceiling as it rises and lowers through the shaft. Music plays and various animations are also displayed on the ceiling. The entire ride takes about 60 seconds.

Disneyland, Anaheim, California

Part of the Haunted Mansion attraction at Disneyland in Anaheim, California, takes place on an elevator. The "stretching room" on the ride is actually an elevator that travels downwards, giving access to a short underground tunnel which leads to the rest of the attraction. The elevator has no ceiling and its shaft is decorated to look like walls of a mansion. Because there is no roof, passengers are able to see the walls of the shaft by looking up, which gives the illusion of the room stretching. The Haunted Mansion attraction at Disney World does not feature this, rather it gives you the illusion it is moving while it remains stationary.

Elevators for Urban Transport

In some towns where terrain is difficult to navigate, elevators are used as part of urban transport systems. Examples:

- Almada, Portugal: *Elevador da Boca do Vento*
- Asansor, Izmir, Turkey
- Ascensores de Valparaíso, urban funicular in Valparaíso, Chile
- Bad Schandau Elevator in Bad Schandau, Germany
- Barcelona, Spain-Elevator and cableway line connecting the port terminal to Montjuic hill
- Bilbao-Casco Viejo Bilbao Metro station (fare-paying elevator connecting upper and lower neighbourhoods, as well as the station)
- Brussels-Marolles, Belgium: "Ascenseur des Marolles", links the upper part of the city to the lower one, from Place Poelaert to Breughel square.
- Coimbra, Portugal: *Elevador do Mercado*
- East Hill Cliff Railway, Hastings, UK
- Genoa, Italy-eleven public elevators
- Hammetschwand Elevator in Bürgenstock, Switzerland

- Jersey City, New Jersey elevator at Bergen Hudson Light Rail station at 9th Street and Palisade Avenue.
- Katarina Elevator in Stockholm, Sweden
- Lisbon, Portugal: *Elevador de Santa Justa*, *Castelo* (planned), *Chiado* (closed), *Município/Biblioteca* (demolished)
- Luxembourg
- Lynchburg, Virginia-Outdoor Public elevator.
- Marburg, Germany-some parts of the historic city core built on higher ground (Uppertown, "Oberstadt" in German) are accessible from the lower street level by elevators. These elevators are unique in servicing also various buildings partially embedded in the steep-sloping terrain.
- Monaco, seven elevators
- Naples, Italy-three public elevators
- Oporto, Portugal: *Elevador da Ribeira*
- Oregon City Municipal Elevator in Oregon City, Oregon, United States
- Salvador, Bahia, Brazil: *Elevador Lacerda*
- Santa Justa Lift in Lisbon, Portugal
- Savannah, Georgia: Public elevators with access to River Street.
- Shanklin Cliff Lift in Shanklin, Isle of Wight
- Skyway in Nagasaki, Japan
- Yalta, Ukraine.

Escalator

An escalator is a moving staircase – a conveyor transport device for carrying people between floors of a building. The device consists of a motor-driven chain of individual, linked steps that move up or down on tracks, allowing the step treads to remain horizontal. Escalators are used around the world to move pedestrian traffic in places where elevators would be impractical. Principal areas of usage include department stores, shopping malls, airports, transit systems, convention centers, hotels, and public buildings.

The benefits of escalators are many. They have the capacity to move large numbers of people, and they can be placed in the same physical space as one might install a staircase. They have no waiting interval (except during very heavy traffic), they can be used to guide people toward main exits or special exhibits, and they may be weatherproofed for outdoor use.

Figure: *Escalators in a Copenhagen Metro station, Denmark, 2007*

Design, Components, and Operation

Operation and Layout: Escalators, like moving walkways, are powered by constant-speed alternating current motors and move at approximately 1–2 feet (0.30–0.61 m) per second. The typical angle of inclination of an escalator to the horizontal floor level is 30 degrees with a standard rise up to about 60 feet (18 m). Modern escalators have single-piece aluminum or steel steps that move on a system of tracks in a continuous loop.

Figure: *"Crisscross" layout*

Figure: *"Multiple parallel" layout*

Escalators have three typical configuration options: parallel (up and down escalators "side by side or separated by a distance", seen often in metro stations and multilevel motion picture theaters), crisscross (minimizes structural space requirements by "stacking" escalators that go in one direction, frequently used in department stores or shopping centers), and multiple parallel (two or more escalators together that travel in one direction next to one or two escalators in the same bank that travel in the other direction).

Escalators are required to have moving handrails that keep pace with the movement of the steps. The direction of movement (up or down) can be permanently the same, or be controlled by personnel according to the time of day, or automatically be controlled by whoever arrives first, whether at the bottom or at the top (the system is programmed so that the direction is not reversed while a passenger is on the escalator).

Design and Layout Considerations: A number of factors affect escalator design, including physical requirements, location, traffic patterns, safety considerations, and aesthetic preferences. Foremost, physical factors like the vertical and horizontal distance to be spanned must be considered. These factors will determine the pitch of the escalator and its actual length. The ability of the building infrastructure to support the heavy components is also a critical physical concern. Location is important because escalators should be situated where they can be easily seen by the general public. In department stores, customers should be able to view the merchandise easily. Furthermore, up and down escalator traffic should be physically separated and should not lead into confined spaces.

Traffic patterns must also be anticipated in escalator design. In some buildings, the objective is simply to move people from one floor to another, but in others there may be a more specific requirement, such as funneling visitors towards a main exit or exhibit. The number of passengers is important because escalators are designed to carry a certain maximum number of people. For example, a single-width escalator travelling at about 1.5 feet (0.46 m) per second can move an estimated 170 persons per five-minute period. The carrying capacity of an escalator system must match the expected peak traffic demand, presuming that passengers ride single file. This is crucial for applications in which there are sudden increases in the number of riders. For example, escalators at stations must be designed to cater for the peak traffic flow discharged from a train, without causing excessive bunching at the escalator entrance.

In this regard, escalators help in controlling traffic flow of people. For example, an escalator to an exit effectively discourages most people from using it as an entrance, and may reduce security concerns. Similarly, escalators often are used as the exit of airport security checkpoints. Such an egress point would generally be staffed to prevent its use as an entrance, as well.

It is preferred that staircases be located adjacent to the escalator if the escalator is the primary means of transport between floors. It may also be necessary to provide an elevator lift adjacent to an escalator for wheelchairs and disabled persons. Finally, consideration should be given to the aesthetics of the escalator. The architects and designers can choose from a wide range of styles and colours for the handrails and balustrades.

Components

Landing Platforms: These two platforms house the curved sections of the tracks, as well as the gears and motors that drive the stairs. The top platform contains the motor assembly and the main drive gear, while the bottom holds the step return idler sprockets. These sections also anchor the ends of the escalator truss. In addition, the platforms contain a floor plate and a combplate. The floor plate provides a place for the passengers to stand before they step onto the moving stairs. This plate is flush with the finished floor and is either hinged or removable to allow easy access to the machinery below. The combplate is the piece between the stationary floor plate and the moving step. It is so named because its edge has a series of cleats that resemble the teeth of a comb. These teeth mesh with matching cleats on the edges of the steps. This design is necessary to minimize the gap between the stair and the landing, which helps prevent objects from getting caught in the gap.

Truss: The truss is a hollow metal structure that bridges the lower and upper landings. It is composed of two side sections joined together with cross braces across the bottom and just below the top. The ends of the truss are attached to the top and bottom landing platforms via steel or concrete supports. The truss carries all the straight track sections connecting the upper and lower sections.

Tracks: The track system is built into the truss to guide the step chain, which continuously pulls the steps from the bottom platform and back to the top in an endless loop. There are actually two tracks: one for the front wheels of the steps (called the step-wheel track) and one for the back wheels of the steps (called the trailer-wheel track). The relative positions of these tracks cause the steps to form a staircase as they move out from under the combplate. Along the straight section of the truss the tracks are at their maximum distance apart. This configuration forces the back of one step to be at a 90-degree angle relative to the step behind it. This right angle bends the steps into a shape resembling a staircase. At the top and bottom of the escalator, the two tracks converge so that the front and back wheels of the steps are almost in a straight line. This causes the stairs to lay in a flat sheetlike arrangement, one after another, so they can easily travel around the bend in the curved section of track. The tracks carry the steps down along the underside of the truss until they reach the bottom landing, where they pass through another curved section of track before exiting the bottom landing. At this point the tracks separate and the steps once again assume a staircase configuration. This cycle is repeated continually as the steps are pulled from bottom to top and back to the bottom again.

Steps: The steps themselves are solid, one piece, die-cast aluminum or steel. Yellow demarcation lines may be added to clearly indicate their edges. In most escalator models manufactured after 1950, both the riser and the tread of each step is cleated (given a ribbed appearance) with comblike protrusions that mesh with the combplates on the top and bottom platforms and the succeeding steps in the chain. Seeberger-or "step-type" escalators featured flat treads and smooth risers; other escalator models have cleated treads and smooth risers. The steps are linked by a continuous metal chain that forms a closed loop. The front and back edges of the steps are each connected to two wheels. The rear wheels are set further apart to fit into the back track and the front wheels have shorter axles to fit into the narrower front track. As described above, the position of the tracks controls the orientation of the steps.

Handrail: The handrail provides a convenient handhold for passengers while they are riding the escalator. In an escalator, the handrail is pulled along its track by a chain that is connected to the main drive gear by a series of pulleys. It is constructed of four distinct sections. At the center of the handrail is a "slider", also known as a "glider ply", which is a layer of a cotton or synthetic textile. The purpose of the slider layer is to allow the handrail to move smoothly along its track. The next layer, known as the "tension member", consists of either steel cable or flat steel tape, and provides the handrail with tensile strength and flexibility. On top of tension member are the inner construction components, which are made of chemically treated rubber designed to prevent the layers from separating. Finally, the outer layer—the only part that passengers actually see—is the cover, which is a blend of synthetic polymers and rubber. This cover is designed to resist degradation from environmental conditions, mechanical wear and tear, and human vandalism.

In the factory, handrails are constructed by feeding rubber through a computer-controlled extrusion machine to produce layers of the required size and type in order to match specific orders. The component layers of fabric, rubber, and steel are shaped by skilled workers before being fed into the presses, where they are fused together.

In the mid-twentieth century, some handrail designs consisted of a rubber bellows, with rings of smooth metal cladding called "bracelets" placed between each coil. This gave the handrail a rigid yet flexible feel. Additionally, each bellows section was no more than a few feet long, so if part of the handrail was damaged, only the bad segment needed to be replaced. These forms of handrail have largely been replaced with conventional fabric-and-rubber railings.

Safety

Safety is also major concern in escalator design. In India where women wear saris, there are heavy chances of getting the *pallu* entangled in the escalator. As a result, a special *sari guard* is built in to most escalators.

There is a risk of feet injuries for children wearing footwear such as Crocs and flip-flops that might get caught in escalator mechanisms.

This was due to the softness of the shoe's material combined with the smaller size of children's feet.

Figure: *Escalators have a grip at their side for passengers aboard to hold.*

Fire protection of an escalator floor opening may be provided by adding automatic sprinklers or fireproof shutters to the opening, or by installing the escalator in an enclosed fire-protected hall. To limit the danger of overheating, ventilation for the spaces that contain the motors and gears must be provided.

Accidents and Litigation

Accidents

There have been reports of people falling off a moving escalator or getting their shoe stuck in part of the escalator; shoe laces are a hazard when loose. Some accidents are caused by improper or unsafe use such as riding the hand rails or by escalator spinning. A few fatal accidents are:

- Eight people died and 30 more were injured on Wednesday, February 17, 1982, when an escalator collapsed on the Moscow Metro. Wrongly set up service brakes were later blamed for the accident.
- 31 people died after a fire, begun in the undercarriage of an MH-type Otis escalator, exploded into the ticketing hall at King's Cross St. Pancras station in 1987.

- On Monday, December 13, 1999, 8-year-old Jyotsna Jethani was killed at New Delhi's international airport. Jethani fell into a gaping hole that resulted from improper maintenance.
- On Saturday, June 15, 2002, Andrea Albright, a 24-year-old J.C. Penney employee in Columbia, Maryland, was critically injured while riding the store's escalator from the first to the second level, and died from her injuries 10 days later. She somehow got her head caught between the escalator rail and a low ceiling. In 2005, her parents sued the property manager, two design firms, and the escalator company for $5 million.
- On New Year's Eve, 2004, escalators at the Taipei City Hall Station kept moving commuters onto the overcrowded island platform. A woman whose hair got caught in the escalator received 20 stitches to the scalp.
- Francisco Portillo, a Salvadoran sushi chef, died after being strangled when his sweatshirt got caught in an escalator at the Porter Square MBTA station in Cambridge, Massachusetts on February 21, 2005. He was allegedly drunk at the time.
- On Saturday, September 13, 2008, an 11-year old boy died after falling off an escalator in Lyngdal, Norway. On Monday, April 20, 2009, a teenage boy died after getting very serious skull injuries after falling off an escalator in Falun, Sweden. On Friday, June 26, 2009, a man died after falling off an escalator in Helsingborg, Sweden. All three were riding the handrail.
- On Tuesday, July 6, 2011, a 13-year old boy has been killed and dozens of people were injured when they were thrown off an escalator that suddenly changed direction in a busy Beijing subway station. In response to concerns regarding China's safety standards, officials have identified the manufacturers of the escalator as a possible reason for the accident. The escalator was built by Otis and was still in its guarantee period.

Lessons of the King's Cross Fire

The King's Cross fire of 1987 illustrated the demanding nature of escalator upkeep and the devices' propensity to collect "fluff" when not properly maintained.

Since the station was part of a public institution (the London Underground) and there was a substantial casualty rate, the incident yielded vociferous public outcry as riders and victims' families demanded the removal of all wooden escalators systemwide. In the official inquiry that followed, the Fennell Report, it was determined that the fire started slowly, smoldered virtually undetected for a time, then exploded into the ticketing hall above in a phenomenon known as the "trench effect." This slow-burning fire, Fennell found, was allegedly kindled by a discarded unextinguished cigarette, which was shown in laboratory tests to be a more powerful ignition source than a lit match. In the escalators' undercarriage, approximately 8,800 kilograms (19,000 lb) of accumulated detritus acted as a wick to a neglected buildup of interior lubricants; wood veneers, paper and plastic advertisements, solvent-based paint, plywood in the ticket hall, and melamine combustion added to the impact of the calamity. Taking this particular situation as an example, one could easily speculate that any accretion of flammable fuels, cloth, or scraps (the "fluff" denoted by Fennell) could likewise lead to a devastating fire.

Figure: *Greenford station escalators (2006)*

Consequentially, older wooden escalators were removed from service in the London Underground, though at least one set remains in operation, at Greenford Station. Additionally, sections of the London Underground that were actually below ground were made nonsmoking; eventually the whole system became a smoke-free zone.

Litigation

In the 1930s, at least one suit was filed against a department store, alleging that its escalators posed an attractive nuisance, responsible for a child's injury. These cases were almost always dismissed. Moreover, continual updating of escalator safety codes facilitated increased levels of consumer safety as well as a reduction in court cases.

Legislation and Escalators

United States: Despite their considerable scope, two Congressional Acts, the Rehabilitation Act of 1973 and the Americans with Disabilities Act of 1990 (ADA), did not directly affect escalators or their public installations. Since Section 504 of the Rehabilitation Act included public transportation systems, for a few years, the United States Department of Transportation considered designs to retrofit existing escalators for wheelchair access. Nonetheless, Foster-Miller Associates' 1980 plan, *Escalator Modification for the Handicapped* was ultimately ignored in favour of increased elevator installations in subway systems. Likewise, the ADA provided more accessibility options, but expressly excluded escalators as "accessible means of egress," advocating neither their removal nor retention in public structures.

Codes and Regulation

In the United States and Canada, new escalators must abide by ASME A17.1 standards, and old/historic escalators must conform to the safety guidelines of ASME A17.3. In Europe, the escalator safety code is EN115.

Key Safety Features Developed Over Time

To enhance passenger safety, newer models of escalators are equipped with one or more of the following safety implementations, as per ASME A17.1 code:

- Antislide devices: Raised circular objects that often stud the escalator balustrade. Sometimes informally called "hockey pucks" due to their appearance, their purpose is to prevent objects (and people) from precipitously sliding down the otherwise smooth metallic surface.
- Combplate impact switches: Stop the escalator if a foreign object gets caught between the steps and the combplate on either end.
- Deflector brush: A long continuous brush made of stiff bristles running up the sides of the escalator just above the step level. This helps deflect garments, shoes, and other items away from the gap between the moving steps and the skirt board.
- Emergency stop button: At each end of the escalator (in some models, also on the balustrade), a large red button can be pressed to stop the device in the event of an emergency. Typically, an alarmed transparent plastic guardplate covers the button; restarting requires turning a key.

- Extended balustrades: Allows riders to grasp the handrail before setting foot on an escalator, to ease customer comfort and stability/equilibrium. (The effect is similar to the flat steps described below.)
- Flat steps: Like a moving walkway, the first two or three steps at either end of the escalator are flat. This gives the passenger extra time to orient him/herself when boarding, and more time to maintain balance when exiting. Longer escalators often have four or more flat steps.
- Handrail inlet switches:. Sensors located at the bottom and top of the unit that guard the handrail termini. If something gets caught in these locations, a hard fault is generated in the controller, and the escalator shuts down automatically.
- Handrail speed sensors: These sensors are usually optical, and monitor how fast the handrail moves. If the sensor notices a speed difference between the handrail and the steps, it sounds an alarm, pauses, and then automatically stops the escalator. In these situations, the escalator must be serviced by authorized personnel before returning to an operable state.
- Missing step detectors: Depending on the manufacturer and model, this sensor is either optical or physical. When a missing step is detected, the escalator automatically shuts down.
- Raised step edges: In some models, a difference in tread height is utilized to keep passengers' feet from the skirt board.
- Safety instructions: A sign, typically posted on both escalator newels at the entrance landing platform. In some situations, safety precautions are posted on walls near the escalator, included on freestanding signs, or—as in some models—printed on the riser surface itself.
- Sensor switch: In automatic-start/stop escalators, this sensor automatically engages the escalator motion when a rider is detected on the first step of the entrance landing platform, and stops the escalator when there are no riders on the unit.
- Step demarcation lights: Either fluorescent or LED lights (traditionally green in colour) located inside the truss. The illumination between the steps improves the passengers' awareness of the step divisions.
- Step demarcation lines: In order to clearly delineate the edges of each individual step, manufacturers offer steps trimmed in yellow, either painted or with plastic inserts.

Safe Riding: Official Safety Foundation Guidelines

While some escalator accidents are caused by a mechanical failure, most can be avoided by following some simple safety precautions. The Elevator Escalator Safety Foundation is a major advocate for safe riding in the United States and Canada, sponsors National Elevator Escalator Safety Week each year, and publishes its own suggestions for safe riding.

History

Inventors and Manufacturers:

Nathan Ames: Nathan Ames, a patent solicitor from Saugus, Massachusetts, is credited with patenting the first "escalator" in 1859, despite the fact that no working model of his design was ever built. His invention, the "revolving stairs", is largely speculative and the patent specifications indicate that he had no preference for materials or potential use (he noted that steps could be upholstered or made of wood, and suggested that the units might benefit the infirm within a household use), though the mechanization was suggested to run either by manual or hydraulic power.

Figure: *Notice on escalators in Spain*

Leamon Souder: In 1889, Leamon Souder successfully patented the "stairway", an escalator-type device that featured a "series of steps and links jointed to each other". No model was ever built. This was the first of at least four escalator-style patents issued to Souder, including two for spiral designs (U. S. Patent Nos. 723,325 and 792,623).

Jesse Wilford Reno, George A. Wheeler, and Charles Seeberger: In 1892, Jesse W. Reno patented the "Endless Conveyor or Elevator." A few months after Reno's patent was approved, George A. Wheeler patented his ideas for a more recognizable moving staircase, though it was never built. Wheeler's patents were bought by Charles Seeberger; some features of Wheeler's designs were incorporated in Seeberger's prototype built by the Otis Elevator Company in 1899.

Reno, a graduate of Lehigh University, produced the first working escalator (he actually called it the "inclined elevator") and installed it alongside the Old Iron Pier at Coney Island, New York in 1896. This particular device was little more than an inclined belt with cast-iron slats or cleats on the surface for traction, and traveled along a 25° incline. A few months later, the same prototype was used for a monthlong trial period on the Manhattan side of the Brooklyn Bridge. Reno eventually joined forces with Otis Elevator Company, and retired once his patents were purchased outright. Some Reno-type escalators were still being used in the Boston subway until construction for the Big Dig precipitated their removal. The Smithsonian Institution considered re-assembling one of these historic units from 1914 in their collection of Americana, but "logistics and reassembly costs won out over nostalgia", and the project was discarded.

Around May 1895, Charles Seeberger began drawings on a form of escalator similar to those patented by Wheeler in 1892. This device actually consisted of flat, moving stairs, not unlike the escalators of today, except for one important detail: the step surface was smooth, with no comb effect to safely guide the rider's feet off at the ends. Instead, the passenger had to step off sideways. To facilitate this, at the top or bottom of the escalator the steps continued moving horizontally beyond the end of the handrail (like a miniature moving sidewalk) until they disappeared under a triangular "divider" which guided the passenger to either side. Seeberger teamed with Otis Elevator Company in 1899, and together they produced the first commercial escalator which won the first prize at the Paris 1900 *Exposition Universelle* in France. Also on display at the *Exposition* were Reno's inclined elevator, a similar model by James M. Dodge and the Link Belt Machinery Co., and two different devices by French manufacturers Hallé and Piat.

Early European Manufacturers: Hallé, Hocquardt, and Piat: Piat installed its "stepless" escalator in Harrods Knightsbridge store on Wednesday, November 16, 1898, though the company relinquished its patent rights to the department store. Noted by Bill Lancaster in

The Department Store: a Social History, "customers unnerved by the experience were revived by shopmen dispensing free smelling salts and cognac." The Harrods unit was a continuous leather belt made of "224 pieces... strongly linked together travelling in an upward direction," and was the first "moving staircase" in England.

Hocquardt received European patent rights for the *Fahrtreppe* in 1906. After the *Exposition*, Hallé continued to sell its escalator device in Europe, but was eventually eclipsed in sales by other major manufacturers.

Major Competitors and Product Nomenclature: In the first half of the twentieth century, several manufacturers developed their own escalator products, though they had to market their devices under different names, due to Otis' hold on the trademark rights to the word "escalator." New York-based Peelle Company called their models the *Motorstair*, and Westinghouse called their model an *Electric Stairway*. The Toledo-based Haughton Elevator company referred to their product as simply *Moving Stairs*.

Manufacturing Mergers and Buyouts: The Playing Field Narrows: Kone and Schindler introduced their first escalator models several decades after the Otis Elevator Co., but grew to dominance in the field over time. Today, they, Mitsubishi, and ThyssenKrupp are Otis' primary rivals.

Schindler now stands as the largest maker of escalators and second largest maker of elevators in the world, though their first escalator installation did not occur until 1936. In 1979, the company entered the United States market by purchasing Haughton Elevator; nine years later, Schindler assumed control of the North American escalator/ elevator operations of Westinghouse.

Kone expanded internationally by acquisition in the 1970s, buying out Swedish elevator manufacturer Asea-Graham, and purchasing other minor French, German, and Austrian elevator makers before assuming control of Westinghouse's European elevator business. As the last "big four" manufacturers held on to the escalator market, KONE first acquired Montgomery Elevator Company, then took control of Germany's Orenstein & Koppel *Rolltreppen*.

Model Development and Design Types

"Cleat-type" Escalators: Jesse Reno's escalators did not resemble modern escalators too closely. Passengers' feet tilted upward at an angle, and the treads consisted of cleated metal (initially) or wood (later models). Reno worked on his own for several years, gaining success with installations from Toronto to Cape Town, South Africa. Similar units of the day by other manufacturers resembled conveyor belts more than moving staircases. For a time, Otis Elevator sold Reno's escalators as their own "cleat-type" escalators.

"Step-type" Escalators: Seeberger's model, bought by Otis, clearly became the first "step-type" escalator, so called after its visual likeness to steps on a regular staircase. The company later combined the best aspects of both inventions (guiding slats and flat steps) and in 1921 produced an escalator similar to the type used today: they called it the "L-type" escalator. It was succeeded by the "M-type", the "O-type", and current models by Otis such as the "NCE-type" escalator.

Spiral Escalators: From Reno to Mitsubishi

Reno, in addition to his notoriety for the first "practical" escalator in public use, also bears the unique distinction of designing the very first escalators installed in any underground subway system – a single spiral escalator at Holloway Road tube station in London in 1906. The experimental device never saw public use, and was forgotten for several decades. The remains of this are now in the London Transport Museum's depot in Acton.

Figure: *A spiral escalator in Times Square, Hong Kong*

Also the first fully operational spiral escalator, Reno's design was nonetheless only one in a series of several similar proposed contraptions. Souder patented two spiral designs, Wheeler drafted spiral stairway plans in 1905, Seeberger devised at least two different spiral units between 1906 and 1911 (including an unrealized arrangement for the London Underground), and Gilbert Luna obtained West German, Japanese, and United States patents for his version of a spiral escalator by 1973. When interviewed for the *Los Angeles Times* that year, Luna was in the process of soliciting "major firms" for acquisition of his patents and company, but statistics are unclear on the outcome of his endeavors in that regard.

The Mitsubishi Electric Corporation was most successful in its development of "spiral" (more "curve" than true spiral) escalators, and has sold them exclusively since the mid-1980s. The world's first "practical" spiral escalator—a Mitsubishi model—was installed in Osaka, Japan, in 1985.

In use, a major planning advantage presented by spiral escalators is that they take up much less horizontal floor space than traditional units, which frequently house large machine rooms underneath the truss.

Etymology

Several authors and historians have contributed their own differing interpretations of the source of the word "escalator", and some degree of misinformation has heretofore proliferated on the Internet. For reference, contradictory citations by seven separate individuals, including the Otis Elevator Company itself, are provided below.

Name Development and Original Intentions: Charles Seeberger trademarked the word "escalator" in 1900, to coincide with his device's debut at the *Exposition Universelle.* According to his own account, in 1895, his legal counsel advised him to name his new invention, and he then set out to devise a title for it on his own. As evidenced in Seeberger's own handwritten documents, archived at the Otis Elevator Company headquarters in Farmington, Connecticut, the inventor consulted "a Latin lexicon" and "adopted as the root of the new word, 'Scala'; as a prefix, 'E' and as a suffix, 'Tor.'" His own rough translation of the word thus created was "means of traversing from", and he intended for the word to be pronounced, (es-CAL-a-tor).

"Escalator" was not a combination of other French or Greek words, and was never a derivative of "elevator" in the original sense, which means "one who raises up, a deliverer" in Latin. Similarly, the root word "*scala*" does not mean "a flight of steps", but is defined by Lewis and Short's *A Latin Dictionary* as the singular form of the plural noun "*scalae*", which denotes any of the following: "a flight of steps or stairs, a staircase; a ladder, [or] a scaling-ladder."

The alleged intended capitalization of "escalator" is likewise a topic of debate. Seeberger's trademark application lists the word not only with the "E" but also with all of the letters capitalized (in two different instances), and he specifies that, "any other form and character of type may be employed... without altering in any essential manner the character of [the] trade-mark." That his initial specifications are ostensibly inconsistent, and since Otis Elevator Co. advertisements so frequently capitalized all of the letters in the word, suppositions about the "capital 'e'" are difficult to formulate.

Derivatives of 'Escalator': The verb "escalate" originated in 1922, and has two uses, the primary: "to climb or reach by means of an escalator" or "to travel on an escalator", and the secondary: "to increase or develop by successive stages; *spec.* to develop from 'conventional' warfare into nuclear warfare." The latter definition was first printed in the *Manchester Guardian* in 1959, but grew to prominent use during the late 1960s and early 1970s.

Loss of Trademark Rights: In 1950, the landmark case *Haughton Elevator Co. v. Seeberger* precipitated the end of Otis' reign over exclusive use of the word "escalator", and simultaneously created a cautionary study for companies and individuals interested in trademark retention. Confirming the contention of the Examiner of Trademark Interferences, Assistant Commissioner of Patents Murphy's decision rejected the Otis Elevator Company's appeal to keep their trademark intact, and noted that "the term 'escalator' is recognized by the general public as the name for a moving stairway and not the source thereof", observing that the Otis Elevator Co. had "used the term as a generic descriptive term...in a number of patents which [had] been issued to them and...in their advertising matter." All trademark protections were removed from the word "escalator", the term was officially genericized, and it fell into the public domain.

Primary uses and Application

Department Stores/Shopping: As noted above, a few escalator types were installed in major department stores (including Harrods) before the *Expo*. Escalators proved instrumental in the layout and design of shopping venues in the twentieth century.

By 1898, the first of Reno's "inclined elevators" were incorporated into the Bloomingdale Bros. store at Third Avenue and 59th Street. This was the first retail application of the devices in the US, and no small coincidence, considering that Reno's primary financier was Lyman Bloomingdale, co-owner of the department store with brother Joseph Bloomingdale.

Public Transportation

The first "standard" escalator installed on the London Underground was a Seeberger model at Earls Court. Noted above, London's Underground installed a rare spiral escalator designed by Reno, William Henry Aston and Scott Kietzman for the Holloway Road Underground station in 1906; it was run for a short time but was taken out of service the same day it debuted. The older lines of the London Underground had many escalators with wooden treads (ca. 1930s) until they were rapidly replaced following the King's Cross fire, noted above.

Figure: *View from bottom of Porter Square escalator, 2010*

Other Applications

Factories and other Industrial Production Environments: In 1905, the American Woolen Company's Wood Mill in Lawrence, Massachusetts (then "the largest single worsted mill in the world") utilized Otis' Seeberger-type "reversible" escalators to carry its workers between floors four times a day. The machines did not run all day:

rather, escalators ran solely to transport employees to/from midday meals and in/out of the mill. In its advertising, Otis Elevator Company hailed this unconventional use for its unique benefits to both workers and owners: "The profitable and practicable feature of the Escalator, from the viewpoint of the owner, is the increased efficiency of each operator due to the elimination of stair climbing."

Military Use: In San Francisco, an escalator at Hunters Point Naval Shipyard was used to convey personnel between the first and third floors. At the time of its construction in 1948, it was touted thus: "[it has the] highest lift of any industrial building in the world. It rises 42 feet."

Escalators were also utilized on aircraft carriers such as the USS *Hornet* (CV-12), to transport pilots from "ready rooms" to the flight deck.

Extant Historic Escalator Models

A few notable examples of historic escalators still in operation are:

Australia:

- Town Hall Railway Station, Sydney, Australia
- Wynyard Railway Station, Sydney, Australia.

Europe:

- St. Anna Pedestrian Tunnel underneath the Schelde in Antwerp, Belgium. This tunnel was opened in 1933.
- Tyne Cyclist and Pedestrian Tunnel, Tyne and Wear, England.

These escalators, manufactured by Waygood Otis in 1951, were "believed to be the longest single lift escalators in the world", at the time of installation. Presumably the first escalators in Britain designed specifically for cyclists, they are also "thought to be still" the longest escalators in the United Kingdom. At most, they may be the longest extant wooden escalators in operation in the world.

- Greenford Station in Greenford, England contains the oldest escalator still in use on the London Underground service. This was the first above ground station to install an escalator to its high levels and one of the only (if not the only) wooden escalators not to be replaced after the fire at Kings Cross station.

North America:

- Macy's Herald Square department store, Otis L-type units with wood treads and replacement metal treads, New York, New York

- Kaufmann's department store (now Macy's), two 16-inch (400 mm) Otis L-type units with original floorplates, several 40-inch (1000 mm) Otis escalators ca. 1950s, Pittsburgh, Pennsylvania
- Westfield San Francisco Centre (formerly The Emporium), chrome-and-glass escalator by Eleanor LeMaire for Otis, San Francisco, California.

Escalators: Superlatives

Longest Systems:

- Central-Mid-Levels escalator: in Hong Kong, tens of thousands of commuters travel each work day between Central, the central business district, and the Mid-levels, a residential district hundreds of feet uphill, using this long distance system of escalators and moving walkways. It is the world's longest outdoor escalator *system* (not a single escalator span), at a total length of 2,600 feet (790 m). It goes only one way at a time; the direction reverses depending on rush hour traffic direction.
- Ocean Park, Hong Kong: a long escalator system connecting two parts of the Park, with an overall length of 730 feet (220 m).

Longest Individual Escalators:

Asia and Europe: Several "metro" or "subway" systems in Central and Eastern Europe feature very long escalators.

Figure: *The longest escalators in the Western Hemisphere, at the Wheaton station, Washington DC Metro*

- In the Park Pobedy station of the Moscow Metro, opened in 2003, the escalators are 126.8 m (63.4 m high), or 740 steps, long, and take nearly three minutes to transit. Deep underground stations in St. Petersburg have escalators up to approximately 142 m long (71 m high).
- The Kiev Metro Kreschatik station's lower-level second exit escalator (a type ËÒ-2, circa 1965), lifts riders 216 feet (66 m), or 743 steps, up a 432-foot (132 m)-long incline.
- The longest escalator in Prague is at the Námìstí Míru station at 290 feet (88 m).
- The longest escalator of a European shopping mall is at MyZeil, Frankfurt, Germany, with a length of 150 feet (46 m).
- The tallest escalator on the London Underground system is at Angel station with a length of 197 feet (60 m), and a vertical rise of 90 feet (27 m).
- The longest wooden escalators in the United Kingdom are at the Tyne Tunnel, with a length of 200 feet (61 m).
- The longest escalator on the Stockholm Metro, and in Western Europe, is at Västra skogen with a length of 220 feet (67 m) and in Helsinki Metro at Kamppi station with a length of 210 feet (64 m).
- The largest "single truss escalator" is in the Bentall Centre in Kingston upon Thames in Greater London, UK. It connects the ground floor with the second floor with only top and bottom supports.

North and South America:

- The longest set of single-span uninterrupted escalators in the Western Hemisphere is at the Wheaton station of the Washington Metro system. They are 230 feet (70 m) long with a vertical rise of 115 feet (35 m), and take what is variously described as 2 minutes and 45 seconds or nearly three-and-a-half minutes, to ascend or descend without walking.
- The longest *freestanding* (supported only at the ends) escalator in the world is inside CNN Center's atrium in Atlanta, Georgia. It rises 8 stories and is 205 feet (62 m) long. Originally built as the entrance to the amusement park The World of Sid and Marty Krofft, the escalator is now used for CNN studio tours.

Shortest Examples

Asia: According to Guinness, the shortest escalator in the world is in the Okadaya Mores shopping mall in Kawasaki, Japan. Its vertical rise is only 32.8 inches (83 cm).

North America: The shortest escalator in the United States is a Schindler unit at the entrance to the JCPenney Department Store in Westfield Garden State Plaza in Paramus, New Jersey.

Notable Spiral Escalator Installations

Asia:

- Wheelock Place, Singapore
- Jeddah Hilton, Saudi Arabia
- Landmark Tower, Japan
- Times Square shopping mall, Causeway Bay, Hong Kong
- Langham Place, Mongkok, Hong Kong
- Lotte World, South Korea
- The Venetian hotel and casino, Cotai, Macau

Figure: *Spiral escalators in the Yokohama Minato Mirai 21, Japan*

- WTC Mangga Dua, Jakarta, Indonesia (the only one in Indonesia)
- Taipei, Taiwan.

North America:

- Wynn Las Vegas, Las Vegas, Nevada, United States
- The Forum Shops at Caesars, Las Vegas, Nevada, United States
- Westfield San Francisco Centre, San Francisco, California, United States—the first such installation in the Western Hemisphere.
- River Rock Casino Resort, Richmond, British Columbia, Canada-the first in Canada.

Moving Walkway

A moving walkway (British English) or moving sidewalk (American English) (colloquially sometimes travelator, horizontal escalator, walkalator, autowalk, movator, people mover) is a slow moving conveyor mechanism that transports people, across a horizontal or inclined plane, over a short to medium distance. Moving walkways can be used by standing or walking on them. They are often installed in pairs, one for each direction.

Figure: *Travelators at Indira Gandhi International Airport, Delhi, India*

History

The first moving walkway debuted at the World's Columbian Exposition of 1893, in Chicago, Illinois. It had two different divisions:

one where passengers were seated, and one where riders could stand or walk. It ran in a loop down the length of a lakefront pier to a casino. Six years later a moving walkway was also presented to the public at the Paris *Exposition Universelle* in 1900. The walkway consisted of three elevated platforms, the first was stationary, the second moved at a moderate speed, and the third at about six miles an hour. These demonstrations likely served as inspiration for some of H. G. Wells' settings mentioned in the "Science Fiction" section below.

The Beeler Organization, a New York City consulting firm, proposed a Continuous Transit System with Sub-Surface Moving Platforms for Atlanta in 1924, with a design roughly similar to the Paris Exposition system. The proposed drive system used a linear induction motor. The system was not constructed.

Figure: *The Great Wharf, Moving Sidewalk*

The first commercial moving walkway in the United States was installed in 1954 in Jersey City, NJ, inside the Hudson & Manhattan Railroad Erie station) at the Pavonia Terminal. Named the "Speedwalk" and built by Goodyear, it was 277 ft (84.5 m) long and moved up a 10 percent grade at a speed of 1.5 mph (2.4 km/h). The walkway was removed a few years later when traffic patterns at the station changed.

The first moving walkway in an airport was installed in 1958 at Love Field in Dallas, Texas. On Jan 1, 1960 Tina Marie Brandon, age 3, was killed on the moving sidewalk.

Figure: *Moving sidewalk, Exposition Universelle, Paris, 1900*

Designs

Moving walkways are built in one of two basic styles:

- Pallet type — a continuous series of flat metal plates join together to form a walkway. Most have a metal surface, though some models have a rubber surface for extra traction.
- Moving belt — these are generally built with mesh metal belts or rubber walking surfaces over metal rollers. The walking surface may have a solid feel or a "bouncy" feel.

Both types of moving walkway have a grooved surface to mesh with combplates at the ends. Also, nearly all moving walkways are built with moving handrails similar to those on escalators.

Pallet-types consists of one-piece, die-cast aluminium pallets. Example dimensions are: widths (between balustrades): between 32 inches (800 mm) and 56 inches (1200 mm), with a speed of 100 feet per minute (.5 metres per second), powered by an AC induction motor.

High-speed Walkways: In the 1970s Dunlop developed the *Speedaway* system. It was in fact an invention by Gabriel Bouladon and Paul Zuppiger of the Battelle Memorial Institute in Geneva (Switzerland). A prototype was built and demonstrated at the Battelle Institute in Geneva in the early 1970s, as can be attested by a (French-speaking) Swiss television program entitled Un Jour une Heure aired in October 1974. The great advantage of the Speedaway, as compared to the then existing systems, was that the embarking/disembarking zone was both wide and slow moving (up to 4 passengers could embark simultaneously, allowing for a large number of passengers, up to 10,000 per hour), whereas the transportation zone was narrower and fast moving.

The entrance to the system was like a very wide escalator, with broad metal tread plates of a parallelogram shape. After a short distance the tread plates were accelerated to one side, sliding past one another to form progressively into a narrower but faster moving track which travelled at almost a right-angle to the entry section. The passenger was accelerated through a parabolic path to a maximum design speed of 15 km/h (9 mph). The experience was unfamiliar to passengers, who needed to understand how to use the system to be able to do so safely. Developing a moving hand-rail for the system presented a challenge, also solved by the Battelle team. The Speedaway was intended to be used as a stand alone system over short distances or to form acceleration and deceleration units providing entry and exit means for a parallel conventional (but fast running) *Starglide* walkway which covered longer distances. The system was still in development in 1975 but never went into commercial production.

Another attempt at an accelerated walkway in the 1980s was the TRAX (*Trottoir Roulant Accéléré*), which was developed by Dassault and RATP and whose prototype was installed in the Paris Invalides metro station. The speed at entry and exit was 3 km/h (2 mph), while the maximum speed was 15 km/h (9 mph). It was a technical failure due to its complexity, and was never commercially exploited.

In the mid 1990s the Loderway Moving Walkway company patented and licenced a design to a number of larger moving walkway manufacturers. Trial systems were installed at Flinders Street Station in Melbourne and Brisbane Airport Australia. These met with a positive response from the public, but no permanent installations were made. This system is of the belt type, with a sequence of belts moving at different speeds to accelerate and decelerate riders. A sequence of different speed handrails is also used. A video of the trials systems can be found at the following link.

In 2002, the first successful high-speed walkway was installed in the Montparnasse—Bienvenüe Métro station in Paris. At first it operated at 12 km/h (7 mph) but due to people losing their balance, the speed was reduced to 9 km/h (6 mph). It has been estimated that commuters using a walkway such as this twice a day would save 15 minutes per week and 10 hours a year.

***Figure:** Experimental 185 metre long high-speed moving walkway on the Paris Métro, France*

Using the high-speed walkway is like using any other moving walkway, except that for safety there are special procedures to follow when joining or leaving. When this walkway was introduced, staff determined who could and who could not use it. As riders must have at least one hand free to hold the handrail, those carrying bags, shopping, etc., or who are infirm, must use the ordinary walkway nearby.

On entering, there is a 10-metre acceleration zone where the 'ground' is a series of metal rollers. Riders stand still with both feet on these rollers and use one hand to hold the handrail and let it pull them so that they glide over the rollers. The idea is to accelerate the riders so that they will be travelling fast enough to step onto the moving walkway belt. Riders who try to walk on these rollers are at significant risk of falling over.

Once on the walkway, riders can stand or walk. Owing to Newton's laws of motion, there is no special sensation of travelling at speed, except for headwind.

At the exit, the same technique is used to decelerate the riders. Users step on to a series of rollers which decelerate them slowly, rather than the abrupt halt which would otherwise take place.

In 2007, a similar high-speed walkway was opened in the newly opened Pier F of Pearson International Airport in Toronto, Canada. This walkway is of the pallet type rather than the belt type. The pallets "intermesh" with a comb and slot arrangement. They expand out of each other when speeding up, and compress into each other when slowing down. The handrailings work in a similar manner. The walkway moves at roughly 2 km/h when riders step onto it, speeds up to approximately 7 km/h for the bulk of the length, and slows to 2 km/h again at the end.

In May 2009 it was announced that because of its unreliability and the number of users having accidents, in 2011 the Parisian high-speed moving walkway will be replaced with a standard moving walkway.

Inclined Moving Walkways: An inclined moving walkway is used in airports and supermarkets to move people to another floor with the convenience of an elevator (namely, that people can take along their suitcase trolley or shopping cart, or baby carriage) and the capacity of an escalator.

Figure: *An inclined moving sidewalk at Beaudry metro station in Montreal, Canada*

The carts have either a brake that is automatically applied when the cart handle is released, strong magnets in the wheels to stay adhered to the floor, or specially designed wheels that secure the cart within the grooves of the ramp, so that wheeled items travel alongside the riders and do not slip away.

The Central-Mid-levels escalator system on Hong Kong Island, Hong Kong also has several inclined moving sidewalks. In Carlton, Victoria, Australia, another inclined moving sidewalk can be found at Lygon Court.

Some department stores instead use Vermaport or Cartveyors—conveying systems that move shopping carts in a similar fashion to an escalator—to transport passengers and their carts between store levels simultaneously.

Inclined moving walkways can also be found at the National Aquarium in Baltimore, Maryland; the international arrivals area of Pierre Elliott Trudeau International Airport in Montreal, Quebec, Canada; Piccadilly Station in Manchester, UK and Ikea in Bristol, UK. Slightly inclined ones can be found at Logan Airport, in Boston, MA.

Applications

Moving walkways are frequently found in the following locations:

Airports: They are popular there because most larger airports require passengers – often with heavy luggage in tow – to walk considerable distances. Moving walkways may be utilized:

- in passageways between concourses and the terminal
- within particularly long concourses
- as a connector between terminals, or
- as access to a parking facility or a ground transport station.

Figure: *A moving walkway at the Port Columbus International Airport, United States.*

Of particular note is the Charles de Gaulle International Airport in Paris, which has several moving walkways inside a series of futuristic suspended tubes.

Museum Exhibits: Moving sidewalks may be used:

- to ensure that a museum exhibit is viewed in a certain sequence
- to provide a particular aesthetic effect
- to make sure the crowd moves through at a reliable pace.

The 1975-76 American Freedom Train did this; they had a moving walkway inside each successive railroad car, thus maximizing the number of people who could view the interior exhibits in the limited time the train was stopped in each town.

The National Gallery of Art in Washington, DC uses a moving walkway to connect the two main galleries.

The Tower of London in London, UK, uses a moving walkway where visitors are passing the cabinets which contain the Crown Jewels.

Zoos: Similar to museums, some zoological park exhibits have a moving walkway to ease guests through an animal display or habitat. An aquarium at the Mall of America does this with a moving walkway made up of specially rounded pallets that enable it to change directions en route. And the San Diego Zoo uses moving ramps not for an exhibit per se, but to help guests ascend steep grades.

Theme Parks: Some amusement park rides, such as continuous-motion dark rides like Disney's Haunted Mansion, make use of a moving sidewalk to assist passengers in boarding and disembarking rides and attractions. Some examples include:

- the Ultra Twister, a roller coaster at the now closed Astroworld in Houston, Texas. (It had a moving walkway with no handrail for passengers to step on prior to boarding their car. The walkway would move at the same speed as the approaching cars, allowing passengers completing the ride to step off and for boarding passengers to enter the car. A loudspeaker announced "Moving conveyor, please watch your step" to warn of the moving walkway.)
- the exit from the Space Mountain attraction at Walt Disney World has a long moving walkway which changes inclination multiple times.
- the exit from the Pirates of the Caribbean attraction at Walt Disney World has an inclined moving walkway leading towards a gift shop.

Theatre: Andrew Lloyd Weber's The Phantom of the Opera (1986 musical) utilizes a travelator for the number 'The Phantom of the Opera' (Act one, scene six), to give the illusion the Phantom and Christine are travelling the catacombs below the Paris Opera House a great distance to the Phantom's lair on the subterranean lake.

Public Transport: Moving walkways are useful for remote platforms in underground subway/metro stations, or assisting with lengthier connections between lines, for example Waterloo Underground Station in London, United Kingdom, and between Central and Hong Kong stations on Hong Kong Island, Hong Kong, as well as between Tsim Sha Tsui and East Tsim Sha Tsui stations in Kowloon, Hong Kong.

Similar walkways exist in Singapore's Bugis MRT Station, Dhoby Ghaut MRT Station and Serangoon MRT Station. In Glasgow's Buchanan Street subway station a moving walkway is used to connect the Subway station with Glasgow Queen Street Station. A moving walkway existed between Spadina station on the Bloor-Danforth subway line and Spadina station on the Yonge–University–Spadina line. Installed in 1978, the series of moving walkways has since been removed (2004) and patrons are now required to walk between the stations.

Urban Areas: Hong Kong is one of the world's most heavily populated cities, and has public escalators that connect many streets.

Paternoster

A paternoster or paternoster lift is a passenger elevator which consists of a chain of open compartments (each usually designed for two persons) that move slowly in a loop up and down inside a building without stopping. Passengers can step on or off at any floor they like. The same technique is also used for filing cabinets to store great amounts of documents or for small spare parts.

History

First built in 1884 by Londoner J. E. Hall as the Cyclic Elevator, the name *paternoster* ("Our Father", the first two words of the Lord's Prayer in Latin) was originally applied to the device because the elevator is in the form of a loop and is thus similar to rosary beads used as an aid in reciting prayers. In another alternative, the word origin could be derived from Czech words *pater* meaning "floors" and *nosit* meaning "to carry".

Figure: *A paternoster in Prague*

Paternosters were popular throughout the first half of the 20th century as they could carry more passengers than ordinary elevators. They were more common in continental Europe, especially in public buildings, than in the United Kingdom. They are rather slow elevators, typically travelling at about 0.3 metres per second, thus improving the chances of getting on and off successfully.

Today, in many countries the construction of new paternosters is no longer allowed because of the high risk of accidents (people tripping or falling over when trying to enter or alight). Five people were killed by paternosters from 1970 to 1993. The elderly, the handicapped and children are the most in danger of being crushed. In 1989, the paternoster in Newcastle University's Claremont Tower was taken out of service after a passenger undertaking an up-and-over journey became caught in the drive chain, necessitating a rescue by the Fire Service. A conventional elevator was subsequently installed in its place. This accident led to an 18-month close-down of all UK paternosters for a safety review, during which additional safety devices were fitted.

In April 2006, Hitachi announced plans for a modern paternoster-style elevator with computer-controlled cars and normal elevator doors to alleviate safety concerns.

Popular Culture

- The movie *Night People*, a 1954 cold war thriller set in post-war Berlin uses a paternoster for comic relief in a scene with Gregory Peck and Buddy Ebsen.
- In the novelization of *Metropolis*, worker 11811 operates the machine controlling a paternoster in the New Tower of Babel; inspired by the machine's name, he continuously mutters a disturbed version of the Lord's Prayer. In the actual film, a paternoster is seen in the scene at the place where Josaphat lives (this scene is only in the 2010 version as it occurs in part of the "lost footage" that was discovered in 2008).
- In German writer Boris Meyn's mystery novel, Die rote Stadt (Rowohlt Taschenbuch Verlag, 7th ed, 2007), lawyer Soren Bischop begins his detective career with the discovery of a bloody corpse in a paternoster. Meyn describes Bischop's reaction as he sees a paternoster for the first time. He observes the compartment disappear and reappear and once he spots the victim, jumps in to help, not knowing if he will have to climb the walls or stand on his head in order to come out the other side.
- In the Gunter Grass novel *Too Far Afield*, numerous scenes are set in an east German government archives building where one of the main characters, who is employed as a courier, rides a paternoster in connection with his duties and lobbies successfully for the paternoster's continued operation following German reunification.
- In the 1985 German film, "Männer", several scenes involve a paternoster. During the closing credits, some of those involved in the film ride the paternoster as their names scroll by.

Surviving Paternosters

Numerous working paternosters are known to survive in Europe (this is an incomplete list):

Austria

- City Hall of Vienna (at stairway 6 near the northern entrance)
- House of Industry, Schwarzenbergplatz 4, Vienna (oldest paternoster in Austria by Anton Freissler)
- Federal Ministry of Economics and Labour, Stubenring, Vienna
- Ministry of Defence, Rossauer Lände 1, Vienna
- Federal Computing Centre, Hintere Zollamtsstraße 4, Vienna

- Versicherungsanstalt für Eisenbahnen und Bergbau (Insurance institution of the railway and mining industries), Linke Wienzeile, Vienna
- The Ringturm (Wiener Städtische Versicherung/Vienna City Insurance Headquarters Building), Schottenring 30, Vienna
- KELAG Zentrale Klagenfurt, Arnulfplatz 2, 9020 Klagenfurt (Kärntner Elektrizitäts Aktiengesellschaft/Carinthian electricity supplier).

Belgium

- A functioning paternoster can be found at the Flemish Parliament in Brussels, Belgium, where it is used as an art display.
- Another paternoster can be found in a building of the Belgian Railways (NMBS) at the station Brussels-Zuid/Midi. It's still used daily.

Czech Republic

- The *Komerèní Banka* building on Václavské námìstí in Prague. (This is a working office and not open to the general public, but it can be seen from the main lobby).
- The Municipality hall of Praha 1 (Vodièkova 18) has a working paternoster open to public combined with two classic lifts, one dedicated to baby trolleys and wheel chairs which are not allowed on the paternoster.
- Ministry of Foreign Affairs, Prague
- Faculty of Law, Charles University, Nám. Curieových 7, Prague
- Czech Technical University in Prague on Dejvice, Technická 2, Prague
- Within the *Lucerna* building in Prague, near the entrance from Štìpánská.
- Office building of KAUÈUK, a.s. in Kralupy nad Vltavou near Prague.
- Ministry of Finance in Prague
- Health center Building on Smíchov, Kartouzská 6, Prague
- Ministry of Agriculture, Prague Florenc
- CEZ (Czech Energy Corp) Jungmanova Street, Prague
- City Courthouse in 2 Prague on Slezska, open to the public (after passing through security)
- Trades Office (Živnostenský úøad), Malinovského Námìstí, Brno

- A working paternoster can be found at the Faculty Of Mechanical Engineering, Brno University of Technology where it is being used by students and faculty staff.
- Bývalý Krajský úøad Zlín (yellow building)
- Office building of Spolek pro chemickou a hutní výrobu (Spolchemie) in Ústí nad Labem
- *New Townhall* on Prokešovo námìstí in Ostrava, which are open to the public.
- SZIF, Hradec Králové, Ulrichovo námìstí 810/4
- Former Building of Rude Pravo Newspapers on Na Florenci street 19, Reception B, Prague 1 (about to be demolished, but occasionally working, for example during Krétakör's performance, during 2011 Praque Quadriennial).

Denmark

- At the seat of the Danish parliament, Christiansborg, there is a working paternoster open to the public.
- Frederiksberg City Hall.
- At Danfoss Nordborg
- At the Axelborg building right across from the Tivoli main entrance
- At KVUC in Copenhagen
- At The Danish Dairy Board in Aarhus.
- At Horsens hospital, The hospital in the city Horsens, there is a working paternoster, but not open to the public.
- At Vejle hospital, The hospital in the city Vejle, there is a working paternoster, but not open to the public.

Finland

- The Finnish house of parliament, the Eduskuntatalo, Helsinki.
- Kansaneläkelaitos office building, Helsinki.(staff only)
- Stockmann department store, Helsinki (staff only)
- Office building in *Yliopistonkatu*, Turku (former headquarters of the Sampo insurance company).

Germany

- Trostbrücke 1, in the Altstadt district of Hamburg (accessible during office hours-no groups and guided tours). A paternoster still in operation and open to general public is in the Bezirksamt

Eimsbüttel (Grindelberg 62/66). Qype's former office building at Deichstraße 29 also has a working Paternoster. Kaiser-Wilhelm-Straße 16 (Publisher Axel Springer) offers at least one paternoster. Ballindamm 25 (shipping company Hapag Lloyd) still has one in use (not open to the public). Stadthausbrücke 8 (authorities ›Stadt-Entwicklungs-Behörde‹) uses a paternoster. Another one being in service can be found in Rathausstraße 7, entrance via Knochenhauertwiete, close to the town hall. Steinhöft 11 (office block ›Slomanhaus‹). There is also a paternoster in the St. Annen 2 building in the historic Speicherstadt, which is not in use at the moment.

- The IG Farben Building in Frankfurt-am-Main. The current occupants of the building, Johann Wolfgang Goethe University, have pledged to maintain and preserve the famous paternosters *"in perpetuity"*.
- Frankfurt, Fleming's Deluxe Hotel the paternoster provides service to six floors and the rooftop restaurant.
- Stuttgart, town hall, Literaturhaus, Universität Stuttgart, Allianz Lebensversicherungs-AG (only for employees), Kaufhof (near main station (only for employees)), Robert Bosch GmbH (Stuttgart-Feuerbach – only for employees), Arbeitsgericht
- Kiel Rathaus, or town hall. One of the best examples in Germany, it is 5 levels and it open to the public.
- Essen Deutsches Haus.
- Mannheim operations building of SCA (only for employees)
- Leverkusen, some at Bayer AG's plant.
- Dortmund, in the vestibule of the Signal-Versicherung building, situated by the junction between the Maerkische Strasse, and the Ostwall.
- Dresden, Alstom Grid/Schnieder Energy (Ex AREVA T&D) building. For staff and authorised visitors only.
- Duisburg, both in the city hall and the internal revenue offices.
- Düsseldorf, in the older of the three Vodafone Global buildings. Currently out of use following an incident; In the Polizeipräsidium (Jürgensplatz 40219).
- Cologne, in the IHK (Industrie-und Handelskammer/Chamber of Industry and Trade) Building (Unter Sachsenhausen 10-26, D-50667 Cologne, Hansahochhaus (housing Saturn, Hansaring, Maybachstraße 115, D-50674 Cologne), WDR HQ (Wallrafplatz

1, D-50667 Cologne (only for employees); Kaufhof (Hohe Straße 41-53, D-50667), Kaufhof Corporate HQ (Leonhard-Tietz-Str., D-50667 Cologne (not open to the public); Volkshochschule Building (near Neumarkt, D-50667 Cologne); Former Felten & Guilleaume Corporate HQ (Schanzenstr. 28, D-51069 Cologne-Mülheim, accessible public office building, 5 Stories); former downtown Bezirksamt „Dischhaus" (Brückenstr., D-50667 Cologne);Bezirksregierung Köln (Regional Government Center Cologne), Entrance: Zeughausstraße 8 (D-50667 Cologne)

- Berlin Foreign Office, Werderscher Markt 1; Finance Ministry, Wilhelmstrasse 97; Agriculture Ministry, Wilhelmstrasse 54; Axel Springer Building, Axel Springer Strasse 65; Bayer Schering Pharma, AG; ART+COM, Kleiststrasse 23-26, 10787 Berlin; (52°302 4.993 N 13°202 39.723 E), rbb (Radio Berlin Brandenburg) Masurenallee 8-14; Rathaus Schöneberg, John-F-Kennedy-Platz; Siemens AG, Siemens Damm (in several buildings).
- Bremen, Baumwollbörse, Wachtstraße 17-24 (near Town Hall); Haus des Reichs, Rudolf-Hilferding-Platz 1
- Wiesbaden, two still in operation in buildings in the industrial park "Infra-Serv Kalle-Albert", Kasteler Straße 45, not accessible to the general public
- Leipzig, new town hall
- Munich, Kaufhof am Marienplatz had a paternoster working for the staff. The building was erected in 1972, so it is one of the last ones ever in Germany. The Polizeipraesidium—the main police station—in the Ettstrasse behind the Frauenkirche has a paternoster, which is accessible to the public. One is in the Sueddeutsche Zeitung Verlagsgebaeude; another in the Hochhaus an der Blumenstrasse.
- Kassel, headquarters of the Wintershall Holding AG, a subsidiary of BASF, not accessible to the general public
- Wuppertal, in the town hall of Barmen and Elberfeld, in the headquarters of Vorwerk (not open to the public), and the fiscal office in Elberfeld
- Augsburg, Finanzamt Augsburg-Stadt, accessible to employees and visitors.

Hungary

- MOL Group's Headquarters in Budapest
- University of Miskolc

- Jahn Ferenc Hospital in Budapest
- MÁV Hospital in Budapest
- Hungarian Television's building in Budapest at Szabadság sqr (Soon to be renovated by new owner, the future of the paternoster is unknown)
- Ministry of Education and Culture in Budapest
- Ministry of Defence in Budapest
- Ministry of Justice in Budapest
- Hungarian Trade Licensing Office in Budapest
- Hospital of Kecskemét
- HQ of the Bkv Zrt. (Budapest public transport company) in Budapest, Akácfa street
- Building of the Hungarian Power Companies Ltd. at Vám u. 5-7., Budapest
- OTP Bank's Headquarters in Budapest, Nádor street
- Former HQ of the Hungarian Post Co. Ltd. at Krisztina krt. 6-8., Budapest
- Hospital of Szigetvár
- County hall (of Csongrád County) in Szeged
- Pesti Központi Kerületi Bíróság (Central District Court of Pest) at Marko u. 25. Budapest
- County Court of Pest County (Pest megyei Bíróság) at Thököly út 97-101. Budapest
- Central Bank of Hungary at Szabadság square 8-9. Budapest.

Italy

- Air Force Ministry, Rome.

Netherlands

- Paternosters are still in operation at the main office of the Corus Steelworks (formerly Hoogovens) in IJmuiden. This remarkable building (by Dudok, 1951) was restored in 1999.
- The office building of Ziggo at Spaarneplein (formerly Main Post Office, architect D.E.C. Knuttel 1919) in The Hague also still is using a Paternoster.
- The Grand Hotel Amrath Amsterdam has a working Paternoster. The building, the Scheepvaarthuis, was originally built as the headquarters for the six leading Amsterdam shipping companies

in 1913 forming the Netherland Line(architect J.M.van der Meij. This Paternoster although not open for use by residents appears to currently being used as a service lift.

- The Philips High Tech campus in Eindhoven had a paternoster in operation until 2006.
- The formerly Main Post Office at the Coolsingel in Rotterdam (architect G.C. Bremer, 1915).
- The formerly Raad van Arbeid/Sociale Verzekeringsbank at the Rhijnspoorplein 1 in Amsterdam (1919). In operation until 2006
- HaKa-building in Rotterdam (architects H.F. Mertens and J.Koeman, 1932). In operation.
- The formerly Belastingdienst at the Puntegaalstraat in Rotterdam (architect H.Hoekstra, 1938/1948). Working Paternoster; not in operation.

Norway

- Oslo: Landbrukets hus (House of Agriculture), Schweigaards gate 34 C. Not open to the public. This is the last remaining operating paternoster lift in Norway.
- Oslo (closed pasternoster lifts): There used to be paternoster lifts at Ullevål hospital (central block, sealed off), the old State Hospital building, the former Aftenposten building at Akersgata, Oslo Lysverker at Solli plass and a couple more.

Poland

- Katowice, the Silesian Parliament at Jagiellonska 25; 14 cabs, 7 floors; built by VEB Aufzugbau Leipzig
- Katowice, office building at Wita Stwosza 7; 12 cabs, 4 floors; built by Flohr (1951: Flohr-Otis, 1989: Otis)
- Wroc³aw, the head office of Bank Zachodni WBK at Rynek 9/ 11; 20 cabs, 10 floors; the paternoster is still in use, yet it is only available to the bank staff
- Gliwice, office building of "Bumar £abêdy" at Mechanikow 9; 14 cabs, 8 floors; build before 1945, only available to the company employees

Russia

- Building E of Moscow Power Engineering Institute, Moscow— non-working
- Ministry of Agriculture, Orlikov Pereulok, Moscow.

Slovakia

- Ministry of Finance, Štefanovièova street, Bratislava
- Ministry of Agriculture, Dobrovièova street, Bratislava
- Ministry of Transport, posts and telecommunications, Nám. slobody, Bratislava
- Ministry of Interior, Pribinova street, Bratislava
- Office building at Popradska @ Moskovska trieda, Košice
- Technical University of Košice
- Chirana Export-Import, Krajinska street, Piešany
- Slovakotex, Jilemnickeho street, Trenèín.

Removed and replaced in 2007 with a modern elevator:

- The Railways of the Slovak Republic HQ, Klemensova street, Bratislava.

Serbia

- One elevator still active, in HQ building of Serbian Railways.

Sri Lanka

- Head office, Ceylon Electricity Board, Colombo. Not open to the public.

Sweden

- Two elevators are still in active service at Norrland's University Hospital in Umeå.
- HSB head office, Kungsholmen, Stockholm. Not open to the public.

Switzerland

- Hôpitaux universitaires de Genève, hospital in Geneva (in use until 2009)
- Vaucher Sport, a sport shop in Bern

Ukraine

- Regional State Administration Building in Uzhhorod

United Kingdom

Some United Kingdom, multi-storey, university buildings were built in the early 1960s and 1970s with paternoster lifts: they included buildings at Aston University; Birmingham University's Gisbert Kapp building (the Department of Electrical and Electronic Engineering, completed in 1971), the Muirhead Tower, and the University Library); Birmingham City University's Baker Building; The Albert Sloman Library at the University of Essex; University of Leicester's Attenborough Building; Leeds University's Roger Stevens building, now closed, Salford University's tower block, now demolished; Sheffield University's Arts Tower, Imperial College's Chemistry Department (removed in the mid 1980s), De Montfort University's Fletcher Building (now replaced with high speed lifts) and James Went Building (now demolished), Oxford University's Biochemistry building and Thom Building (housing the Department of Engineering Science), and Newcastle University. Until the late 1980s, St. Thomas' Hospital, Westminster had a paternoster for staff use, whiles one administrative building at AEE Winfrith had one until the late 1990s.

- The Arts Tower at the University of Sheffield contains a 38-car paternoster. The building is a teaching block and not specifically open to the public, but the paternoster can be seen from the front door. It is the tallest in the UK. It is currently under renovation.
- Attenborough Tower at the University of Leicester.
- A seven floor Paternoster survives in *E block* at the Ericsson (formerly Marconi) site in Beeston, Nottinghamshire. Employees were banned from going around the bottom or over the top following an incident a few years ago, when abuse caused by a group of visitors shaking the car had caused the car to get stuck at the bottom. The lift has been out of action since November 2007, and is unlikely to be put back into service.
- Rolls-Royce's seven storey tower block on Victory Road in Derby. The award-winning building housing this (designed by Rolls-Royce in-house architect Andrew Carr) has been demolished, and the paternoster scrapped.
- Staff in the main ward building of Northwick Park Hospital, Harrow, Middlesex, have access to a paternoster in the main ward block. This is regularly maintained and is frequently used by staff instead of the nearby conventional lifts due to its speed in transferring between adjacent floors.
- The Dental Hospital in Birmingham has one which used to be for staff use, until maintenance costs forced its closure in 2007.
- In Scotland, a working paternoster serves seven floors of the Pontecorvo Building (former Department of Genetics) at the University of Glasgow. The building is not open to the public. A

paternoster was installed there on construction, in 1966–67 (by architects Basil Spence & Partners) because each floor has a small area and it was anticipated that staff and students would make many short journeys. This expectation has been fulfilled, and the paternoster is considered to have been a very valuable device. Occupants of the Pontecorvo Building are currently being relocated to allow its demolition.

- There is a paternoster at Technology House, the headquarters of Boxclever, in Bedford, which was switched off on February 11, 2008 for health and safety reasons
- There is a paternoster at Chadwick House, an office building at Birchwood Park near Warrington. Although covered over during re-refurbishments in 2005 due to maintenance costs, the paternoster is still operable if uncovered.
- There is a disused paternoster at Marks & Spencer in Liverpool. The lift was used until the late 1990s and was covered up due to health and safety concerns and rising maintenance costs. It is still fully in place behind access panels.
- There is a disused paternoster in Marks & Spencer Pantheon, London, which is covered up.
- There is a disused paternoster in the former Elliott Brothers research laboratories in Borehamwood, later renamed GEC, Marconi, and now the Elstree Business Centre. This paternoster was used in an episode of *The Unmutual Prisoner*, and taken out of service and covered up in 2001.

Hotel Energy Management

Hotel Energy Management is the practice of controlling procedures, operations and equipment that contribute to the energy use in a hotel operation. This can include electricity, gas, water or other natural resources. Because hotels can have complicated operations and extensive facilities they utilize many different types of energy resources. Hotel energy usages are tracked and classified by the U.S. Department of Energy and statistics are regularly published in the Energy Information Administration annual reports.

Modern practices to control energy usage includes contributions by the guests themselves which has been popularized by information cards requesting guests to save water by letting hotel housekeeping staff know if they would care to re-use towels and bed linens. Some celebrities endorse this practice and some for-profit companies such as

Project Planet distribute or sell these kind of materials and or procedures to hotel operators. This reduces the amount of water and/ or cleaning substances used by the hotel laundry department which also reduces the expense to the property owner or manager.

Recently consultants have developed entire organizations around advising hotels where they are operating inefficiently or using more energy than necessary. Some of them participate by providing the products to implement their advice for a share of the cost savings. These companies have proliferated over the previous years as public and business energy concerns grow and are known as ESCO's (Energy Saving COmpanies).

Other practices include using infrared motion sensors and door contacts to control the heating and air conditioning systems (HVAC) when guests leave them on and leave the room or leave open balcony doors or windows. While energy saving practices are commonplace in Europe and Asia, American guests often do not understand these ideas or mistake the products to be cameras or an invasion of privacy. Because of this the use of these products are not widespread however they can be seen more and more.

Industrial Laundry

Large institutions that require a constant flow of clean linen, working-clothing or uniform, will often employ the services of an industrial laundry. Hospitals, prisons and hotels, for instance, will usually have their own laundry departments. The organized collection, laundering and timely delivery of textiled service ware is essential to the operation of the institution. Employees in uniforms reassure customers that they represent the company. From day-to-day counter work to service representatives making residential calls, customers trust uniformed employees and rely on them for dependable and positive reinforcement.

Stages of Operation

When linen is sent to be laundered, it goes through six stages. The first three stages are called "soiled side" operations, since they occur before the linen is actually washed. The last three are called "clean side" operations, since they involve the handling of clean linen.

Soiled Retrieval

In this step, the institution's linens are collected by laundry personnel and returned to the laundry facility. Members of the institution's housekeeping staff will place the soiled linen at a collection point, usually by dropping it down a laundry chute. Laundry workers will then collect the soiled linen, place it in carts reserved for soiled linen and transport it to the laundry facility. Linen retrieval poses a problem, especially in health care institutions. Soiled linen can be contaminated with bloodborne and airborne pathogens. For this reason, employees who retrieve soiled linen are required to use personal protective gear and standard safety precautions. This problem is especially prevalent in hospitals. Prior to sorting, the linen must be covered to prevent the spread of airborne germs.

Soil Sorting

At this stage, the retrieved linen is unloaded and sorted according to item type. Different items often require different washing formulas. Also, later stages in the process require the linen to be pre-sorted, since it is handled batch by batch. Heavy or biohazardous stains such as blood and feces may require longer wash times and stronger formulas. Thus it is inadvisable to mix different items of linen in the same wash batch. Large institutions often use a production-line method for soil sorting, with several full-time employees assigned to the task.

Figure: *Soil sorting*

Since soiled linen may be contaminated with biohazards or sharp objects, employees involved in the sorting process are required to use personal protective equipment and standard safety precautions.

Smaller items tend to "hide" among larger items. For this reason, some sorting goes on during the washing, processing and packaging stages.

Washing

This is the stage in which the laundry is actually washed. The sorted linen is weighed according to the washing machine's load limit. Large washing machines are used, usually operated by a certified washer operator. The washer operator loads and unloads the washer, decides what is to be washed according to the laundry's schedule, and monitors the chemical levels in the water. Since modern tunnel washers monitor their own chemical levels and unload linen directly into the laundry's "clean area", the operator is required only to load the linen.

Figure: *Tunnel washer*

Proper washing depends on five factors: Water quality, mechanical Agitation, Time, Chemical concentration and Heat. Washer operators use the acronym WATCH. These five factors work together. The purer the water and the fresher the chemicals, the cleaner the laundry will be. Mechanical action exposes the surface area of the linen to the water and chemicals, ensuring that the item is thoroughly soaked. Mechanical also tends to dislodge stains. Heat helps the chemicals to react with the stains. The longer the item is exposed to heat, chemicals and mechanical action, the cleaner it will be.

Over the past twenty years, many industrial laundries have switched from conventional washers to tunnel washers, also called continuous-batch washers. Since tunnel washers don't have to be stopped for loading and unloading of linen, they provide a more continuous flow of clean laundry. Higher-volume facilities, which may process over 15,000 pounds of linen per day, often rely heavily on tunnel washers.

Processing

In this stage, the clean linen is dried, ironed and folded. Some items, such as towels and blankets, are put through a dryer until they are no longer damp, then sent to mechanical folders. "Wetwork" items, such as sheets, are sent through steam-powered ironers which dry, press and fold them.

Dryers use hot air and mechanical action to evaporate the moisture and chemicals from the linen prior to folding. Heated air is forced through pores into a spinning central cylinder called the drum. As the cylinder constantly spins, the linen inside tumbles, exposing the surface area to heat which evaporates the moisture. The air temperature must be carefully controlled. If it isn't hot enough, the linen won't be thoroughly dried. If it is too hot, the linen may overdry, damaging the product and creating a fire hazard.

Ironers use heavy steam-heated rollers to dry the linen while pressing out wrinkles.

Folders use mechanical action to fold the linen into shapes that are easily stored and handled. Folders come in two varieties: large-piece for blankets and other large items, and small-piece for smaller items such as towels or pads. The more compact the shape into which the item is folded, the greater the amount of linen that can be packed into a limited storage space.

Some items, such as wash cloths, may be too small to be handled mechanically. These items must be packaged by hand.

Packaging

In this step, the processed linen is prepared for delivery. Individual orders are filled, based on the needs and requests of the laundry's customers, then sent to the laundry's main distribution points and storage areas. Linen not used for orders is placed in storage areas, giving the facility a reserve of clean laundry.

Distribution

In this step, trained delivery people transport the clean linen back to the customers. This is a skilled position, since the delivery person must have a thorough knowledge of both laundry operation and the principles of good customer service. In hospitals, delivery people must be familiar with patient relations, confidentiality policies and hospice. Large institutions will usually employ several full-time delivery people.

Occupational Hazards

The most common accidents in industrial laundries involve chemical exposure, sharp objects left in soiled linen, slips from wet floors, exposure to pathogens in contaminated linen, and body parts being stuck in machinery. While these problems can usually be avoided by standard precautions and a little common sense, they can and do happen. Production workers have a saying: "Common sense isn't that common."

Exposure to soil and pathogens can be limited by two things. One, of course, is the use of personal protective equipment: barrier gowns, gloves, eyewear, foot coverings and face masks. These items should be worn when handling soiled linen. Infections can also be eliminated by proper hand-washing with antibacterial soap. Employees should wash their hands after handling any linen, whether soiled or clean.

Since the noise levels in industrial laundries can be quite high, earmuffs and disposable earplugs are often issued. Hearing protection is essential.

Exposure to chemicals is also common. Since washers require a constant stream of detergent, bleach and other chemicals, the supply must be constantly replenished. Laundries are required to provide a material safety data sheet, or MSDS, for all chemicals used in the facility. Many laundries require their machine operators to be familiar with HAZMAT, if not fully certified.

With the constant workload and harsh working conditions, employees can easily become short-tempered. This occasionally leads to problems with violence and workplace bullying. For this reason, laundry managers must be competent disciplinarians, ready to deal with employees who have attitude problems.

Laundry machines use high-pressure steam and dangerous chemicals. Poor maintenance can cause injuries such as severe burns and chemical exposures. Hoses, steam lines and other machine parts must be checked and replaced regularly.

Production Problems

Communication: Like any good business, a laundry's operation depends on good communication. Customers must file their orders in a timely manner. Delivery people and order fillers must keep records of the types and quantities of linens used. Managers must be informed of production difficulties and attitude problems. Any breakdown in communication will hinder the laundry's productivity.

Cross-contamination

Clean linen and soiled linen should never be mixed. For this reason, most laundry facilities have two major work areas, the "soiled area" and the "clean area". These areas are usually separated by a wall. Separate carts are designated for clean and soiled linen. Linen usually passes from the soiled area to the clean area through the washers. Any clean linen that comes into contact with soiled linen or with carts used to transport soiled linen is considered soiled and must be re-washed. Laundry workers who handle soiled linen are required to wash their hands before working with clean linen.

Wet Linen Storage

Wet or soiled linen that is allowed to sit for an extended period of time may become permanently wrinkled. Worse, wet linen stored in a humid area may mildew, requiring replacement.

Dust

Dust can and does settle on clean linen. For this reason, clean linen left on shelves and in delivery carts should be covered. While many laundries use dust covers specifically made for this purpose, others will improvise, using sheets or blankets.

Cart Space

Every laundry, regardless of size, has a limited amount of cart space for storing linen. For this reason, the laundry's carts must be constantly recycled. The moment a cart is emptied, it is returned to the laundry to be filled with another order. If it is designated for soiled linen, it should be emptied at the laundry facility, then sent back to the collection point for another load.

Replacement Linens

Each trip through the wash cycle places wear and tear on the linen. Thus, a major laundry facility needs a constant stream of new linens coming in to replace worn-out items. Items that are not too badly damaged may be set aside for something other than their original purpose. (Permanently stained or torn blankets, for instance, may be used to line floor areas being waxed.) However, they will still need to be replaced in the linen stream.

Maintenance

From its major computerized machines down to the wheels on its carts, every laundry facility depends on mechanical and electric devices. These devices require a range of constant maintenance by skilled and certified technicians. Poorly maintained equipment can limit productivity and may even cause or contribute to injuries.

Rework

As in any business, any job that was not done properly the first time must be redone. Items that weren't thoroughly cleaned must be rewashed. Orders that were filled using the wrong supplies must be re-filled. These are two of the many examples of rework in a laundry.

Overstuffing

In recent years, it has become standard practice in prisons for prisoners to deposit personal laundry in mesh bags. The advantage of this system is that the mesh bags keep personal items separate in large loads during the wash cycle. The disadvantage is that prisoners tend to overstuff the bags. This inhibits mechanical agitation while preventing water and chemicals from reaching soiled linen. The result is poorer quality linen.

Tunnel Jams

If tunnel washers have one noteworthy defect, it is the tendency for the tunnel to become blocked when the washer is overloaded. When the tunnel is blocked, the washer must be stopped and allowed to drain, then the blockage must be removed manually. A tunnel jam may cost the laundry several hours of production time. Operators can prevent tunnel jams by paying strict attention to the washer's load limits.

Kitchen

A kitchen is a room or part of a room used for cooking and food preparation.

In the West, a modern residential kitchen is typically equipped with a stove, a sink with hot and cold running water, a refrigerator and kitchen cabinets arranged according to a modular design. Many households have a microwave oven, a dishwasher and other electric appliances. The main function of a kitchen is cooking or preparing food but it may also be used for dining and entertaining.

Cafeteria

A cafeteria is a type of food service location in which there is little or no waiting staff table service, whether a restaurant or within an institution such as a large office building or school; a school dining location is also referred to as a dining hall or canteen (in UK English). Cafeterias are different from coffeehouses, although that is the Spanish meaning of the English word.

Instead of table service, there are food-serving counters/stalls, either in a line or allowing arbitrary walking paths. Customers take the food they require as they walk along, placing it on a tray. In addition, there are often stations where customers order food and wait while it is prepared, particularly for items such as hamburgers or tacos which must be served hot and can be quickly prepared. Alternatively, the patron is given a number and the item is brought to their table. Sometimes, for some food items and drinks, customers collect an empty container, pay at the check-out, and fill the container after the check-out. Free second servings are often allowed under this system. For legal purposes (and the consumption patterns of customers), this system is rarely or never used for alcoholic beverages in the USA.

Customers are either charged a flat rate for admission (as in a buffet), or pay at the check-out for each item. Some self-service cafeterias charge by the weight of items on a patron's plate.

As cafeterias require few employees, they are often found within a larger institution, catering to the clientele of that institution. For example, schools, colleges and their residence halls, department stores, hospitals, museums, military bases, prisons, and office buildings often have cafeterias.

At one time, upscale cafeteria-style restaurants dominated the culture of the Southern United States, and to a lesser extent the

Midwest. There were several prominent chains of them: Bickford's, Morrison's Cafeteria, Piccadilly Cafeteria, S&W Cafeteria, Apple House, K&W, Britling, Wyatt's Cafeteria, and Blue Boar among them. Currently two midwest chains still exist, Sloppy Jo's Lunchroom and Manny's, both located in Illinois. There were also a number of smaller chains, usually in and around a single city. These institutions, with the exception of K&W, went into a decline in the 1960s with the rise of fast food and were largely finished off in the 1980s by the rise of "casual dining". A few chains — notably Luby's and Piccadilly Cafeterias (which took over the Morrison's chain), continue to fill some of the gap left by the decline of the older chains. Many of the smaller Midwestern chains, such as MCL Cafeterias centered around Indianapolis, are still very much in business.

The world's largest non-military cafeteria is in the Brody Complex at Michigan State University.

History

Perhaps the first self-service restaurant (not necessarily cafeteria) in the United States was the Exchange Buffet in New York City, opened September 4, 1885, which catered to an exclusively male clientele. Food was purchased at a counter, and patrons ate standing up. This represents the predecessor of two formats: the cafeteria, described below, and the automat.

During the 1893 World's Columbian Exposition in Chicago, an entrepreneur named John Kruger built an American version of the smörgåsbords he had seen while travelling in Sweden. Emphasizing the simplicity and light fare, he called it the "Cafeteria"-Spanish for "coffee shop". The exposition attracted over 27 million visitors (half the US population at the time) in six months, and it was initially through Kruger's operation that America first heard the term and experienced the self-service dining format.

Meanwhile, in everyday, hometown America, the chain of Childs Restaurants was quickly growing from about 10 locations in New York City (in 1890), to hundreds across the United States and Canada (by 1920). Childs is credited with the critical innovation of adding trays and a "tray line" to the self-service format, which they introduced in 1898 at their 130 Broadway location. Childs did not change its format of sit-down dining, however. This was soon the standard design for most Childs Restaurants-and many imitators-from coast-to-coast, and ultimately the dominant design for cafeterias.

It has also been said that the "cafeteria craze started in May 1905, when a woman named Helen Mosher opened a humble downtown L.A. restaurant where people chose their food at a long counter and carried their own trays to their tables." California does have a long and rich history in the cafeteria format-most notably the many Boos Brothers Cafeterias, and also Clifton's and Schaber's. However, the facts do not warrant the "wellspring" characterization that some have ascribed to the region. The earliest cafeterias in California were opened at least 12 years after Kruger's Cafeteria, and Childs already had several dozen locations scattered around the country. Finally, Horn & Hardart, an automat format chain (only slightly different from the cafeteria), was also well established in the mid-Atlantic region before 1900.

Between 1960 and 1980, the popularity of cafeteria format restaurants was gradually overcome by the emergence of the fast food restaurant and fast casual restaurant formats.

Other Names

A cafeteria in a U.S. military installation is known as a chow hall, a mess hall, a galley, mess decks or, more formally, a dining facility, whereas in common British Armed Forces parlance, it is known as a cookhouse or mess. Students in the USA often refer to cafeterias as lunchrooms, though breakfast as well as lunch is often eaten there. Cafeterias serving university dormitories are sometimes called dining halls or dining commons. A food court is a type of cafeteria found in many shopping malls and airports featuring multiple food vendors or concessions, although a food court could equally be styled as a type of restaurant as well, being more aligned with public, rather than institutionalised, dining.

Some monasteries, boarding schools and older universities refer to their cafeteria as a refectory. Modern-day British cathedrals and abbeys, notably in the Church of England, often use the phrase refectory to describe a cafeteria open to the public. Historically, the refectory was generally only used by monks and priests. For example, although the original 800-year-old refectory at Gloucester Cathedral (the stage setting for dining scenes in the Harry Potter movies) is now mostly used as a choir practice area, the relatively modern 300-year-old extension, now used as a cafeteria by staff and public alike, is today referred to as the refectory.

A cafeteria located in a television studio is often called a commissary. NBC's commissary, The Hungry Peacock, was often joked about by Johnny Carson on The Tonight Show.

College Cafeteria

A college cafeteria is a term in the United States that denotes a cafeteria that is designed to serve college students at the university. In the UK the word *refectory* is often used. Also see the different meanings of the word college around the Anglosphere. These cafeterias can be a part of a residence hall or in a separate building. Many of these colleges employ their own students to work in the cafeteria. The amount of meals served to students varies from school to school, but is normally around 20 meals per week. Like normal cafeterias, a person will have a tray to select the food that they want, but instead of paying money, they pay beforehand by purchasing a meal plan.

The method of payment for college cafeterias is commonly in the form of a meal plan, whereby the patron pays a certain amount at the start of the semester and the details of the plan are stored on a computer system. Student ID cards are then used to access the meal plan. A meal plan is not necessary to eat at a college cafeteria however. Meal plans can vary widely in their details to best fit the needs of the students. Typically, the college tracks the student's usage of their plan by counting either the number of pre-defined meal servings, points, dollars, or number of buffet dinners. The plan may give the student a certain number of any of the above per week or semester and they may or may not roll over to the next week or semester.

Many schools offer several different options for using their meal plans. The main cafeteria is usually where most of the meal plan is used but smaller cafeterias, cafés, restaurants, bars, or even fast food chains located on campus may accept meal plans. A college cafeteria system often has a virtual monopoly on the students due to an isolated location or a requirement that residence contracts include a full meal plan. It is not uncommon for the entire food service operation to be outsourced to a managed services company such as Aramark, Sodexo and Compass Group (under the Scolarest name in the United Kingdom).

Restaurant

A restaurant prepares and serves food and drink to customers in return for money. Meals are generally served and eaten on premises, but many restaurants also offer take-out and food delivery services. Restaurants vary greatly in appearance and offerings, including a wide variety of the main chef's cuisines and service models.

While inns and taverns were known from antiquity, these were establishments aimed at travelers, and in general locals would rarely eat there. Modern restaurants are dedicated to the serving of food, where specific dishes are ordered by guests and are prepared to their request. The modern restaurant originated in 18th century France, although precursors can be traced back to Roman times.

A restaurant owner is called a *restaurateur*; both words derive from the French verb *restaurer*, meaning "to restore". Professional artisans of cooking are called chefs, while preparation staff and line cooks prepare food items in a more systematic and less artistic fashion.

History

In Ancient Rome, thermopolia (singular thermopolium) were small restaurant-bars which offered food and drinks to the customer. A typical thermopolium had L-shaped counters into which large storage vessels were sunk, which would contain either hot or cold food. They are linked to the absence of kitchens in many dwellings and the ease with which people could purchase prepared foods. Besides, eating out was also considered an important aspect of socialising.

In Pompeii, 158 thermopolia with a service counter have been identified across the whole town area. They were concentrated along the main axes of the town and the public spaces where they were frequented by the locals.

Food catering establishments which may be described as restaurants were known since the 11th century in Kaifeng, China's northern capital during the first half of the Song Dynasty (960–1279). With a population of over 1,000,000 people, a culture of hospitality and a paper currency, Kaifeng was ripe for the development of restaurants. Probably growing out of the tea houses and taverns that catered to travellers, Kaifeng's restaurants blossomed into an industry catering to locals as well as people from other regions of China. Stephen H. West argues that there is a direct correlation between the growth of the restaurant businesses and institutions of theatrical stage drama, gambling and prostitution which served the burgeoning merchant middle class during the Song Dynasty.

Restaurants catered to different styles of cuisine, price brackets, and religious requirements. Even within a single restaurant much choice was available, and people ordered the entree they wanted from written menus. An account from 1275 writes of Hangzhou, the capital city for the last half of the dynasty:

> *"The people of Hangzhou are very difficult to please. Hundreds of orders are given on all sides: this person*

wants something hot, another something cold, a third something tepid, a fourth something chilled; one wants cooked food, another raw, another chooses roast, another grill".

The restaurants in Hangzhou also catered to many northern Chinese who had fled south from Kaifeng during the Jurchen invasion of the 1120s, while it is also known that many restaurants were run by families formerly from Kaifeng.

Types of Restaurants

Restaurants range from unpretentious lunching or dining places catering to people working nearby, with simple food served in simple settings at low prices, to expensive establishments serving refined food and wines in a formal setting. In the former case, customers usually wear casual clothing. In the latter case, depending on culture and local traditions, customers might wear semi-casual, semi-formal, or even in rare cases formal wear.

Typically, customers sit at tables, their orders are taken by a waiter, who brings the food when it is ready, and the customers pay the bill before leaving. In finer restaurants there will be a host or hostess or even a maître d'hôtel to welcome customers and to seat them. Other staff waiting on customers include busboys and sommeliers.

Restaurants often specialize in certain types of food or present a certain unifying, and often entertaining, theme. For example, there are seafood restaurants, vegetarian restaurants or ethnic restaurants. Generally speaking, restaurants selling food characteristic of the local culture are simply called restaurants, while restaurants selling food of foreign cultural origin are called accordingly,

Restaurant Regulations

Depending on local customs and the establishment, restaurants may or may not serve alcohol. Restaurants are often prohibited from selling alcohol without a meal by alcohol sale laws; such sale is considered to be activity for bars, which are meant to have more severe restrictions. Some restaurants are licensed to serve alcohol ("fully licensed"), and/or permit customers to "bring your own" alcohol (BYO/BYOB). In some places restaurant licenses may restrict service to beer, or wine and beer.

Restaurant Guides

Restaurant guides review restaurants, often ranking them or providing information for consumer decisions (type of food, handicap accessibility, facilities, etc.). In 12th century Hangzhou (mentioned above as the location of the first restaurant), signs could often be found posted in the city square listing the restaurants in the area and local customer's opinions of the quality of their food. This was an occasion for bribery and even violence. One of the most famous contemporary guides, in Western Europe, is the Michelin series of guides which accord from 1 to 3 stars to restaurants they perceive to be of high culinary merit. Restaurants with stars in the Michelin guide are formal, expensive establishments; in general the more stars awarded, the higher the prices. The main competitor to the Michelin guide in Europe is the guidebook series published by Gault Millau. Unlike the Michelin guide which takes the restaurant décor and service into consideration with its rating, Gault Millau only judges the quality of the food. Its ratings are on a scale of 1 to 20, with 20 being the highest.

In the United States, the Forbes Travel Guide (previously the Mobil travel guides) and the AAA rate restaurants on a similar 1 to 5 star (Forbes) or diamond (AAA) scale. Three, four, and five star/diamond ratings are roughly equivalent to the Michelin one, two, and three star ratings while one and two star ratings typically indicate more casual places to eat. In 2005, Michelin released a New York City guide, its first for the United States. The popular Zagat Survey compiles individuals' comments about restaurants but does not pass an "official" critical assessment. In the United States Gault Millau is published as the *Gayot* guide, after founder Andre Gayot. Its restaurant ratings use the same 20 point system, and are all published online.

The Good Food Guide, published by the Fairfax Newspaper Group in Australia, is the Australian guide listing the best places to eat. Chefs Hats are awarded for outstanding restaurants and range from one hat through three hats. The Good Food Guide also incorporates guides to bars, cafes and providers. *The Good Restaurant Guide* is another Australian restaurant guide that has reviews on the restaurants as experienced by the public and provides information on locations and contact details. Any member of the public can submit a review.

Nearly all major American newspapers employ food critics and publish online dining guides for the cities they serve. A few papers maintain a reputation for thorough and thoughtful review of restaurants to the standard of the good published guides, but others provide more of a listings service.

More recently Internet sites have started up that publish both food critic reviews and popular reviews by the general public. Their major competition comes from bloggers, particularly publishers of food blogs, also called foodies. These writers and publishers represent the common dining aficionado rather than the gourmet, and thus do not provide "official" reviews, but nonetheless are capable of garnering large, loyal followings.

Economics

United States: As of 2006, there are approximately 215,000 full-service restaurants in the United States, accounting for $298 billion, and approximately 250,000 limited-service (fast food) restaurants, accounting for $260 billion.

One study of new restaurants in Cleveland, Ohio found that 1 in 4 changed ownership or went out of business after one year, and 6 out of 10 did so after three years. (Not all changes in ownership are indicative of financial failure.) The three-year failure rate for franchises was nearly the same.

Canada: There are 86,915 commercial foodservice units in Canada, or 26.4 units per 10,000 Canadians. By segment, there are:

- 38,797 full-service restaurants
- 34,629 limited-service restaurants
- 741 contract and social caterers
- 6,749 drinking places.

Fully 63% of restaurants in Canada are independent brands. Chain restaurants account for the remaining 37%, and many of these are locally owned and operated franchises.

Chapter 6

Property Manager Overview

A property manager is a person or firm charged with operating a real estate property for a fee, when the owner is unable to personally attend to such details, or is not interested in doing so. The property may be individual title owned or it may be owned under sectional title, share block company owned and may be registered for residential, commercial office and retail or industrial use.

Overview of Responsibilities

Letting & leasing on behalf of a landlord Typical duties expected of a property manager include finding/evicting and generally dealing with tenants, home repair, home improvement, cleaning, garden maintenance, landscaping and snow removal, to be coordinated with the owner's wishes. Such arrangements may require the property manager to collect rents, and pay necessary expenses and taxes, making periodic reports to the owner, or the owner may simply delegate specific tasks and deal with others directly.

A property manager may arrange for a wide variety of services, as may be requested by the owner of the property, for a fee. Where a dwelling (vacation home, second home) is only periodically occupied, the property manager might arrange for heightened security monitoring, house-sitting, storage and shipping of goods, and other local sub-contracting necessary to make the property comfortable when the owner is in residence (utilities, systems operating, supplies and staff on hand, etc). Property management can also include commercial properties where the property manager may operate the business, as well as managing the property. Some jurisdictions may require a property manager to be licensed for the profession.

The property manager has a primary responsibility to the landlord and a secondary responsibility to the tenant. The relationship the property manager has with the landlord and with the tenant are crucial in forming the expectations of both parties to the lease since both parties will seek and expect certain rights and benefits out of it.

Owner Expectations

The owner of a property expects the property manager to:

- carry out the owner's instructions, control costs and maximize revenue to maintain a stabilized cash flow as a return on capital invested (commonly referred to as the capitalization rate or the cap. rate)
- exercise control over the building to safeguard the capital invested, provide a duty of care through proper maintenance of the building
- be professional and well informed on Fair Housing laws and property management practices and procedures
- enhance the value of the property by making improvements that will increase its market value, retain and enhance pride of ownership.

Tenant Expectations

The tenant of a property expects the property manager to:

- ensure the "quiet enjoyment" of the premises—an assurance that the premises will be able to be used and enjoyed for the intended purposes without interference from the landlord and/ or other tenants (save for emergencies)
- provide comfort—-a living environment that is properly heated, cooled and ventilated with as many amenities as possible compatible with the rental level
- provide security and safety—the ability to live and/or work in a building in which there are no inherent defects or conditions that might be hazardous to health or to property
- provide status—-accommodation and facilities that meet socio-economic and cultural standards for the tenants and their guests.

Professional Designations

Building Owners and Managers Association (BOMA International) offers industry-standard designations that certify the training to Property Managers:

- Real Property Administrator (RPA)
- Facilities Management Administrator (FMA)
- Systems Maintenance Administrator (SMA)
- Systems Maintenance Technician (SMT).

Institute of Real Estate Management (IREM);

- Certified Property Manager (CPM)
- Accredited Residential Manager (ARM)
- Accredited Commercial Manager (ACM)
- Accredited Management Organization (AMO).

Manufactured Housing Institute (MHI);

- Accredited Community Manager (ACM)
- Professional Housing Consultant (PHC).

National Apartment Association (NAA) has the following designations:

- Certified Apartment Manager (CAM)
- Certified Apartment Property Supervisor (CAPS).

National Association of Residential Property Managers (NARPM) offers designations to certify ethical and professional standards of conduct for property managers:

- Residential Management Professional (RMP)
- Master Property Manager (MPM)
- Certified Support Specialist (CSS)
- Certified Residential Management Company (CRMC).

State-specific designations:

- California-Certified Community Association Manager (CCAM)
- Florida-Community Association Manager (CAM)
- Minnesota-Certified Community Association Manager (CCAM)
- Minnesota-Certified Residential Manager (CRM).

Commercial Property

The term commercial property (also called investment or income property) refers to buildings or land intended to generate a profit, either from capital gain or rental income.

Definition

Commercial property includes office buildings, industrial property, medical centers, hotels, malls, retail stores, shopping centers, farm land, multifamily housing buildings, warehouses, and garages. In many states, residential property containing more than a certain number of units qualifies as commercial property for borrowing and tax purposes.

Commercial real estate is commonly divided into four categories:

Categories of Commercial Real Estate

Category	Examples
Retail	medical centers, hotels, malls, retail stores, shopping centers, public housesOffice office buildings
Industrial	industrial property, office/warehouses, garages, distribution centers
Multifamily (apartments)	multifamily housing buildings

Of these, only the first three are classified as being commercial buildings. Residential Income Property may also be used to mean Multifamily Apartments.

Top Tips for Investing in an Emerging Commercial Market

1. Know your goals
2. Restrategise and regroup
3. Reduce your personal debt
4. Pay down your owner-occupied residence
5. Research & know the market
6. Understand the cycle
7. Look for opportunities.

According to Real Capital Analytics, a New York real estate research firm, more than $160 billion of commercial properties in the U.S. are now in default, foreclosure or bankruptcy. No significant change is expected in the market. In Europe, approximately half of the €960 billion of debt backed by European commercial real estate is expected to require refinancing in the next three years, according to PropertyMall, a UK based commercial property news provider.

Preparing to Buy a Commercial Property

Purchasing a business or commercial property can be complex and daunting, especially if it is your first business venture. Below are some key questions to ask when buying a business or property.

1. What am I looking for?
2. How much is it worth?
3. How does the process work?

4. How do leasehold, freehold going concern and freehold investment yields or multipliers work or differ – the calculation to value or capitalise the net income or net surplus before owner/managers salaries to arrive at the value of the business or property?
5. Has the "Add Back" calculation been applied to the financial accounts to achieve the notional bottom line prior to applying the correct current market multiplier for the business or property – this changes depending on location, length of lease, condition of property, timing of next rent review etc?
6. How long has the lease term got to go, how long before the next rent review, is there rights of renewal on the lease, is there variations to the original lease?

Maintenance, Repair, and Operations

Maintenance, repair, and operations (MRO) or Maintenance, Repair and Overhaul involves fixing any sort of mechanical or electrical device should it become out of order or broken (known as repair, unscheduled or casualty maintenance). It also includes performing routine actions which keep the device in working order (known as scheduled maintenance) or prevent trouble from arising (preventive maintenance). MRO may be defined as, "All actions which have the objective of retaining or restoring an item in or to a state in which it can perform its required function. The actions include the combination of all technical and corresponding administrative, managerial, and supervision actions."

MRO operations can be categorised by whether the product remains the property of the customer, i.e. a service is being offered, or whether the product is bought by the reprocessing organisation and sold to any customer wishing to make the purchase. (Guadette, 2002)

The former of these represents a closed loop supply chain and usually has the scope of maintenance, repair or overhaul of the product. The latter of the categorisations is an open loop supply chain and is typified by refurbishment and remanufacture. The main characteristic of the closed loop system is that the demand for a product is matched with the supply of a used product. Neglecting asset write-offs and exceptional activities the total population of the product between the customer and the service provider remains constant

Engineering

In telecommunication, and engineering in general, the term maintenance has the following meanings:

Any activity – such as tests, measurements, replacements, adjustments and repairs — intended to retain or restore a functional unit in or to a specified state in which the unit can perform its required functions.

For material — all action taken to retain material in a serviceable condition or to restore it to serviceability. It includes inspection, testing, servicing, classification as to serviceability, repair, rebuilding, and reclamation.

For material — all supply and repair action taken to keep a force in condition to carry out its mission.

For material — the routine recurring work required to keep a facility (plant, building, structure, ground facility, utility system, or other real property) in such condition that it may be continuously used, at its original or designed capacity and efficiency for its intended purpose.

Manufacturers and Industrial Supply Companies often refer to MRO as opposed to Original Equipment Manufacture (OEM). OEM includes any activity related to the direct manufacture of goods, where MRO refers to any maintenance and repair activity to keep a manufacturing plant running.

Industrial supply companies can generally be sorted into two types:

- the ones who cater to the MRO market generally carry a broad range of items such as fasteners, conveyors, cleaning goods, plumbing, and tools to keep a plant running.
- OEM supply companies generally provide a smaller range of goods in much larger quantities with much lower prices, selling materials that will be regularly consumed in the manufacturing process to create the finished item.

Maintenance Types

Generally speaking, there are two types of maintenance in use:

- Preventive maintenance, where equipment is maintained before break down occurs. This type of maintenance has many different variations and is subject of various researches to determine best and most efficient way to maintain equipment. Recent studies have shown that Preventive maintenance is effective in preventing age related failures of the equipment. For random failure patterns which amount to 80% of the failure patterns, condition monitoring proves to be effective.

- Corrective maintenance, where equipment is maintained after break down. This maintenance is often most expensive because worn equipment can damage other parts and cause multiple damage.

Preventive Maintenance

Preventive maintenance is maintenance performed in an attempt to avoid failures, unnecessary production loss and safety violations. As equipment cannot be maintained at all times, some way is needed to decide when it is proper to perform maintenance. Normally, this is done by deciding some inspection/maintenance intervals, and sticking to this interval more or less affected by what you find during these activities. The result of this is that most of the maintenance performed is unnecessary; it even adds substantial wear to the equipment. Also, you have no guarantee that the equipment will continue to work even if you are maintaining it according to the maintenance plan.

The effectiveness of a preventive maintenance schedule depends on the RCM analysis which it was based on, and the ground rules used for cost-effectivity.

Planned Maintenance

Planned Preventative Maintenance ('PPM') or more usual just simple Planned Maintenance (PM) or Scheduled Maintenance is any variety of scheduled maintenance to an object or item of equipment. Specifically, Planned Maintenance is a scheduled service visit carried out by a competent and suitable agent, to ensure that an item of equipment is operating correctly and to therefore avoid any unscheduled breakdown and downtime.

Together with Condition Based Maintenance, Planned maintenance comprises preventive maintenance, in which the maintenance event is preplanned, and all future maintenance is preprogrammed. Planned maintenance is created for every item separately according to manufacturers recommendation or legislation. Plan can be based on equipment running hours, date based, or for vehicles distance travelled. Good example of PM program is car maintenance. After so many kilometers or miles oil should be changed, parts renewed,...

Planned maintenance has some advantages over Condition Based Maintenance such as:

- easier planning of maintenance and ordering spares,
- costs are distributed more evenly,
- no initial costs for instruments for supervision of equipment.

Disadvantages are:

- less reliable than equipment with CBM
- more expensive due to more frequent parts change.

Parts that have scheduled maintenance at fixed intervals, usually due to wearout or a fixed shelf life, are sometimes known as time-change interval, or TCI items.

Corrective Maintenance

Corrective maintenance is probably the most commonly used approach, but it is easy to see its limitations. When equipment fails, it often leads to downtime in production. In most cases this is costly business. Also, if the equipment needs to be replaced, the cost of replacing it alone can be substantial. It is also important to consider health, safety and environment (HSE) issues related to malfunctioning equipment.

Corrective maintenance can be defined as the maintenance which is required when an item has failed or worn out, to bring it back to working order. Corrective maintenance is carried out on all items where the consequences of failure or wearing out are not significant and the cost of this maintenance is not greater than preventive maintenance.

MRO Software

In many organizations because of the number of devices or products that need to be maintained or the complexity of systems, there is a need to manage the information with software packages. This is particularly the case in aerospace (e.g. airline fleets), military installations, large plants (e.g. manufacturing, power generation, petrochemical) and ships.

These software tools help engineers and technicians in increasing the system availability and reducing costs and repair times as well as reducing material supply time and increasing material availability by improving supply chain communication.

As MRO involves working with an organization's products, resources, suppliers and customers, MRO packages have to interface with many enterprise business software systems (PLM, EAM, ERP, SCM, CRM).

One of the functions of such software is the configuration of bills of materials or BOMs, taking the component parts list from engineering (eBOM) and manufacturing (mBOM) and updating it from "as delivered" through "as maintained" to "as used".

Another function is project planning logistics, for example identifying the critical path on the list of tasks to be carried out (inspection, diagnosis, locate/order parts and service) to calculate turnaround times (TAT).

Other tasks that software can perform:

- Planning operations,
- Managing execution of events,
- Management of assets (parts, tools and equipment inventories),
- Knowledge-base data on:
    - o Maintenance service history,
    - o Serial numbered parts,
    - o Reliability data: MTBF, MTTB (mean time to breakdown), MTBR (mean time between removals),
    - o Maintenance and repair documentation and best practices,
    - o Warranty/guarantee documents.

Many of these tasks are addressed in Computerized Maintenance Management Systems (CMMS). Data standards have been developed around these activities, most notably EAMXML and MIMOSA.

MRO Goods

MRO goods are typically defined as any goods used in the creation of a product but not in the final product itself. Examples include:

- the machinery used to make a product
- spare parts for the machinery that creates the product, and
- items used to maintain the facility in which the product is made.

Chapter 7

Lease Systems

A lease is a contract calling for the lessee (user) to pay the lessor (owner) for use of an asset. A rental agreement is a lease in which the asset is tangible property. Leases for intangible property could include use of a computer program (similar to a license, but with different provisions), or use of a radio frequency (such as a contract with a cell-phone provider). A gross lease is when the tenant pays a flat rental amount and the landlord pays for all property charges regularly incurred by the ownership from lawnmowers and washing machines to handbags and jewelry.

A cancelable lease is a lease that may be terminated solely by the lessee or solely by the lessor. A non-cancelable lease is a lease that cannot be so terminated. In common parlance, "lease" may connote a non-cancelable lease, whereas "rental agreement" may connote a concealable lease.

The lease will either provide specific provisions regarding the responsibilities and rights of the lessee and lessor, or there will be automatic provisions as a result of local law. In general, by paying the negotiated fee to the lessor, the lessee (also called a tenant) has possession and use (the rental) of the leased property to the exclusion of the lessor and all others except with the invitation of the tenant. The most common form of real property lease is a residential rental agreement between landlord and tenant. The relationship between the tenant and the landlord is called a tenancy, and the right to possession by the tenant is sometimes called a leasehold interest. A lease can be for a fixed period of time (called the term of the lease) but (depending on the terms of the lease) may be terminated sooner.

A lease should be contrasted to a license, which may entitle a person (called a licensee) to use property, but which is subject to termination at the will of the owner of the property (called the licensor). An example of a licensor/licensee relationship is a parking lot owner and a person who parks a vehicle in the parking lot. A license may be seen in the form of a ticket to a baseball game. The difference would be that if possession is subject to ongoing, recurrent payments and is generally not subject to termination except for misconduct or nonpayment, it is a lease; if it's a one-time entrance onto someone else's property, it's probably a license. The seminal difference between a lease and a license is that a lease generally provides for regular periodic payments during its term and a specific ending date. If a contract has no ending date then it may be in the form of a *perpetual license* and still not be a lease.

Under normal circumstances, owners of property are at liberty to do what they want with their property (for a lawful purpose), including dealing with it or handing over possession of the property to a tenant for a limited period of time. If an owner has surrendered possession to another (i.e., the tenant) then any interference with the quiet enjoyment of the property by the tenant in lawful possession is itself unlawful.

Similar principles apply to real property as well as to personal property, though the terminology would be different. Similar principles apply to sub-leasing, that is the leasing by a tenant in possession to a sub-tenant. The right to sub-lease can be expressly prohibited by the main lease, sometimes referred to as a "master lease".

History

Over the centuries, leases have served many purposes and the nature of legal regulation has varied according to those purposes and the social and economic conditions of the times. Leases, for example, were mainly used for agricultural purposes until the late 18th century and early 19th century when the growth of cities in industrialised countries had made leases an important form of landholding in urban areas.

The modern law of landlord and tenant in common law jurisdictions retains the influence of the common law and, particularly, the *laissez-faire* philosophy that dominated the law of contract and property law in the 19th century. With the growth of consumerism, consumer protection legislation recognised that common law principles, which assume equal bargaining power between the contracting parties, create hardships when that assumption is inaccurate. Consequently reformers have emphasised the need to assess residential tenancy laws in terms of protection they provide to tenants. Legislation to protect tenants is now common.

General Terms

A Lease is a legal contract, and thus enforceable by all parties under the Contract Laws of the applicable jurisdiction. But, since it also represents a conveyance of possessory rights to real estate, it is a hybrid sort of contract that involves qualities of a deed. Some specific kinds of leases may have specific clauses required by statute depending upon the property being lease, and/or the jurisdiction in which the agreement was signed or the residence of the parties.

Common elements of a lease include:

- Names of the parties of the agreement.
- The starting date and duration of the agreement.
- Identifies the specific object (by street address, VIN, or make/ model,serial number) being leased.
- Provides conditions for renewal or non-renewal.
- Has a specific consideration (a lump sum, or periodic payments) for granting the use of this object.
- Has provisions for a security deposit and terms for its return.
- May have a specific list of conditions which are therein described as Default Conditions and specific Remedies.
- May have other specific conditions placed upon the parties such as
    - o need to provide insurance for loss
    - o restrictive use
    - o which party is responsible for maintenance.

All kinds of personal property (e.g.: cars, furniture,...) or real property (raw land, apartments, single family homes, and business property (including wholesale and retail)) may be leased. As a result of the lease, the owner (lessor) grants the use of the stated property to the lessee.

Types of Tenancies

Fixed-term Tenancy or Tenancy for Years

A fixed-term tenancy or tenancy for years lasts for some fixed period of time. It has a definite beginning date and a definite ending date. Despite the name "tenancy for years", such a tenancy can last for any period of time—even a tenancy for one week may be called a tenancy for years. At Common law the duration did not need to be certain, but could be conditioned upon the happening of some event, (e.g., "until the crops are ready for harvest" or "until the war is over"). In many jurisdictions that possibility has been partially or totally abolished.

A fixed term tenancy comes to an end automatically when the fixed term runs out or, in the case of a tenancy that ends on the happening of an event, when the event occurs. If a holdover tenant remains on the property after the termination of the lease, s/he may become a tenant at sufferance because the lessor/landlord has suffered (or allowed) the tenant to remain as a tenant instead of evicting him or her. Such a tenancy is generally "at will," meaning the tenant or the landlord may terminate it at any time, upon the providing of proper statutory notice.

Periodic Tenancy

A periodic tenancy also known as a tenancy from year to year, month to month, or week to week, is an estate that exists for some period of time determined by the term of the payment of rent. An oral lease for a tenancy of years that violates the Statute of Frauds (by committing to a lease of more than — depending on the jurisdiction — one year without being in writing) may actually create a periodic tenancy, depending on the laws of the jurisdiction where the leased premises are located. In many jurisdictions the "default" tenancy, where the parties have not explicitly specified a different arrangement, and where none is presumed under local or business custom, is a month-to-month tenancy.

Either the landlord or the tenant may terminate a periodic tenancy when the period or term is nearing completion, by giving notice to the other party as required by statute or case law in the jurisdiction. Neither landlord nor tenant may terminate a periodic tenancy before the period has ended, without incurring an obligation to pay for the months remaining on the lease. Either party must give notice if it intends to terminate a tenancy from year to year, and the amount of notice is either specified by the lease or by state statute. Notice is usually, but not alway, at least one month, especially for the year to year periodic tenancy. Durations of less than a year must typically receive notice equal to the period of the tenancy-for example, the landlord must give a month's notice to terminate a tenancy from month to month. However, many jurisdictions have increased these required notice periods, and some have reduced the capacity of a landlord to use them drastically.

For jurisdictions that have local rent control laws, a landlord's ability to terminate a residential tenancy is substantially reduced. For example, in California, the cities of Los Angeles, Santa Monica, West Hollywood, San Francisco, and Oakland have "rent stabilization ordinances" that limit a landlord's ability to terminate a periodic tenancy, among other restrictions.

The notice must also state the effective date of termination, which, in some jurisdictions, *must* be on the *last day* of the payment period. In other words, if a month-to-month tenancy began on the 15th of the month, in a jurisdiction with a *last day* requirement the termination could not be effective on the 20th of the following month, even though this would give the tenant more than the required one month's notice.

Tenancy at Will

A *tenancy at will* is a tenancy which either the landlord or the tenant may terminate at any time by giving reasonable notice. Unlike a periodic tenancy, it isn't associated with a time period. It may last for many years, but it could be ended at any time by either the lessor or the lessee for any reason, or for no reason at all. Proper notice, as always with landlord/tenant law, must be given, as set forth in the state's statutes. If there is no formal lease, the tenancy at will is the one that usually exists. In rare cases it may occur where the tenancy is not for consideration. Under the modern common law, a tenancy at will without compensation is very rare, partly because it comes about only if the parties expressly agree that the tenancy is for no rent, commonly where a family member is allowed to live in a home (a nominal consideration may be required) without any formal arrangements. In most residential tenancies for a fixed term, for consideration, the tenant may not be removed except for cause, even if there is no written lease. (However, an oral lease for more than 12 months is not enforceable if the statute of frauds in the jurisdiction includes leases of more than 12 months.) Many residential leases convert to "at will" tenancy subject to 30-days notice. Alternatively, a tenancy at will (without a specific time limit) may exist for a temporary period where a tenant wishes to take possession of a property and the landlord agrees, but there is insufficient time in which to negotiate and complete a new lease. In this case, the tenancy at will is terminated as soon as a new lease is negotiated and signed. The parties may also agree on the basis that if the parties fail to enter into a new lease within a reasonable time period, then the tenant must vacate the premises.

If a lease exists at the sole discretion of the landlord, the law of the jurisdiction may imply that the tenant is granted, by operation of law, a reciprocal right to terminate the lease at will. However, a lease that explicitly exists at the will of the tenant (e.g. "for as long as the tenant desires to live on this land") generally does not imply that the landlord may terminate the lease; rather, such language may be interpreted as granting the tenant a life estate or even a fee simple.

A tenancy at will is broken, again by operation of law, if the:

- Tenant commits waste against the property;
- Tenant attempts to assign the tenancy;
- Tenant uses the property to operate a criminal enterprise;
- Landlord transfers his/her interest in the property;
- Landlord leases the property to another person;
- Tenant or landlord dies.

The specifics of these rules differ from jurisdiction to jurisdiction.

Subject to any notice required by law, a tenancy at will also comes to an end when either the landlord or the tenant acts inconsistently with a tenancy. For example, the changing of locks by the landlord is an indication of the end of the tenancy, as is the vacation of the premises by the tenant. However, in some jurisdictions, such as California, a landlord is prohibited from using a "self help" remedy, such as changing the locks, to terminate a tenancy, particularly a residential tenancy. Doing so may constitute a "constructive eviction" and expose the landlord to civil and criminal liability.

Tenancy at Sufferance

A *tenancy at sufferance* (sometimes called a *holdover tenancy*) exists when a tenant remains in possession of a property after the expiration of a lease, and until the landlord acts to eject the tenant from the property. Although the tenant is technically a trespasser at this point, and possession of this type is not a true estate in land, authorities recognize the condition in order to hold the tenant liable for rent. The landlord may evict such a tenant at any time, and without notice.

The landlord may also impose a new lease on the holdover tenant. For a residential tenancy, this new tenancy is month to month. For a commercial tenancy of more than a year, the new tenancy is year to year; otherwise it is the same period as the period before the original lease expired. In either case, the landlord can raise the rent, so long as the landlord has told the tenant of the higher rent before the expiration of the original lease.

Formalities

Formal requirements for a lease are determined by the law and custom of the jurisdiction in which real property is located. In the case of personal property, it is determined by the law and custom of the jurisdiction in which the rental agreement is made.

A tenancy for a duration greater than one year must be in writing in order to satisfy the Statute of Frauds.

Term

The term of the lease may be fixed, periodic or of indefinite duration. If it is for a specified period of time, the term ends automatically when the period expires, and no notice needs to be given, in the absence of legal requirements. The term's duration may be conditional, in which case it lasts until a specified event occurs, such as the death of a specified individual. A periodic tenancy is one which is renewed automatically, usually on a monthly or weekly basis. A tenancy at will lasts only as long as the parties wish it to, and may be terminated by either party without penalty.

It is common for a lease to be extended on a "holding over" basis, which normally converts the tenancy to a periodic tenancy on a month by month basis. It is also possible for a tenant, either expressly or impliedly, to give up the tenancy to the landlord. This process is known as a "surrender" of the lease.

Rent

Rent is a requirement of leases in some common law jurisdiction, but not in civil law jurisdiction. In England it was held in the case of *Ashburn Anstalt v Arnold* that rent was not a requirement for there to be a lease, however the court will more often construe a licence where no rent is paid as it is seen as evidence for no intention to create legal relationship. There is no requirement for the rent to be a commercial amount. "Pepper corn" rent or rent of some nominal amount is adequate for this requirement.

Car Rental

In addition to the above, a car rental agreement may include various restrictions on the way a renter can use a car, and the condition in which it must be returned. For example, some rentals cannot be driven off-road, or out of the country, or towing a trailer, without specific permission. In New Zealand you may have to specifically endorse a promise that the car will not be driven onto Ninety-Mile Beach (because of the hazardous tides).

There will certainly be a requirement to show a driver's license, and only those drivers appearing on the contract may be authorized to drive. It may include an option to purchase auto insurance (motor insurance, UK), if the renter does not already have a policy to cover rentals—another important consideration for multiple drivers. Some agencies may even require a bond payable if the car is not returned in order, often held in the form of a credit-card authorization—voided if the car is returned per agreement. A renter should be advised that he or she will be responsible for any parking or traffic violations incurred upon the vehicle during the rental period. There should also be advice on handling thefts, accidents, break-downs, and towing.

Further terms may include added fees for late returns, drop-off at a different location, or failure to top up the petrol immediately before the return.

Finally, there may be provisions for making a non-refundable deposit with a booking, terms for payment of the initial period (with discounts, vouchers, etc.), extended periods, and any damages or other fees that accrue prior to the return.

Real Estate Rental

A rental agreement is often called a lease, especially when real estate is rented. In addition to the basics of a rental (who, what, when, how much), a real estate rental may go into much more detail on these and other issues. The real estate may be rented for housing, parking a vehicle(s), storage, business, agricultural, institutional, or government use, or other reasons.

- Who: The parties involved in the contract, the lessor (sometimes called the owner or landlord) and the lessee (sometimes called the renter or tenant) are identified in the contract. A housing lease may specify whether the renter is living alone, with family, children, room-mate, visitors. A rental may delineate the rights and obligations of each of these. For example, a "sub-let" to a stranger might not be permitted without permission of the landlord. This also applies to whether or not pets may be kept by the renter. On the other hand, the renter may also have specific rights against intrusions by the landlord (or other tenants), except under emergency circumstances. A renter is in possession of the property, and a landlord would be trespassing upon the renter's rights if entry is made without proper notice and authority (e.g., 24 hours' notice, daytime, knock first, except for emergency repairs, in case of fire, flood, etc.).

- What: Rented real estate may include all or part of almost any real property, such as an apartment, house, building, business office(s) or suite, land, farm, or merely an inside or outside space to park a vehicle, or store things. The premises rented may include not only specific rooms, but also access to other common areas such as off-street parking, basement or attic storage, laundry facility, pool, roof-deck, balconies, etc. The agreement may specify how and when these places may be used, and by whom. There may be detailed description of the current condition of the premises, for comparison with the condition at the time the premises are surrendered.
- When: the term of the rental may be for a night (e.g., a hotel room), weeks, months, or years. There may be statutory provisions requiring registration of any rental that could extend for more than a specified number of years (e.g., seven) in order to be enforceable against a new landlord.

  A typical rental is either annual or month-to-month, and the amount of rent may be different for long-term renters (because of lower turnover costs). Leaving a long-term lease before its expiration could result in penalties, or even the cost of the entire agreed period (if the landlord is unable to find a suitable replacement tenant, after diligent pursuit). If a tenant stays beyond the end of a lease for a term of years (one or more), then the parties may agree that the lease will be automatically renewed, or it may simply convert to a tenancy at will (month-to-month) at the pro-rated monthly cost of the previous annual lease. If a tenant at will is given notice to quit the premises, and refuses to do so, the landlord then begins eviction proceedings. In many places it is completely illegal to change locks on doors, or remove personal belongings, let alone forcibly eject a person, without a court order of eviction. There may be strict rules of procedure, and stiff penalties (triple damages, plus attorneys' fees) for violations.
- How much: Rent may be payable monthly, annually, or in advance, or as otherwise agreed. A typical arrangement for tenancy at will is "first and last month's rent" plus a security deposit. The "last month's rent" is rent that has yet to be earned by the landlord.

Deposit

The security deposit is often handled as an escrow deposit, owned by the tenant, but held by the landlord until the premises are surrendered in good condition (ordinary wear and tear excepted). In some states, the landlord must provide the tenant with the name and account number of the bank where the security deposit is held, and pay annual interest to the tenant. Other regulations may require the landlord to submit a list of pre-existing damage to the property, or forfeit the security deposit immediately (because there is no way to determine whether a prior tenant was responsible).

Insurance

In order to rent or lease in many apartment buildings, a renter (also referred to as a "lessee") is often required to provide proof of renters insurance before signing the rental agreement. There is a special type of the homeowners insurance in the United States specifically for renters — HO-4. This is commonly referred to as renter's insurance or renter's coverage. Similar to condominium coverage, referred to as a HO-6 policy, a renter's insurance policy covers those aspects of the apartment and its contents not specifically covered in the blanket policy written for the complex. This policy can also cover liabilities arising from accidents and intentional injuries for guests as well as passers-by up to 150' of the domicile. Renter's policies provide "named peril" coverage, meaning the policy states specifically what you are insured against. Common coverage areas are:

- Fire or Lightning
- Windstorm
- Smoke
- Vandalism or Malicious Mischief
- Theft
- Accidental Discharge of Water.

Additional events including riot, aircraft, explosion, smoke, hail, falling objects, volcanic eruption, snow, sleet, and weight of ice may also be covered.

Land Lease

A land lease or ground lease is a lease in which the tenant rents and uses the land, but owns the temporary or permanent buildings and other objects placed upon it.

Sublease

In real estate law, sublease (or, less formally, sublet) is the name given to an arrangement in which the lessee in a lease assigns the lease to a third party, thereby making the old lessee the sublessor, and the new lessee the sublessee, or subtenant. This means they are renting the property and renting it out at the same time. For example, the owner of an office building may lease the whole building to a management company. This company may then sublease parts of the building to other people. The management company is said to *sublet* the property to the individual tenants by means of a sublease. In this event, the management company (which was previously the lessee under the original lease) becomes the sublessor, and the individual tenants are subtenants or sublessees.

The sublessor remains liable to the original lessor for any damage to the property and for payment of rent. Often the original lessee requires a lower rent payment from the sublessee than what he or she may have originally paid, leaving a partial amount of the rent left up to the original lessee.

It is sometimes illegal to charge the subtenant more than the original amount in the sublessee's contract (for instance, in a rent control situation where the rental amount is controlled by law). Subletting of social housing is generally illegal, whatever the rent charged to the subtenant; in the UK it is officially described as a category of housing fraud.

A sublease can also apply to vehicles as an alternate type of car rental. In a vehicle sublease, a lessee or vehicle owner can assign a lease to a third party and by way of contractual agreement for specific dates. Although this arrangement is not popular, it is a growing trend in the travel industry as a less expensive alternative for travelers and locals.

Head Lease

A head lease is a lease between a tenant and a landlord in which overall contractual responsibility is given to one identifiable tenant called the head lessee. This form of lease normally relates to an entire building which is multi-tenanted and subleased, and is usually for a longer term than the subleases.

Leasing

Leasing is a process by which a firm can obtain the use of a certain fixed assets for which it must pay a series of contractual, periodic, tax deductible payments.

The lessee is the receiver of the services or the assets under the lease contract and the lessor is the owner of the assets. The relationship between the tenant and the landlord is called a tenancy, and can be for a fixed or an indefinite period of time (called the term of the lease). The consideration for the lease is called rent. A gross lease is when the tenant pays a flat rental amount and the landlord pays for all property charges regularly incurred by the ownership from lawnmowers and washing machines to handbags and jewellry.

Under normal circumstances, a freehold owner of property is at liberty to do what they want with their property, including destroy it or hand over possession of the property to a tenant. However, if the owner has surrendered possession to another (the tenant) then any interference with the quiet enjoyment of the property by the tenant in lawful possession is unlawful.

Similar principles apply to real property as well as to personal property, though the terminology would be different. Similar principles apply to sub-leasing, that is the leasing by a tenant in possession to a sub-tenant. The right to sub-lease can be expressly prohibited by the main lease.

Formality

A tenancy for years greater than 1 year must be in writing in order to satisfy the Statute of Frauds.

Term

The term of the lease may be fixed, periodic or of indefinite duration.

If it is for a 'tenancy for years', the term ends automatically when the period expires, and no notice needs to be given, in the absence of legal requirements.

The term's duration may be conditional, in which case it lasts until some specified event occurs, such as the death of a specified individual.

A periodic tenancy is one which is renewed automatically, usually on a monthly or weekly basis.

A tenancy at will lasts only as long as the parties wish it to, and be terminated without penalty by either party.

It is common for a lease to be extended on a "holding over" basis, which normally converts the tenancy to a periodic tenancy on a month by month basis.

Rent

Rent is a requirement of leases in common law jurisdiction, but not in civil law jurisdiction. There is no requirement for the rent to be a commercial amount. "Pepper corn" rent or rent of some nominal amount is adequate for this requirement.

Real Estate

There are different types of ownership for land but, in common law states, the most common form is the 'fee simple absolute', where the legal term *fee* has the old meaning of real property, i.e. real estate. An owner of the 'fee simple' holds all the rights and privileges to that property and, subject to the laws, codes, rules and regulations of the local law, can sell or by contract or grant, permit another to have possession and control of the property through a lease or tenancy agreement. For this purpose, the owner is called the lessor or landlord, and the other person is called the lessee or tenant, and the rights to possess and control the land are exchanged for some payment (called 'consideration' in legal English), usually a monthly rent. The acceptance of rent by the landowner from a tenant creates (or extends) most of the rights of tenancy even without a written lease (or beyond the time limit of an expiring lease). Although leases can be oral agreements that are periodic, i.e. extended indefinitely and automatically, written leases should always define the period of time covered by the lease. In the 1930s, the British government introduced infinite leases, only to remove the power to create these in the early 1990s. A lease may be:

- a fixed-term agreement, in other words one of these two:
  - for a specified period of time (the "term"), and end when the term expires;
  - conditional, i.e. last until some specified event occurs, such as the death of a specified individual; or
- a periodic agreement, in other words renewed automatically
  - usually on a monthly or weekly basis
  - *at will*, i.e. last only as long as the parties wish it to, and be terminated without penalty by either party.

Because ownership is retained by the lessor, he or she always has the better right to enforce all the contractual terms and conditions affecting the use of the land. Normally, the contract will be *express* (i.e. set out in full and, hopefully, plain language), but where a contract is silent or ambiguous, terms can be *implied* by a court where this would make commercial sense of the transaction between the parties. One important right that may or may not be allowed the lessee, is the ability to create a sublease or to assign the lease, i.e. to transfer control to a third party. Hence, the builder of an office block may create a lease of the whole in favour of a management company that then finds tenants for the individual units and gives them control.

Under common law, a lease should have three essential characteristics:

1. A definite term (whether fixed or periodic)
2. At a rent
3. confer exclusive possession.

Tangible Personal Property

An owner can allow another the use of a vehicle (such as vehicle leasing of a car, a truck or an airliner) or a computer either for a fixed period of time or at will. This can be a simple leasing transaction, or it can be a transaction intended to allow the user the right to buy the item at some future time.

- In a simple lease (rental) of a car, the lessee pays the lessor a rental for the use of the car during the agreed period which may be a few days (e.g. for a holiday trip) or longer where it is more economic to pay for use rather than pay for the ownership of an asset of depreciating value. Normally, only the lessee will be allowed to use the vehicle and, in such a case, the lessee has possession and control. But, the lessor could be an employer who allows a third person the use of the car to visit clients.
- In a lease with the possibility of purchase, O could allow P to lease the car for a specified period of time. If all the rental payments are made in full, P will then be allowed to buy the car at the contractual purchase option price. In a consumer lease subject to the federal Consumer Leasing Act and the Truth in Lending Act, the purchase option price can not be a "bargain" purchase, that is, it cannot be less than the originally estimated fair market value. A "bargain" purchase creates an installment sale, to which the Truth in Lending Act (TILA) applies including the standardized disclosures, most importantly the Annual Percentage Rate (APR). Typically, the vehicle dealer or other personal property seller offers the leasing terms and contract of a third party finance company. Hence, O leases the vehicle to P, and upon execution of the contract simultaneously sells ownership of the car to F and assigns the lease contract to F. It is standard for the contractual terms to prohibit P from parting with possession or control of the car to another (if P does part with possession, this can be a theft of the car from F).

There are two principal types of leasing, depending upon the party taking the risk of the value of the vehicle (or other leased property) at lease end. In the U.S. this is called Closed-end leasing. In other jurisdictions, it is called hire purchase, *lease purchase* or finance leasing. These transactions are complicated. The most common problem arises when O makes specific representations as to the quality and reliability of the car to P during the initial negotiations. If what is said induces P to buy the car from O, those representations would usually be enforceable against O. But, in this transaction, O first sells the car to F who makes no representations to P. The laws vary from state to state on the extent to which P might be allowed a remedy if the car proves to be of poor quality.

To clarify the concept, the owner of tangible movables has the power to keep possession and only to transfer control. This may be for:

- short-or long-term storage (e.g. leaving a passport with hotel staff or depositing valuable property in a bank vault — a hotel or bank holding property is a bailee); or
- for delivery purposes (e.g. using a carrier to transport goods to a specific destination); or
- it may be a form of mortgage — a pawnshop holds a pledge over the goods deposited until the money lent is repaid.

Leasing is a common method by which airlines acquire their aircraft, usually from companies specialised in the field of Commercial Aircraft Sales and Leasing. Aircraft leasing transactions are typically divided into finance leasing and operating leasing.

Leasing is also used for ships, in which case the agreement is structured as a bareboat charter.

Businesses often choose to lease rather than buy office equipment, including computers. Since office equipment depreciates rapidly, leasing can be more cost-efficient than ownership.

In addition, more and more unconventional items are becoming available for lease, such as handbags and luxury watches.

Real Property

Whether it is better to lease or buy land will be determined by each state's legal and economic systems. In those countries where acquiring title is complicated, the state imposes high taxes on owners, transaction costs are high, and finance is difficult to obtain, leasing will be the norm. But, freely available credit at low interest rates with minimal tax disadvantages and low transaction costs will encourage land ownership. Whatever the system, most adult consumers have, at some point in their lives, been party to a real estate lease which can be as short as a week, as long as 999 years, or perpetual (only a few states permit ownership to be alienated indefinitely). For commercial property, whether there is a depreciation allowance depends on the local state taxation system.

If a lease is created for a term of, say, ten years, the monthly or quarterly rent is a fixed cost during the term. The term of years may have an asset value for balance sheet purposes and, as the term expires, that value depreciates. However, the apportionment of relief as between business expense and depreciating asset is for each state to make (all that is certain is that the lessee cannot have a double allowance).

Private Property

Rental, tenancy, and lease agreements are formal and informal contracts between an identified landlord and tenant giving rights to both parties, e.g. the tenant's right to occupy the accommodation for an agreed term and the landlord's right to receive an agreed rent. If one of these elements is missing, only a tenancy at will or bare licence comes into being. In some legal systems, this has unfortunate consequences. When a formal tenancy is created, the law usually implies obligations for the lessor, e.g. that the property meets certain minimum standards of habitability. With a bare licence, some states do not imply any significant lessee protections.

A tenancy agreement can be made up of:

- *express terms*. These include what is in the written agreement (if there is one), in the rent book, and/or what was agreed orally (if there is clear evidence of what was said).
- *implied terms*. These are the standard terms established by custom and practice or the minimum rights and duties formally implied by law.

Commercial Property

Generally speaking in the modern US legal framework, commercial real property leases fall into one of just a few categories: Office, Retail, Warehouse, Ground, and a catch-all hybrid often referred to as "Mixed Use". Each has certain typical characteristics, although Ground leases may differ somewhat, taking on some characteristics of Retail leasing when associated with a retail project, like a shopping center; and although Mixed Use projects can vary greatly depending upon the various inclusions and the size of the overall project, among other things. It is widely appreciated by those who specialize in commercial leasing, including the business side and the legal side, that, other than hybrids such as Mixed Use project leasing, Retail leasing can have the most complexity.

Mixed Use projects often have elements of most or all of the other categories, not infrequently including a hotel, office building, ground floor retail with residential condominium above and a parking garage. The interplay of all these different components with each other and the underlying property documents which describe, define, and control their interactions, operation and management, as well as the division of costs for the operation of the site, are typically very complex.

Retail leasing often requires the parties to address issues typically not addressed at all in other types of commercial leasing which have no retail component.

These additional challenges include such topics as exclusives and restrictive covenants, radius restrictions on near-by self-competition, co-tenancy, no-build areas and visibility corridors, parking ratio assurances, signage concerns (including pylons, monuments, and criteria), CAM and CAM caps and controls (including the "cumulative" and "non-cumulative" concepts), continuous operating covenants, and much more.

Advantages

For businesses, leasing property may have significant financial benefits:

- Leasing is less capital-intensive than purchasing, so if a business has constraints on its capital, it can grow more rapidly by leasing property than it could by purchasing the property outright.
- Capital assets may fluctuate in value. Leasing shifts risks to the lessor, but if the property market has shown steady growth over time, a business that depends on leased property is sacrificing capital gains.
- Because of investments which are done with leasing, new businesses are formed. Furthermore, unemployment in that country is decreased.
- Leasing may provide more flexibility to a business which expects to grow or move in the relatively short term, because a lessee is not usually obliged to renew a lease at the end of its term.

- In some cases a lease may be the only practical option; such as for a small business that wishes to locate in a large office building within tight locational parameters.
- Depreciation of capital assets has different tax and financial reporting treatment from ordinary business expenses. Lease payments are considered expenses, which can be set off against revenue when calculating taxable profit at the end of the relevant tax accounting period.

Disadvantages

For businesses, leasing property may have significant drawbacks:

- A net lease may shift some or all of the maintenance costs onto the tenant.
- If circumstances dictate that a business must change its operations significantly, it may be expensive or otherwise difficult to terminate a lease before the end of the term. In some cases, a business may be able to sublet property no longer required, but this may not recoup the costs of the original lease, and, in any event, usually requires the consent of the original lessor. Tactical legal considerations usually make it expedient for lessees to default on their leases. The loss of book value is small and any litigation can usually be settled on advantageous terms. This is an improvement on the position for those companies owning their own property. Although it can be easier for a business to sell property if it has the time, forced sales frequently realise lower prices and can seriously affect book value.
- If the business is successful, lessors may demand higher rental payments when leases come up for renewal. If the value of the business is tied to the use of that particular property, the lessor has a significant advantage over the lessee in negotiations.

International Usage

The practice of leasing is well established in most countries of the world.

However the benefits (in particular the tax benefits) to the lessee and lessor will vary widely depending on national accounting standards and tax regulations. These largely divide into countries observing:

- Legal Form: the lessors legal ownership of the property,
- Substance: the lessee legal right to use the property.

National accounting standards vary in the tests that decide if the lease is a:

- Capital or Finance lease, which is considered a financing transaction-as the lessor has less of the risks of ownership, such as the value of the equipment in future years.
- Operating lease, whose term is short compared to the useful life of the asset, where the lessee does not have to show the lease on their balance sheet.

Chapter 8

Rainwater Harvesting

Rainwater harvesting is the accumulating and storing, of rainwater for reuse, before it reaches the aquifer. It has been used to provide drinking water, water for livestock, water for irrigation, as well as other typical uses given to water. Rainwater collected from the roofs of houses, tents and local institutions, can make an important contribution to the availability of drinking water.It can supplement the sub soil water level and decrease urban greenery. Water collected from the ground, sometimes from areas which are especially prepared for this purpose, is called Stormwater harvesting.

In some cases, rainwater may be the only available, or economical, water source. Rainwater harvesting systems can be simple to construct from inexpensive local materials, and are potentially successful in most habitable locations. Roof rainwater can't be of good quality and may require treatment before consumption. As rainwater rushes from your roof it may carry pollutants in it such as the tiniest bit of mercury from coal burning buildings to bird feces. Although some rooftop materials may produce rainwater that is harmful to human health, it can be useful in flushing toilets, washing clothes, watering the garden and washing cars; these uses alone halve the amount of water used by a typical home. Household rainfall catchment systems are appropriate in areas with an average rainfall greater than 200 mm (7.9 in) per year, and no other accessible water sources (Skinner and Cotton, 1992). Overflow from rainwater harvesting tank systems can be used to refill aquifers in a process called groundwater recharge, though this is a related process, it must not be confused with Rainwater harvesting.

Figure: *Rainwater capture and storage system at the Monterrey Institute of Technology and Higher Education, Mexico City.*

There are a number of types of systems to harvest rainwater ranging from very simple to the complex industrial systems. The rate at which water can be collected from either system is dependent on the plan area of the system, its efficiency, and the intensity of rainfall (i.e. annual precipitation (mm per annum) x square meter of catchment area = litres per annum yield)... a 200 square meter roof catchment catching 1,000mm PA yields 200 kLPA.

Basic Configuration

Rainwater harvesting systems channel rainwater that falls on to a roof into storage via a system of gutters and pipes. The first flush of rainwater after a dry season should be allowed to run to waste as it will be contaminated with dust, bird droppings etc. Roof gutters should have sufficient incline to avoid standing water. They must be strong enough, and large enough to carry peak flows. Storage tanks should be covered to prevent mosquito breeding and to reduce evaporation losses, contamination and algal growth. Rainwater harvesting systems require regular maintenance and cleaning to keep the system hygienic.

Subsurface Dyke

A subsurface dyke is a barrier impermeable to water that is placed underground to control the groundwater flow in an aquifer, and to raise the water table.

Although the total amount of water on Earth is generally assumed to have remained virtually constant, the rapid growth in population, together with the extension of irrigated agriculture and industrial development, are putting stress on the quality and quantity aspects of natural system. The sub-surface dyke constructed at Krishi Vigyan Kendra, Kannur at Panniyur near Taliparamba under Kerala Agricultural University with the support of ICAR as part of demonstrating rain water harvesting technologies has become a living example for an effective method for ground water conservation. The success story of the sub-surface dyke has demonstrated that it is one of the most feasible methods for the conservation and exploitation of the ground water resources of the state. The dyke is now the largest rainwater harvesting system in the region.

The subsurface dyke at Krishi Vigyan Kendra, Kannur under Kerala Agricultural University with the support of ICAR, has become an effective method for ground water conservation by means of rain water harvesting technologies. The sub-surface dyke has demonstrated that it is a feasible method for conserving and exploiting the groundwater resources of the Kerala state of India. The dyke is now the largest rainwater harvesting system in that region.

Subsurface dyke is a structure that is built in an aquifer with the intention of obstructing the natural flow of ground water, thereby raising the ground water level and increasing the amount of water stored in the aquifer.

Construction

A trench was made across the valley portion of the undulating topography of the farm down to the bed rock. Three layers of plastic sheets were spread on the wall of the trench from ground level to the bed rock level. The plastic sheet on the wall measured 40m in length with a maximum depth of 8 m. It obstructs the flow of sub surface water raising water table in the catchment area.

Benefits

The dyke was constructed in the 25 hectare farm of Krishi Vigyan Kendra Kannur in 2007 to solve the problem of water scarcity. The experience of KVK indicated that subsurface dyke was an efficient barrier to arrest the subsurface flow of water and conserve ground water. The rate of depletion of drainable water in the catchment area due to the typical undulating topography could be efficiently arrested by the dyke. The dyke resulted in the maintenance of higher water table in the catchment area for a longer period of time. There is an existing dug out pond with top length of 12 m, width 8m a depth 5m in the upstream side of the dyke. The pond is the only source of water in the KVK farm. The pond, which usually gets dried up in the summer is now maintaining a high water table throughout the year as the dyke ensures an incessant supply of water to the pond. Weekly data on the ground water level were recorded using water level recorder. The data showed that significantly higher level of water table was maintained in the catchment area (upstream area) compared to down stream area. Taking into account the mean depth of soil as 2 m the catchment area as 1.5ha (the actual area is 15 ha) and the drainable porosity as 10%, the total water storage capacity of the dyke would be 3000 m3. The crops cultivated in the catchment area would be benefited by way of constant capillary feeding of the rhizosphere. Kerala receives, on an average, more than 3000mm of rainfall per annum which is concentrated to the months of June to October. Due to the typical undulating topography of the state, the excess rain received is mostly lost through runoff. Immediately on cessation of rains subsurface water drains off along the slope resulting in poor retention of water in the catchment area. In spite of the heavy rainfall received in Kerala, the state experiences severe drought during summer months due to inefficient utilisation of rain water. In a state like Kerala, where the pressure on land is very high surface storage of water in large reservoirs with their adverse ecological impact is not an economic proposition. Alternatively, structures like subsurface dyke are most ideal for in situ conservation of rainfall received in a watershed.

Siting

The ideal location for the dyke is a well defined, wide, greatly sloping valley with a narrow outlet having limited thickness of loose soil or porous rock on the top with massive or impervious rock below . Subsurface dyke has many advantages. It does not require additional surface reservoir. There is no loss of agricultural land. There is minimum evaporation loss since the storage is subsurface. There is no siltation and loss of reservoir capacity. The cost of maintenance is negligible. It is environment-friendly.

Other water harvesting technologies

The other rainwater harvesting technologies demonstrated at KVK include stone pitched contour bunds, dry rubble check dams, protection of seasonal spring by afforestation, moisture conservation pits, sprinkler and drip irrigation and roof water harvesting system.

Groundwater Recharge

Rainwater may also be used for groundwater recharge, where the runoff on the ground is collected and allowed to be absorbed, adding to the groundwater. In the US, rooftop rainwater is collected and stored in sump.

Advantages in Urban Areas

Rainwater harvesting can (a) assure an independent water supply during water restrictions, that is though somewhat dependent on end use and maintenance, (b)usually of acceptable quality for household needs and (c) renewable at acceptable volumes despite forecast climate change (CSIRO, 2003). It produces beneficial externalities by reducing peak storm water runoff and processing costs. In municipalities with combined sewer systems, reducing storm runoff is especially important, because excess runoff during heavy storms leads to the discharge of raw sewage from outfalls when treatment plant capacity cannot handle the combined flow. RH systems are simple to install and operate. Running costs are negligible, and they provide water at the point of consumption. We are consuming this water for our basic needs.

Rain water harvesting law Some states have water law in favour of land owners, and some states own all water rights, leaving you only water rights they are willing to grant through permits. For example, in Colorado you may not catch, collect or harvest rain water from your roof unless you first buy a permit.

Quality

As rainwater may be contaminated due to pollutants like microscopic germs etc., it is often not considered suitable for drinking without treatment. However, there are many examples of rainwater being used for all purposes — including drinking — following suitable treatment.

Rainwater harvested from roofs can contain human, animal and bird faeces, mosses and lichens, windblown dust, particulates from urban pollution, pesticides, and inorganic ions from the sea (Ca, Mg, Na, K, Cl, SO_4), and dissolved gases (CO_2, NO_x, SO_x). High levels of pesticide have been found in rainwater in Europe with the highest concentrations occurring in the first rain immediately after a dry spell; the concentration of these and other contaminants are reduced significantly by diverting the initial flow of water to waste as described above. The water may need to be analysed properly, and used in a way appropriate to its safety. In the Gansu province for example, harvested rainwater is boiled in parabolic solar cookers before being used for drinking. In Brazil alum and chlorine is added to disinfect water before consumption. So-called "appropriate technology" methods, such as solar water disinfection, provide low-cost disinfection options for treatment of stored rainwater for drinking.

System Sizing

It is important that the system is sized to meet the water demand throughout the dry season. Generally speaking, the size of the storage tank should be big enough to meet the daily water requirement throughout the dry season. In addition, the size of the catchment area or roof should be large enough to fill the tank.

Around the World

- Currently in China and Brazil, rooftop rainwater harvesting is being practiced for providing drinking water, domestic water, water for livestock, water for small irrigation and a way to replenish ground water levels. Gansu province in China and semi-arid north east Brazil have the largest rooftop rainwater harvesting projects ongoing.
- In Rajasthan, India rainwater harvesting has traditionally been practiced by the people of the Thar Desert. There are many ancient water harvesting systems in Rajasthan which have now been revived
- In Bermuda, the law requires all new construction to include rainwater harvesting adequate for the residents.
- The U.S. Virgin Islands have a similar law.
- In the Indus Valley Civilization, Elephanta Caves and Kanheri Caves in Mumbai rainwater harvesting alone has been used to supply in their water requirements.

- In Senegal and Guinea-Bissau, the houses of the Diola-people are frequently equipped with homebrew rainwater harvesters made from local, organic materials.
- In the United Kingdom water butts are often found in domestic gardens to collect rainwater which is then used to water the garden. However, the British government's Code For Sustainable Homes encourages fitting large underground tanks to new-build homes to collect rainwater for flushing toilets, washing clothes, watering the garden and washing cars. This reduces by 50% the amount of mains water used by the home.
- In the Irrawaddy Delta of Myanmar, the groundwater is saline and communities rely on mud-lined rainwater ponds to meet their drinking water needs throughout the dry season. Some of these ponds are centuries old and are treated with great reverence and respect.
- Until 2009 in Colorado, water rights laws almost completely restricted rainwater harvesting; a property owner who captured rainwater was deemed to be stealing it from those who have rights to take water from the watershed. Now, residential well owners that meet certain criteria may obtain a permit to install a *rooftop precipitation collection system* (SB 09-080). Up to 10 large scale pilot studies may also be permitted (HB 09-1129). The main factor in persuading the Colorado Legislature to change the law was a 2007 study that found that in an average year, 97% of the precipitation that fell in Douglas County, in the southern suburbs of Denver, never reached a stream—it was used by plants or evaporated on the ground. In colorado you cannot even drill a water well unless you have at least 35 acres. In New Mexico, rainwater catchment is mandatory for new dwellings in Santa Fe.
- Kerala, India,
- In Australia rainwater harvesting is typically used to supplement the reticulated mains supply. In south east Queensland, households that harvested rainwater doubled each year from 2005 to 2008, reaching 40% penetration at that time (White, 2009 (PhD)).
- In Beijing, some housing societies are now adding rain water in their main water sources after proper treatment.

Bibliography

Amram, M.: *Value Sweep: Mapping Corporate Growth Opportunities*, Harvard Business School Press, NY, 2002.

Ardenne, R.: *German Exploitation of Belgium*, Brookings Institution, Washington, 1942.

Barris, J., & Garcia-Almirall, P.: *A Density Function of the Appraisal Value*, European Real Estate Society 2011 – Eindhoven, The Netherlands, Best Paper on Real Estate Valuation, 2011.

Barris, J.: *An Expert System for Appraisal by the Method of Comparison*, UPC, Barcelona, 2008.

Bastiat, Frédéric: *Economic Harmonies,* W. Hayden Boyers, trans.; George B. de Huszar, ed. Liberty Fund, 1850.

Bauer, Yehuda: *The Negotiations between Nazis and Jews 1933-1945*, Liania Levi, Paris, 1996.

Baum, A., Nunnigton, N., & Mackmin, D.: *The Income Approach to Property Valuation,* Estates Gazette, London, 2011.

Bethell, Tom: *The Noblest Triumph: Property and Prosperity through the Ages*, St. Martin's Press, New York, 1998.

Brown, G., & Matysiak, G.: *Real Estate Investment: A Capital Market Approach*, Financial Times, London, 1999.

Clark, Mona: *Interpersonal Skills for Hospitality Managers*, London, Chapman Hill, 1995.

De Soto, Hernando, and Francis Cheneval: *Realizing Property Rights*, Ruffer & Rub., NY, 2006.

De Soto, Hernando: *The Other Path*, Harper & Row, NJ, 1989..

González, N., Moll, L., & Amanti, C.: *Funds of knowledge: Theorizing Practices in Households, Communities, and Classrooms*, Lawrence Erlbaum Associates, New Jersey, 2005.

Hayward, R.: *Valuation: Principles into Practice,* Estates Gazette, London, 2008.

Hoffman, Edward: *Project Management Success Stories: Lessons of Project Leaders*, New York, John Wiley & Son, 2000.

Holloway, J. C. : *Labour, Vocational Education and Training, in W. Pompl and P. Lavery,* Tourism in Europe - Structures and Developments, Oxford, CAB International, 1993.

Ireland, Lewis: *Quality Management for Projects and Programs*, Upper Darby, PMI, 1991.

Isaac, D., & O'Leary, J.: *Property Valuation Principles,* Palgrave MacMillan, London, 2012.

Kane, S., Linne, M. and Johnson, J.: *Practical Applications in Appraisal Valuation Modeling*, Appraisal Institute, Chicago, 2004.

Lock, Dennis: *Project Management,* New York, Wiley, 1996.

Lin, G. C. I. and S. V. Nagalingam: *CIM Justification and Optimisation*. CRC Press, NY, 2000.

Lowenstein, R.: *When Genius Failed: The Rise and Fall of Long-Term Capital Management*, Random House, NJ, 2001.

Lum, L.: *Personal Investing: An Interactive Approach with Access Certificate*, South-Western Educational Publishing, US, 2003.

Moore, M.: *Community Capacity Assessment: A Guide for Developing an Inventory of Community-level Assets and Resources*, New Mexico Children, Youth and Families Department, Santa Fe, NM, 1994.

Palda, Filip: *Pareto's Republic and the New Science of Peace* 2011, Cooper-Wolfling, NY, 2011.

Pipes, Richard: *Property and Freedom*, Knopf Doubleday, New York, 1999.

Reilly, F. K. and K. C. Brown: *Investment Analysis and Portfolio Management,* South-Western Educational Publishing, US, 2003.

Samuel Noah Kramer. *From the Tablets of Sumer: Twenty-Five Firsts in Man's Recorded History*. Indian Hills: The Falcon's Wing Press, 1956.

Simons, Robert: *When Bad Things Happen to Good Property,* Environmental Law Institute, Washington, DC, 2007.

Sullivan, Arthur; Steven M. Sheffrin: *Economics: Principles in action*, Pearson Prentice Hall, Upper Saddle River, New Jersey, 2003

U.S. Department of Transportation: *Roads and Streets Maintenance Management System: A Manual for Decentralized and Local Agencies,* Federal Highway Administration, Office of Operations, Washington, DC, 1985.

Vanier, D.J.: *Asset Management from "A" to "Z",* Institute for Research in Construction, National Research Council Canada, Ottawa, Canada, 1998.

Wiedemer, J. P. and J. E. Goeters: *Real Estate Investment, 6e*. South-Western Educational Publishing, US, 2003.

Index

❑❑❑